On the Line

"
Trust your instruments, not your body, the modern pilot is always told, but this beast is best felt.

Michael Collins **"**

Words & Images
Andy Kirkpatrick

On the Line

TRS Manual

Andy Kirkpatrick

WARNING

Climbing is dangerous

Enthusiasm is **no substitute** for **knowledge** and **experience**

This manual is designed to equip climbers with the skills necessary to stay safe. However, rock climbing and mountaineering are inherently dangerous activities, and thus, this manual is intended for experienced rock climbers and mountaineers only.

No one should undertake climbing without the appropriate training or equipment and must assume personal responsibility for mastering the correct techniques and employing sound judgement. I strongly recommend that every climber seek instruction from a qualified professional if they are uncertain about any aspect of this manual.

By utilising the information contained within this manual, you acknowledge that its content might be outdated or inaccurate, and you agree that the author cannot be held liable for any damages arising from the use of this manual.

This book provides valuable information on subjects covered, including climbing, abseiling, and anchoring. It is specifically tailored for individuals actively engaged in rock climbing.

All content in this book, including text, graphics, images, exercises, techniques, and references to third-party materials, is for informational and educational purposes only.

The author and publisher of this book shall bear no liability or responsibility to any reader or third party for any injury or damage resulting from the application of the information provided in this book.

Admin

Margin Call

When you write a book like this, you need to write it less like an actual living, breathing, creative person but more like a lawyer, and so any humour found within the main text is there by accident (climbing, like German humour, is no laughing matter, as is tea). As this book features a lot of white space at the margins, I thought I'd scribble in a few of my own words, thoughts, ideas and reflections along the way. If they're ignored, it will not affect the value of this book; instead, they are there as little thumbnail thoughts that might be of value to someone. Also, I spent many of my school days being told off for drawing in the margins rather than doing the work on the lines, so this is perhaps a two-finger salute to all my old teachers.

Target Reader

I regard top rope soloing technique as an advanced-level skill; therefore, this book is intended for experienced climbers. I assume that readers are familiar with the basics, can operate safely on a crag or mountainside, and understand how to use standard climbing equipment.

If you believe the topics discussed in this book surpass your current abilities, I advise you to stop reading. Instead, consider other books (refer to the appendix) and prioritise mastering the basics.

Should you identify gaps in your expertise, I strongly recommend enrolling in a climbing course, becoming a member of a climbing club, or hiring a professional instructor to address those deficiencies.

If you candidly recognise your limitations yet wish to explore this book, understanding what you're unfamiliar with can be enlightening. However, always bear in mind that reading is no substitute for practical experience.

Reading Instructions

This book demands careful perusal and is designed to be read sequentially. Nevertheless, many will likely use it as a reference for specific queries. Certain sections might necessitate multiple readings, and to emphasise crucial points, I've employed repetition. I recommend initially concentrating on the sections you grasp with ease, then revisiting more challenging parts later. Approach your learning progressively, advancing only when you feel confident and well-anchored.

Weights & Measures

I know the only country to land a man on the moon used inches and feet. But being a European, I have to go with the metric system. There are also some measurements that are particular only to climbers in a certain geographical area, for example, to a Brit, a 60 cm sling is 4 feet, a 120 cm is 8 feet, and a 240 cm is 16 foot. What you call a sling at your own crag may be different, but I'm not interested in angry emails on the subject (this is a book, not an internet forum).

Feedback & Updates

Any feedback or questions can be forwarded via my website at www.andy-kirkpatrick.com (there are no dumb questions, just people dumb enough not to ask for help).

Contents

0
Book

08	Nomenclature
12	Forward
15	Introduction
19	Condensed
21	Basics
25	Safety
227	Final Thoughts
229	Last Word
231	**Appendix**
233	Certs
243	Limbic Hijack
246	Index

31
Devices

33	The Perfect Device
43	**Mechanics**
45	Eccentric
59	Rocker-Arm
69	Lever
75	Inertia
79	Wedge
83	ABD
91	GMD
95	Hitches
99	**Device Focus**
101	Petzl Shunt
107	Petzl Croll S
109	Petzl Micro/Nano Traxion
113	Petzl ASAP
115	Camp Goblin
117	Taz Lov3
119	Trango Vergo
121	CT RockNwall
123	Petzl Mini Traxion

125
Equipment

127	Karabiners
133	Quick-Links
137	Rope & Cord
141	Lanyards
143	Chest Slings
147	Link Cord
149	TRS Ropes
153	Rope Protection
156	Other Gear

159
System

161	Attachment
177	One Rope System
181	Two Rope System
185	Pseudo Leading
187	Top Rope TRS
189	Rope-Ballast
193	Catastrophe-Knots
197	Rigging
209	Sub Anchors
217	Escape

Nomenclature

When writing on technical subjects, particularly when misunderstandings could result in fatalities, an agreed-upon language is essential. One should avoid outdated terms and ambiguous words with multiple interpretations. I have endeavoured to use modern and universal terms, even if that means overriding geographical preferences, such as using the European term 'top rope' rather than the 'bottom rope', which is used by some. I trust the reader will understand the rationale behind this choice.

Let's begin with the terminology for belaying a climber from a rope running through a high anchor, with both climber and belayer starting from the ground. In this book, I will employ the European term 'top rope' (**TR**) (✎ 01) over the alternative 'bottom rope'.

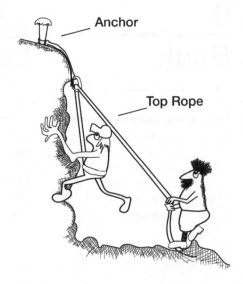

Fig. 01

'Top Rope soloing' (self-belay from a line attached to a high anchor) can be abbreviated as **TRS**.

Rather than using the term 'cam' to describe the part of a device that interfaces with the rope, I will refer to it as '**the jaw**' (✎ 02) to sidestep confusion with camming actions.

Belay assist devices, such as the Petzl GriGri, Edelrid Eddy, and Kong Vergo, are denoted as assisted braking belay devices (**ABD**).

A belay tube used in plaquette style or guide mode will be termed a 'guide mode device' (**GMD**).

We will dispense with the outdated terms 'jumaring' or 'jumar'. In their place, I will employ terms like '**ascender**', 'rope clamp', and '**rope climbing**'.

The terms 'Prusik' and 'Prusik loop' will give way to '**friction hitch**' and '**hitch cord**'.

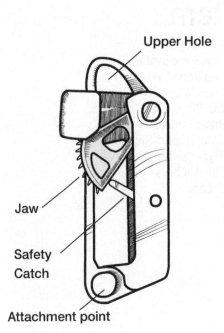

Upper Hole

Jaw

Safety
Catch

Attachment point

Fig. 02

A 'Progress Capture Device' (**PCD**) encapsulates most rope devices that climb a rope, whereas 'Progress Capture Pulleys' (**PCP**) pertains to pulleys with integrated rope clamps.

'**Quick-link**' is used to describe Maillon Rapides, non-hinged locking shackles, while the term '**connector**' will sometimes replace 'karabiner' when referencing the device's connection to the climber, given the diverse methods available for this purpose.

The '**climbing-line**' (✐ 03) designates the rope serving as the primary safety measure, the one that bears the load during a fall. The '**safety-line**' is a secondary rope, engaged only if the primary TRS device fails.

The widely-recognised 'Single Rope Technique' (**SRT**) term 're-belay' has been supplanted by the term '**re-anchor**'.

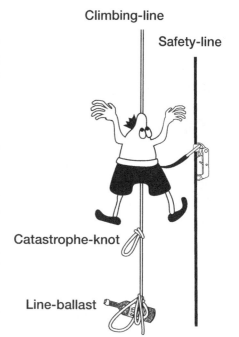

Climbing-line

Safety-line

Catastrophe-knot

Line-ballast

Fig. 03

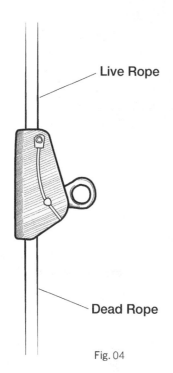

Live Rope

Dead Rope

Fig. 04

The '**live rope**' (✐ 04) pertains to the loaded, or potentially loaded, segment of the climbing-line. Conversely, the '**dead rope**' refers to the slack portion below a loaded device.

For clarity, I will eschew the terms 'single rope' and 'double rope', favouring 'one rope' or 'two ropes' instead, so as to preclude confusion with CE/UIAA rope labelling.

A TRS device that glides effortlessly up and down the rope is described as '**self-trailing**'.

A device that allows the rope to pass through without the user's intervention is classified as '**self-tending**'.

Lastly, all knot names and device model names are capitalised to enhance clarity.

I will use 'one', rather than 'you' which feels odd, but sounds better in a legal case.

On TRS

- Most people don't die, apart from those that do.

- *There are lots of ways to do it; there is only one way to do it.*

- *It's really safe; it's not really safe; it's really not safe (well, out of 34,456,568 conflicting posts, someone must be right).*

- *Seventy-three and a third different people will tell you that fourteen and a half varied methods, some possibly even including mystical incantations, work for them.*

- *Someone will recommend a method they don't use but would have used theoretically five years ago despite not having climbed since Denali in '79.*

- *47 people will tell you that various previous posters have a death wish and are 'GONNA DIE!!!'*

- *A pedant will complain about the capital letters, spelling and excessive punctuation.*

- *A genuine master in pedantry will then correct the previous pedant's grammar.*

- *Someone will post a link to the dated Lyon Equipment report or the Petzl website to demonstrate that Shunts are a death trap waiting to happen.*

- *Someone else will state they've used a Shunt since before they were invented, and they aren't going to change.*

- *At that point, a link to a video will be posted that shows <insert latest famous climber> ignoring absolutely everything anyone has said about redundancy and working a route using just a GriGri.*

- *The thread will diverge to solo lead climbing and the mythical Wren Silent Partner.*

- *Various people will return to the topic and recommend a Troll Rocker (camming ascender) as the best thing for your back-up, far safer than the 'deadly' Shunt and smoother than the awkward Microcender that Petzl now recommends.*

- *9 posters will race to remind everyone that Troll no longer exists but ISC now make them.*

- *A bright spark will mention that DMM's equivalent is the 'Buddy'.*

- *Finally, common sense will prevail, and someone tell you from personal experience that it is just all too much hassle and it's just far easier to find a proper buddy to climb with.*

Mark Stevenson (ex-engineer), giving advice on TRS, UKC Forum 2014.

Mine Alone

I have spent much of my adult life self-belay top roping. In many ways, it has facilitated my life as a professional climber and has been the linchpin tactic used in most of the hardest trad and sport new routes in Scotland over the past 25 years. As an introvert who likes climbing on cold, wet and windy crags in a corner of the UK with no real climbing scene and on projects that require many days of brushing, trying, and refining, I just couldn't have done without it.

I owe my wife and friends a huge debt of gratitude for enduring a few years of cold belays and endless 'down a bit, up a bit'. Ultimately, I had to realise that my big projects were mine alone. No one who wanted to climb the same routes as me was around, and I needed a sustainable solution to that big problem. Today, I rarely need a belay more than once on any rock climb up to E11. Self-belay does all the heavy lifting for me. Dangerous as it is, it also keeps me safe. I can always have just one more top rope session to ensure I have moves dialled before a poorly protected lead. If I needed a belay every time, I might be tempted to go for it too early. Doing just that caused me my first broken ankle.

Although self-belaying has afforded me endless freedom to explore the deep adventure of hard projecting on rock, it has a significant downside, exposure to risk. Now, I could easily go full-on 'industrial rope access' and double up on ropes, devices and generally go belt and braces for every part of the system, but I choose not to, instead going for a simpler system with mitigation in place for its hazards. This is a very personal choice that all climbers have to make, and the main thing is to understand the choices being made. This book will help you to pick and choose from the selection of benefits, hazards and strategies to mitigate them and, therefore, strike a balance you are happy with. It's the book that would have saved me from exposure to risk as a self-belay novice I was fortunate to get away with.

Like many, I started out with the device I was already familiar with: the GriGri. On a session in 2004 working the crux move of what soon became Scotland's first 8c, I nearly blew it with two simple mistakes. The first mistake was using a rope 2mm too skinny, which I got away with initially. I fell repeatedly from the crux move for an hour straight. Aware that the big drop knee move I was doing was making me fall off into a sideways dive, I took a notion to tie an overhand in the dead rope in case my chest pressed on the locking mechanism as I fell. For some unknown reason, I pulled up a lot of slack and tied the overhand well below me.

As it turned out, it wasn't the sideways dive that got me. On the very next attempt, as I moved my foot in preparation for the crux, the dead rope ended up sitting across my foot. As I pinged off for the umpteenth time, my foot kicked upwards and flicked a loop of dead rope into the air. It was the wrong moment for the already light dead rope to be momentarily weightless. The GriGri didn't lock, and I dropped like a stone, just touching the ground on the stretch of the rope, hard up against my stopper knot. I did not see that one coming.

Right away, I switched to the Shunt. More importantly, I started to pay attention not only to the limitations of that device but also to the whole system. As I did so, I gradually learned to self-belay on any angle, including massive horizontal roofs, complex traverses and alpine north faces. I also learned to offset the hazards of single ropes, solo devices and poor trad placements with careful (but mostly simple) mitigation strategies. Yet I've still nearly killed myself a couple of times since. It's often the simple stuff that gets you. Last year, I grabbed the rope I'd just fixed to a tree just to use for balance to identify the best spot to throw it over the edge of the crag below. But I accidentally grabbed the bottom end of the rope. I almost lost my balance and toppled over the forty-metre crag below. There is much to be said for taking your time and being methodical, no matter your set-up. I reminded myself of this in more colourful language as I scrabbled to my feet, holding clumps of heather under white knuckles.

The need for this book is underlined every time I observe online discourse on self-belay top roping. All too often, devices or methodologies are discussed in binary terms as 'safe' or 'dangerous'. This line of thinking is itself a red flag. Moreover, some potential hazards of both devices and rope set-ups do not seem evident to some experienced climbers. I occasionally detect outsourcing of concern over these hazards to equipment manufacturers and away from the climber trusting their life to the system. This is not a recipe for happy and healthy climbing.

Soloing is hazardous, rope or no rope. Accepting this is the first step to being a safer and more efficient climber. Anticipation and mitigation are the name of the game, and this book will be an invaluable tool in the box. At least with soloing, the ball is always in your court. My worst injuries in climbing were caused by my belayer dropping me while belaying an easy sport route with a GriGri.

Whether you are new to self-belay top roping or a die-hard veteran, you'll have something to learn from this book, as I certainly have. Building a solid foundation of knowledge of rope systems is critical, but those foundations always require further strengthening and updating to allow you to confidently tackle the endless complex scenarios that the mountains will throw at you.

Dave Macleod, Scotland (2023)

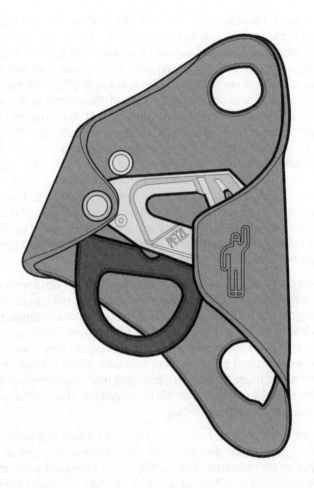

Fig.05

Introduction

✏ 05

In the late '80s, the Petzl Croll became a popular option for climbers who didn't want to use the Shunt, which already had a reputation for being a tricky TRS device.

Margin Call

One question that I get asked a lot is, "How do you do the drawings in your books?" Perhaps I'm a control freak, or I'm cheap and don't want to pay an illustrator (a bit of both), but I've done all the illustrations in every book since Psychovertical in 2006. The reason I illustrate all my books, which makes them 50% more work, is that line drawings are much more precise than photos; plus, when drawing the illustrations, I can see gaps in what I've written. They both inform each other. The images are hand drawn, but with a mouse, using Adobe Illustrator, so that's the answer. As a side note, the images on pages 10 and 11 are a homage to my hero Sheridan Anderson.

Climbers have been top rope soloing for over fifty years, but the technique has never been fully ratified by the climbing community — or its technical brain trusts — meaning a safe way to top rope solo has never been established. Why? No one wanted to put their names to anything related to ropes and soloing. Sure, there were ways to do it, but no one wanted to leave behind a paper trail, information and techniques, that led back to them. Instead, information was passed on by word of mouth. Although imperfect, this worked pretty well.

This lack of information changed with the arrival of the internet. Overnight, the subject went from just whispers to a deafening din. But with no gatekeepers or editors with any accredited technical expertise, this explosion of information only made things more dangerous. This book is my attempt to rectify this.

To most climbers, hanging a rope down a climb and then using some kind of ascender seemed easy enough to work out. It was figure-outable. You worked something out, then tweaked it after each close call or near-death experience.

Early in my climbing life, top rope soloing was a necessary evil as I lacked climbing partners. I would hitch to a crag, set up a rope, and climb. Free soloing was an option, but I soon realized I'd probably kill myself if I kept it up.

One early near miss involved climbing a classic called Great North Road, in an old quarry, on a snowy day. I was wearing my plastic mountaineering boots and no doubt imagined myself on some alpine North face, high in the clouds. Close to the top, climbing around a small overhang, I looked down, expecting to see my rope running smoothly through my Shunt, and then to the bottom. But instead, I saw a huge loop hanging from my Shunt. If I slipped, I'd have taken a fifty-foot fall. This was my first 'Oh shit!' moment. That moment just before a climber dies, when they have total clarity about why they're about to die. Slipping a hand from an ice-cold jam, I spotted the problem was the middle mark of the rope, fashioned by me with electrical tape; it had jammed in the Shunt. With shaking fingers, I squeezed the Shunt, and the rope whipped through it.

I was saved.

I had many other close calls, like having the sheath of my rope abrade over an edge, a device unclipping itself, plus the all-time classic human error of attaching my device upside down.

It was teaching myself to big wall climb that forced me to do a lot of top rope soloing, generally by pseudo lead soloing, which meant rope soloing with the back-up of my shunt on a top rope. This security was vital, as I had no idea about big walls, aid climbing, or rope soloing. This was before the age of the web.

All that was many decades ago. Top rope soloing became less important as I found others to climb with and no longer had to cultivate these obscure skills. During my evolution as a climber, I went from shunting solos on small gritstone lines to soloing El Cap five times (plus thirty more with partners). And although I occasionally dabbled in top rope soloing, I pretty much forgot about it for many years.

Then something odd happened around when writing my lead-roped soloing book, "Me, Myself & I". More people started top rope soloing. Why there should be a mini-boom in this oddest, and most anti-social of activities could be the exact reason behind the explosion in bouldering, in that there was an increasing number of climbers who could not find partners. Especially those who worked irregular hours.

I also think that more and more climbers were interested in climbing beyond their pay grade, leaving their lane of weakness and trying more challenging climbs alone on a top rope just for fun. Thirdly, I also wonder if a generation of climbers who have grown up in a self-checkout world just don't like climbing with other people but prefer the company of things.

And so, almost overnight, questions on TRS exploded on internet forums, YouTube, and social media groups. There are now even online training courses.

Although I'd written a book — I suppose, the book — on rope soloing, I was increasingly concerned about how many people assumed there was a settled science of top rope soloing rather than it being a potentially hazardous activity. I saw people developing solutions for problems that were more dangerous than the problems themselves, often providing overly complicated set-ups that were confusing or incorrectly applied.

There's also a common misapprehension among climbers, where they frequently assume that expert rock climbers are de facto experts in safe climbing techniques. Most often, the opposite is true, as very good climbers can often rely on their climbing skill and strength to save them from bad technique. The novice climber only has these techniques to fall back on — literally.

I heard more and more stories of near-death accidents. Many were due to user error, while others demonstrated the shortcomings of what had once been deemed safe working practices. Because the Petzl Shunt was designed as a rappelling back-up device, its use in situations beyond the intended application resulted in many TRS accidents. For this reason, the Petzl Shunt was slowly phased out as a TRS device recommended by real experts.

At the same time, companies that had once market devices suitable for for lead and top rope soloing began to distance themselves from the activity, declaring that such a practice was too dangerous to recommend a device for. For legal purposes, their position was a reasonable safeguard.

However, this "Just Don't Do It" stance contradicted thirty years of experience indicating that TRS can be done safely. As the zero-tolerance attitude of companies provided no useful alternatives to the Petzl Shunt, many climbers continued using it. Some persisted to an early grave.

During this time, I tried to fill the void by writing a couple of articles on my website that aimed to clarify the method, equipment, and safety back-ups I'd used, which led others to perceive me as some kind of expert on the subject when I wasn't.

In September 2021, I heard about an accident where a climber, Craig F, had his Shunt completely detach from his rope. At the time, I assumed it had to be some kind of user error, like when a climber forgets to properly tie in, climbs a route, and then plummets to the ground after clipping the chains. However, it was later demonstrated that a properly connected Shunt can become inverted and detach itself from the rope.

Since Craig's incident, there has been renewed research into safe and non-restrictive methods of top rope soloing, as well as the questioning of established dogmas. Although the increased interest has finally led to some good articles on the subject, I felt that this technique still deserved a deeper dive, plus, having . This has led to a three-year slow burn of drawing together all my worthwhile knowledge on top rope soloing and putting it into a foundational text.

I repeat, I'm no expert in top rope soloing, but who would want to be? Rather, I'm just interested in getting it all down on paper to hopefully help climbers, both novice and experienced, stay a little safer when playing alone.

Andy Kirkpatrick 2023

Fig.06

Condensed

"If I had more time, I would have written a shorter letter."

Cicero

 06
Condensed milk.

One word
Redundancy.

One Sentence
Employ two TRS devices, rig ropes correctly, and study how devices and systems fail and accidents happen.

One Paragraph
Safe TRS technique requires a primary and secondary TRS device, bombproof anchors, and a solid grasp of rope climbing, rappelling, self-rescue, and rope technique.

One Half of a page
Top rope soloing, also known as TRS, is a climbing technique in which a climber ascends a rock or ice climb alone, without a belayer at the bottom, using a self-belaying system.

In this method, the climbing rope or ropes are anchored securely at the top of the climb and hung down the route. The climber then attaches to the climbing-line as their primary fall protection. This is designed to catch a fall and allows the climber to ascend safely under their own power; the device is not used for direct progress.

A second device is then attached to the climbing-line or a second safety-line to act as back-up and redundancy in case the primary device fails. Traditionally, climbers used only a single device and employed catastrophe-knots on the climbing-line, but this has proven to be dangerous and has led to incidents.

During the climb, the self-belay devices move up the rope as the climber progresses, providing back-up protection in case of a fall. TRS allows solo climbers to climb with a higher degree of safety compared to free soloing, where no ropes or protection are used.

However, top rope soloing requires specific training and expertise to ensure safety and the proper execution of the technique. It's vital to understand that not all ascenders are the same, and eccentric, rocker-arm, and lever action devices each have their own unique ways of working, or failing to work.

The climber must also study how to escape the system and have a solid grasp of modern rope rigging techniques, including self-rescue in various scenarios.

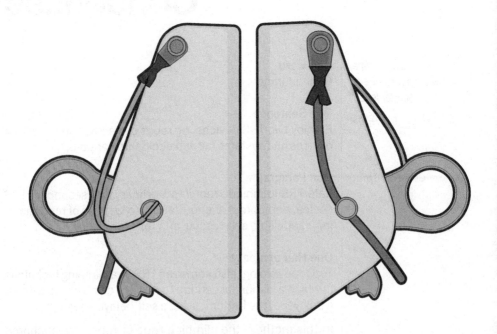

Fig.07

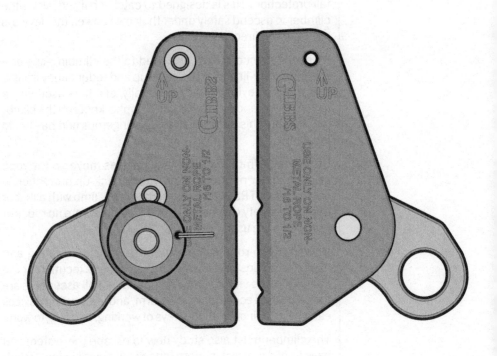

Fig.08

Basics

Top rope soloing, also known as self-lining or Shunting, is a self-belay technique that allows an individual to climb on a top rope without a partner. Such climbs are generally single-pitch, as the climb must be accessible from the top in order to build an anchor. Unlike free soloing, if the top rope soloist falls, they should be caught by the climbing-line (as would be the case when top roping with a partner).

Why do climbers top rope solo?

 07

The unique first-generation Gibbs lever action ascender, invented by Charles Gibbs in the 1965. The Gibbs ascender was one of the first really effective rope-friendly TRS devices on the market, having several advantages over the more established eccentric Jumar design by Adolph Jüsi and Walter Marti.

For the majority of climbers, TRS is a way to climb when no climbing partners are available. Traditionally, such climbers worked strange hours in professions similar to firefighters, strippers, and the like. These days, more people seem to work irregular hours, which may also explain the burgeoning popularity of this activity. In addition, TRS is a convenient method of climbing, where the soloist can climb unencumbered by the weight of a rack and does not have to worry about placing protection or taking turns with partners.

As climbing ethics evolved, pre-practising routes became more common. Many climbers will now employ TR methods (both partnered and solo) to push their grades or head point death routes. Top roping is now a popular and effective method for becoming a more capable climber.

 08

Gibbs #1, the current iteration of the classic design, has always been of marginal interest in vertical sports such as climbing, mountaineering, and caving. Its primary market has been industrial rope access, rescue, and arboriculture. Today, the Gibbs still retains its position as a specialist niche rope grab for industry and rescue, boasting unique features such as variants made in stainless steel or models capable of handling 19 mm ropes.

TRS is also used as a training tool, used as a way to train climbing fundamentals with an extra degree of security, such as leading, placing protection, ascending ropes, self-rescue, or rappelling.

What does it entail?

To carry out the safest top rope solo possible, the climber first builds a solid anchor at the top of a climb. From this, they suspend either a single climbing-line or a climbing and safety-line. Both lines are rated as single ropes and although dynamic ropes can be used, low stretch ropes (AKA static/ semi-static) work best.

The climber then connects one or two TRS devices to the climbing-line. Or, in the case of a two-rope system, the climber connects a secondary device to the safety-line.

If the climber falls, they will be checked by their primary TRS device. If this device fails, the climber's fall will then be checked by their secondary device. In the absence of a secondary device, the climber will have to depend on some form of catastrophe-knot.

If the soloist cannot climb unassisted to the top, they will either climb the rope or rappel back to the ground.

Margin Call

One contentious aspect of TRS, a subject full of contention, is the name itself. Firstly, is a 'top rope' actually being employed, or is it actually a 'fixed rope'? Next, is the climber climbing solo? When someone rappels or climbs a rope, are they climbing solo? No, they're climbing a rope or rappelling. Also, the term 'solo' is perhaps a form of stolen valour, plus it can easily lead to confusion with LRS or lead rope soloing, which is dangerous. In the UK, a common term used for this was 'Self Lining,' which was very appropriate, as you're by yourself, and you're climbing a fixed-line. Another term was 'Shunting,' but that's outdated, although a climber does sort of 'shunt' up the rope if they're not skilled. If I had my way, this form of climbing would be labelled as 'Fixed Rope Climbing' or FRC. But my intention with this book was not to engage in a war of semantics with every climber on the planet, each of whom will have their own view on the subject, but rather to make peace with a contentious part of climbing.

Is it safe?

Climbing, like Formula One racing or bullfighting, is not a safe sport. Well-tested climbing systems with multiple layers of redundancy can be - and are - compromised by human error and sometimes plain bad luck.

The one advantage, and disadvantage, of solo climbing is that it only involves one person, so the errors can either be reduced by at least fifty percent – or doubled.

There are also Black Swan events that can afflict an unlucky soloist, in which unprecedented catastrophic failure occurs. It is for this reason that the soloist employs multiple layers of redundancy and back-up so that all their eggs are not in the same basket.

TRS climbing should be viewed as potentially more dangerous than lead or traditional top rope climbing due to its increased complexity and reliance on a chain of life-supporting elements. These include ropes, devices, and their systematic integration.

What level of skill do I need?

TRS requires a climber to understand all the fundamentals, such as knots, anchors, placing protection, rappelling, and general cliff safety.

Anyone who can set up traditional top rope anchors or rappels should be able to rig up a TRS system. But are they safe to climb on?

Many climbers lack knowledge in rope climbing (jumaring) techniques, which form the core of TRS. Rope climbing is not a common climbing skill unless the climber is a caver, big wall climber, arborist or industrial rope access technician. So investing time in developing and practicing such skills is an important step.

Next, novice climbers may lack self-rescue skills, like transferring from a loaded TRS device to a descender. This might sound easy, but the key is not to die doing it when it goes wrong.

Next comes the climber's route-finding and route-choosing experience: being able to pick the correct and safe routes to TRS. This will take time, but the routes a novice climber would wish to tackle, such as slabs and direct features, tend to be ideal for TRS.

Melding skill and experience are what really counts. The theory is no match for reality, which is always far more sweaty, brutal, and scary. If a climber finds themselves out of their depth, then move back to shallow waters. Novice climbers should not rush it. They should nail the basics before the basics nail them.

TRS versus lead rope soloing

One of the primary drivers for writing a book on Top Rope Soloing (TRS) was the urge to update my lead rope soloing book, "Me, Myself & I," in 2021. I had written MY&I in 2014, focusing mainly on solo lead climbing multi-pitch routes and big walls, with just one paragraph touching on TRS for training. That paragraph simply suggested learning to lead solo while using a TRS system, which I described involving a single Petzl Micro Traxion. This approach was standard for climbers in 2014 but not in 2021.

During the rewrite of the book, I thought it necessary to expand this paragraph into a larger section, a full review of TRS and how to do it safely. Unfortunately, the more I wrote, the more complex the subject became. More importantly, there were multiple points at which lead and top rope soloing diverged, with one contradicting the other. While both involved ropes, solo climbers, and rock, they were often fundamentally and dangerously incompatible. Both subjects needed their own independent manuals.

Lead rope soloing requires a totally different approach and understanding compared to TRS, and mixing them up could lead to a tragic outcome. Nevertheless, I view TRS as a good entry into lead soloing, as both demand a very high degree of skill, problem-solving, pre-emption, and equipment proficiency.

TRS sucks

Although some climbers just love TRS for its own sake, enjoying the low risk solitude, most rightly view it more as a means to an end. Climbing is not meant to be a solitary activity, but a sport built around camaraderie, competition, shared ambitions, shared experiences, and — not wanting to sound like a hippy — witnessing each others journey of growth. Or, its opposite, i.e. taking the piss out of each other.

So, master TRS, but don't become too anti-social, and end up neglecting the things that make climbing what climbing is.

Fig.09

Safety

 09

Since TRS is typically a solitary endeavour, many climbers first encounter the technique while watching videos of their climbing heroes head-pointing state-of-the-art climbs. If you're the strongest climber in the world, you might assume that you're also the best, right? That the methods they use are the best ones? However, the techniques on display often break many of the fundamental rules of "staying alive" covered in this book. For instance, using only one device, relying on thin climbing ropes, and having a general "it'll be alright" approach to one's safety. Most of the time, things go as planned, but the top climbers tend not to share the times when they don't. And, unfortunately, those occasions when things don't go as planned are more frequent than one might think.

Rather than tuck this away at the back, I thought I'd lay down some safety basics first, as the number one reason for writing this book, and for climbers to read it, is to be safe.

Failure Points

One feature of this book is the concept of failure points, which are basically the things that can jeopardise a climber. Each section of the book will feature numerous sections on failure points, and these should be studied very carefully; generally, they've been written in blood.

Below is an example of how even the most benign action, like clipping an ascender into a belay loop, may have several failure points:

- The locker is cross-loaded between the ascender and the belay loop.
- The locker has not been locked shut.
- The karabiners nose is hooked onto the ascender rather than clipped into it.
- The ascender is not correctly aligned, inhibiting its ability to lock onto the rope.
- The ascender is upside down.
- The ascender frame is fractured.
- The jaw on the ascender is dirty and stiff, iced up, or its teeth are worn or damaged, potentially leading to failure.
- The rope and jaw are not set correctly, with the safety catch not fully engaged.
- The rope is too thin for the device.
- The locker is not clipped into the belay loop but rather the leg retention tab, racking loop, or leg loop.
- The ascender is a cheap sweatshop eBay imitation. It may look like a life supporting device for bottomless caves and the biggest walls, but really, it's only for cosplay.
- Everything is actually solid and safe; only the climber forgot to fasten their harness.

Of course, in real life, the number of failure points when climbing is almost limitless. So, climbers should constantly check for potential failure points to keep them at bay. Making this a ritual will ingrain the practice into a life-saving habit. The immediate consequence of a failure point can range from comical to tragic. We tell funny story about the former but can die from the latter, but both are lessons that will inform others, either because we look foolish, or because we're dead.

Mistakes are inevitable, regardless of a climber's skill level. This book aims to cultivate thinking strategies on TRS systems to identify critical failure points and reduce the common risks where fatal mistakes are known to occur.

Two-point Rule

The most crucial rule to follow when using any rope technique at height, be it top rope soloing, rappelling, or roped climbing, is the two-point rule, an iron law that's written in blood. Much of the traditional TRS technique breaks this law, and I hope this book will change that. Therefore, I'm establishing the two-point rule as the foundation of this book.

The rule is simple, meaning it's impossible to forget, even when terrified. The only excuses for not following the rule are cutting corners, laziness, or negligence.

When suspended from a rope, the climber must maintain no fewer than two connection points.

These points can consist of karabiners, knots, rope devices, and friction hitches, each designed to keep the climber connected to their life-support umbilical: the rope. This rule applies to rope climbing, rappelling, hanging belays, anchors and self-rescue, but not to lead climbing, as the climber will often only have one connection when tied into the lead rope. A climber using a double rope system would not break the rule, which is why a double rope system is much safer (in my opinion).

Cliff Safety

Due to their geological formation, such as erosion, glaciation, weathering or faulting, the top of a cliff, crag or wall can be a risky place to work. Loose rock, dirt, grit or sand tend to abound, often set at an angle that will funnel any fall over the edge. And so a climber should never become too complacent when working on the edge of significant drops.

Complacency is one of the primary culprits in climbing accidents and no one should ever be "not afraid" of heights, as it's not about an irrational fear of heights, but a rational fear of their consequence. I know individuals who have slipped on gravel to their deaths, tripped over ropes, even been blown over the edge by a gust of wind, and none were afraid of anything.

Margin Call

Anyone who undertakes a high-risk activity like climbing must embrace the concept of self-agency: your capacity to make decisions and act independently of others. It's okay to refer to what has been learned or instructed, the rules of the game, the laws of the land, and nature, but the buck stops with you. Don't make dangerous, blind choices and blame others when they don't work out; instead, think for yourself and act in your— and others'— best interest. The worst indictment of someone who makes a high-risk mistake is "I just didn't think," which generally means they didn't think for themselves but instead acted like a brainless robot. Sticking to what others may do will keep you safe, but sometimes it might kill you. You're your own judge and jury, but reality passes the sentence. Another key to self-agency is also taking responsibility for your actions; don't blame others for your mistakes, as that way, you'll never learn anything and will just keep making mistakes.

Bravado, or a fragile ego, or the fear of looking "too safety conscious" is also a potential killer, but no one looks more foolish than someone careless enough than to fall off the top of a cliff. Always balance out how you feel about things now, with how you'd feel waiting for the mountain rescue team to arrive and shovel you up.

Rather than a climber inching towards the edge to build an anchor, pulling on tree roots and slipping and sliding on stone ball bearings, it's safer to set an anchor away from the edge, connect to the rope, and then establish a secondary solid re-anchor, either at the edge or on the face, rather than searching hazardously for something sturdy. This higher anchor also means a climber can remain secure while de-rigging the lower one.

Really, cliff safety is about starting out being slow and ultra safe, and slowly, over time, stripping it back until one is on the right side of no-longer safe, which is safe enough.

Pre-flight Check

With no one to conduct buddy checks or spot critical errors, the climber must establish a routine when climbing alone. This routine should include the following points:

- Check for the rope running over abrasive edges, but best practice is always to pad the rope or edge every time.

- Ensure the climbing-line runs directly to the anchor and isn't caught on a ledge, flakes or bushes. This can be verified in several ways, but walking back from the climb while holding the rope's end should confirm that it leads to the top. Note that climbers should only have life-supporting ropes connected to life-supporting top anchors hanging down the climb, and nothing else. Disconnected ropes are a pathway to a disconnected future. If a rope isn't be used, coil it up or stick it in a rope bag.

- The climber must carry the necessary equipment to escape the system, including a belay device, hitch cords, and lockers.

- Always visually check that all connectors are done up, devices are locked shut and correctly oriented, and the rope(s) are directed properly.

- Fully weight both TRS devices before climbing. This checks the device's orientation, ensures connectors are secure, and verifies that the rope is correctly rigged.

- While fully weighting the rope, ensure that the rope's weight is set above ground level.

| ## Take it Slow

A lack of respect for climbing, substituting cool complacency for level-headed diligence and relying on positive thinking instead of healthy paranoia, is a quick path to disaster. Moving up and down a climbing-line is relatively simple as long as climbers don't cut corners. They should stick to safe working practices and understand that adhering to safety protocols doesn't hinder progress but can make things more efficient. If a climber wishes to grasp what "slow" truly means, they should visit a spinal injuries ward.

Where it becomes risky is in the transitions, like escaping from the system, rappelling from the anchor, and especially starting from the ground. It's in these moments mistakes often happen, as the climber might not be fully engaged.

To prevent costly mistakes, deliberately move at a measured pace. Think more, observe more, and remember that every action, no matter how minor, has a consequence. Ensure it's a positive one. A bomb disposal approach is recommended: don't rush, avoid panic, steer clear of carelessness, and simply do what's necessary to complete the task safely.

Suspension syndrome

A potentially fatal result of hanging in ones harness for too long, as might happen if a climber is left hanging in space on an overhanging climb, and fails to self-rescue, is suspension syndrome. How long does it take? A climber can fall unconscious with 15 to 45 minutes, and once unconscious, cardiac arrest can take place soon after. An unconscious climber might also be asphyxiated by a neck cord, or die of exposure.

Suspension syndrome is not fully understood, but involves an imbalance in blood flow to the legs. A hanging climber's leg loops do not restrict blood flow from the heart, which travels via the arteries down the front on the leg, but they do compress the veins at the back of the legs, which move blood back to the heart. This imbalance, and pooling of blood in the legs, can lead to rapid onset unconsciousness and death. Both high and low temperatures can exacerbate this issue.

The only real way to overcome this issue is not to become a victim of it, which means having both the equipment and skill to climb the rope and escape the hang. This includes both carrying the tools to resolve this, as well as a back-up plan in case you drop them. If a climber does become trapped on the rope, and must wait for help (or death), keeping the blood flow moving in both legs is key, so leg lifts, bicycling, or flips and brief inverting can all help to keep the blood flowing until rescued.

🖉 10

Suspension syndrome (also known as suspension trauma and harness hang syndrome) is well-known in industrial rope access but not in climbing, even though it has been the cause of many deaths, including rappelling accidents and crevasse falls. A climber with a basic level of skill in technical rope systems should be able to avoid this condition by employing simple rope climbing techniques to regain the anchor long before the risk of suspension syndrome arises. The real danger occurs when an inexperienced climber becomes stuck on the rope while attempting to escape the system or gets entangled with a catastrophe-knot or a jammed back-up hitch while rappelling. The primary cause of such issues is often a lack of essential tools such as friction cords, slings, and ascenders to address a minor problem before it escalates into a life-threatening situation.

🖉 11

Understanding how the harness leg loops can impact blood flow to and from the heart is crucial in preventing suspension syndrome. Once you grasp this concept, you can take appropriate action if you find yourself trapped in such a situation.

🖉 12

Keeping the blood flowing is critical to avoiding suspension syndrome. There are several ways to achieve this, but the essential principle is to keep moving until rescue arrives.

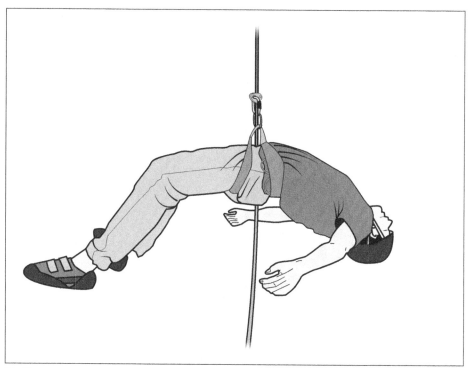

Fig.10

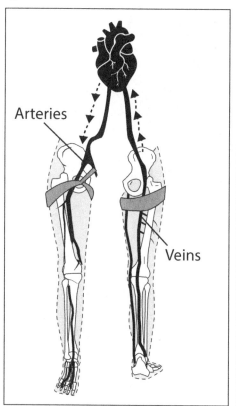

Arteries

Veins

Fig.11

Fig.12

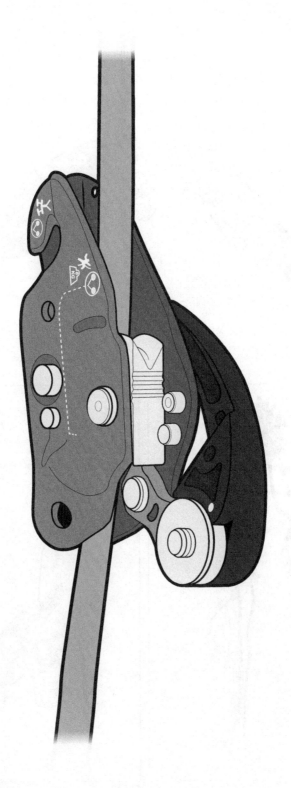

Fig.13

DEVICES

 13
Taz LOV3

Margin Call

The first TRS device I bought – in fact, the first climbing device I ever bought – was a Petzl Shunt. I was on the dole at the time, living on £24 a week, so it was a big deal. I'd hitchhiked 80 miles from the squat I was living in, out to a village climbing shop, nestled below a gritstone crag. The idea was to buy the Shunt, then head up the hill to top-rope some classics. I vividly remember going into the shop, where the Shunt was on the wall display, the assistant getting it down, me handing over the cash, and holding it in my hands for the first time. Gathering my stuff, I marched up to the hill to the crag, excited for a week of top-rope solo, or at least until I had to 'sign on' again. Upon arriving at the base of the crag, with all my gear on my back — tent, sleeping bag, etc.— I dumped it all out on the ground, only to realize, to my dismay, that I had forgotten to bring my rope.

If you've ever perused climbing forums and sought out threads about TRS, it quickly becomes evident that climbers are deeply fixated on finding the perfect TRS device, then enthusiastically sharing their discovery with others. In such discussions, accompanied by arguments and sometimes heated exchanges typical of online forums, there is often no consideration given to the individual's experience and skill level. Instead, you'll encounter a stream of declarations that Device X is the ultimate TRS tool, while Device Y is sub par.

In these conversations, there is often little analysis of why Device X is deemed superior to Device Y, or how the advantages of one may inadvertently expose the user to unforeseen risks. Ironically, the device that appears to be less feature-rich is often the safer choice, while those that provide a heightened sense of freedom in climbing can do so at the expense of safety, almost resembling free soloing.

It's crucial to recognize that no TRS device operates in isolation from the user's skill, experience, and overall climbing knowledge, and the systems that bring it all together.

In this section of the book, I will delve into what the perfect device would have to do; the mechanics of the primary TRS devices that climbers may encounter in their quest for the perfect tool; and end by focusing on a few devices that demand extra attention for both commendable and concerning reasons within the context of TRS.

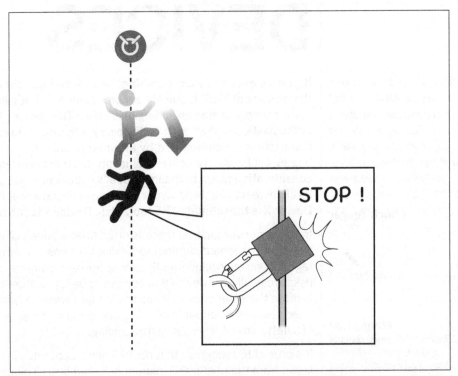

Fig. 14

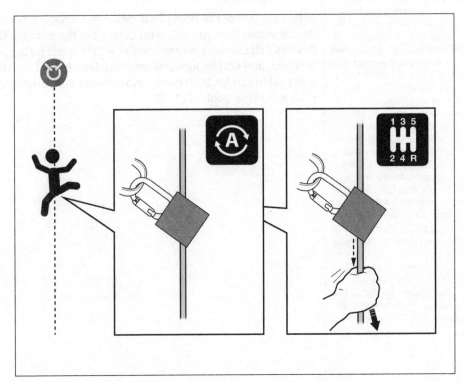

Fig. 15

The Perfect Device

"The real problem is not whether machines think, but whether men do."

B. F. Skinner

 14

The No. 1 job of a TRS device is to safeguard the climber's life.

 15

The ideal device is one that travels along the rope without needing assistance from the climber, known as self-tending. So you either have devices with automatic drive, or manual.

Free soloing is as far as one can get from being gear-dependent. Beyond chalk bag and rock boots, the climber just steps off the deck and climbs. Top rope soloing, however, is not like free soloing; it's all about the systems. So much so that until a solid TRS system is developed, the climber will feel in service to the system rather than the other way around. But believe me, it gets better.

So let's start with the trickiest item on the TRS equipment list, the top rope solo device.

TRS techniques employ a matrix of important elements shared with traditional climbing systems: ropes, anchors, back-ups, escape systems etc. But in TRS, the keystone piece is the device employed to keep the climber safe, saving their ass in a fall.

In an ideal world, such an important device would be designed, manufactured, and tested for TRS, stocked on a shelf, bought, the in-depth instructions studied, and then used with total safe certainty. Unfortunately, this is not the case.

No one has designed, manufactured, or tested such a device, and few would stock them if they did. Instead, manufacturers make rope tools that align or overlap with the top rope soloists, but not specifically for it. This creates a moral dilemma and endless online debate, touching on legality, redress, blowback and responsibility; what is the best tool, and what if someone kills themselves using it?

Some of the solutions offered by manufacturers, who can see the demand, are filtered via their legal teams, producing solutions that are one hundred percent safe for the company to recommend but only halfway to being a practical solution.

Then there are the solutions, both old and new, shared by climbers, both expert and novice, in which there is the opposite issue: one hundred percent function, but only halfway safe.

What is to be done?
I myself have tended to go down this latter route in the past, both employing and recommending the systems I was taught at the beginning of my own climbing life, the Petzl Shunt, which had served me and others well, at least most of the time. But times change, and now I take a different view. Give it another few years, and that view will have changed again.

16
The greater the lag in locking, the greater the risk of panic grabbing.

 17
In order to avoid rope damage, a TRS device must have a grabbing action that dissipates the energy of the falling climber. This is generally achieved by having the device slip rather than squeeze the rope to death.

But fundamentally, there are no TRS devices that should be recommended by me or anyone else, only devices that a skilful and careful climber chooses to use.

Fundamentally, any device a climber might use for TRS will void its warranty on being used as a TRS device.

Before looking for the best device on the market, it's vital to know what such a device would look like. Here's my wish list. Note that several points that counteract each other:

■ **Life-supporting** ⊠05
Safeguard the user if they fall while climbing. This may seem like a no-brainer and the number one reason for employing such a device. Still, people often see this feature as less critical than others.

The perfect device will have a zero failure rate, meaning it catches the climber every time, meaning it's a high-quality, fully functioning mechanical device. For example, a 5 mm Auto-block will do the job most of the time, but what would be the failure rate over a thousand falls, and what would the consequence be of that failure?

Zero failure is only approachable when a device is used correctly, manufacturer's instructions followed, and is in perfect working order. Of course, zero failure is an ideal, not a certainty, and a one-in-a-million failure is always a possibility, or one in a hundred if human error is included. **This is why the focus of this book is on a system, not the device, the system designed to soak up terminal failure.**

What is important is that a solid and confident working relationship is established with the device, as a TRS climber who feels their asshole pucker up each time they fall is not going to be a TRS climber for long (which may be a good thing).

■ **Self-tending** ⊠06
Allow the climber to move upwards on the rope without requiring manual feeding, snagging, or undue friction. This is vital for many reasons, the obvious being that it simply allows the climber to use both hands to climb. A device that needs the rope to be constantly pulled through and that keeps sticking is not conducive to climbing mindfulness. Remember, the device should give the impression that the climber is free soloing (only without the downfall of dying) not harassed by it, and pissed off.

■ **Instant Lock** ⊠07
The device grabs the rope with minimal lag. This is important in establishing confidence in a device, as undue lag can

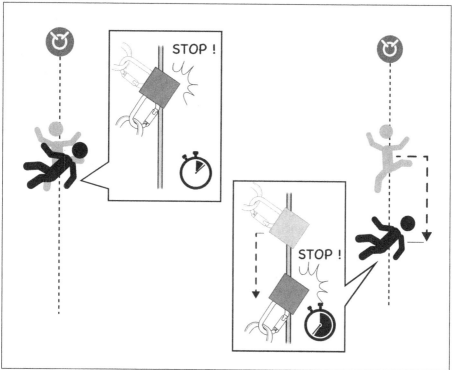

Fig.16

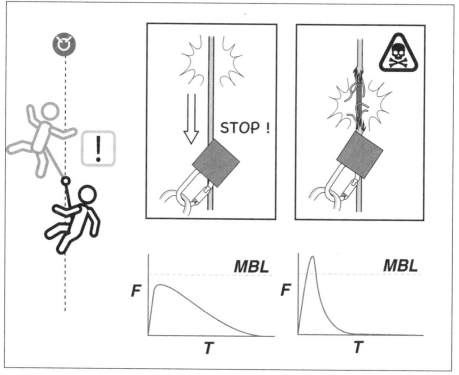

Fig.17

18
The ability to manoeuvre a device up and down can be important, but note that doing so could lead to a panic grab failure.

 19
A dead man's handle is designed to stop a train if the driver lets go. However, with a TRS device, grabbing hold in panic can cause the device to fail to lock at all, which only further intensifies the panic grip.

 20
The ideal device is one that moves up and down the rope with ease until it is fully weighted. This is crucial on pitches that involve some level of traversing.

make climbers panic-grab the device or rope. What affects lag is the way the device is designed to engage the rope, such as how much it rotates before locking, with some devices requiring zero rotation, while others, a hundred and eighty degrees. Another factor is the time needed to overcome a sprung action, one reason why some climbers disable the spring in their assisted breaking devices. Another lag comes from the travel of a connector in a belay loop, which is why a chest sling is often used. The downside of reduced lag is the device engages the moment the climber reverses their upward progress, which can be very restrictive and is a good example of competing priorities.

■ **Factor-2 Proof** ☒ 08
Designed to withstand a catastrophic factor 2 fall without breaking the device or cutting the rope. This is important because sooner or later, the climber is going to make a mistake. Luckily, all the devices here are tested for this kind of eventuality.

■ **Reverse Gear** ☒ 09
Can the device go backwards? Sometimes a climber will want to disengage the device's jaw with one hand in order to reverse and climb down a little. Devices with smooth jaws make this easy, not so with toothed jaws that need a bit more practice. Note, this short-term device disabling can be very dangerous if using a single device, as a fall while disabling the jaw could lead to a ground fall, as a reversing of the 'deadman's handle' can come into effect, where in a panic the climber does not let go of the jaw.

■ **Panic-Proof** ☒ 10
The device will engage even if grabbed by the climber in panic, either before or after loading. A vital feature if the climber wants to avoid 'panic-grabbing' failure or increased lag when the climber retards the action of the device by grabbing at the rope. This also includes capture by the thighs or armpits.

■ **Rope-path**
The ideal device has a rope pathway that incurs minimal friction, so straight through the device with no angles or deviations. This is a key point to why many devices work well, while others do not, especially ABDs.

■ **Bidirectional** ☒ 11
It only grabs the rope when the climber fully weights the device. Beyond safety, this is one of the most important features of a perfect device. A sprung ascender, especially one using an eccentric jaw featuring teeth, is designed to only

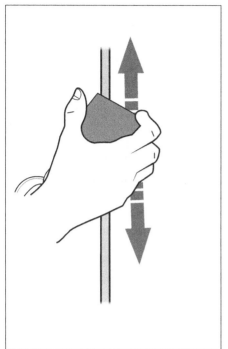

Fig. 18

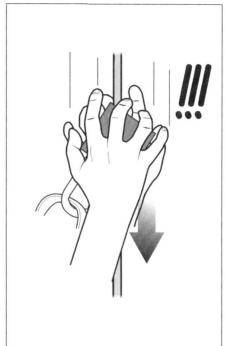

Fig. 19

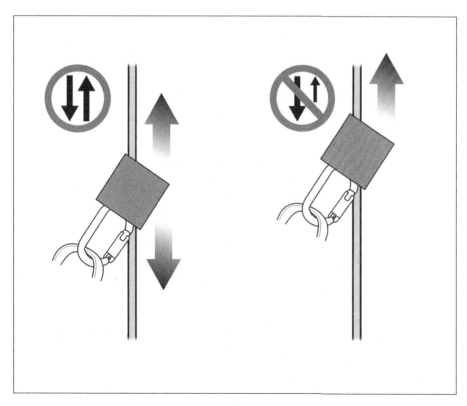

Fig. 20

21
Often overlooked, many devices will fail to lock if pressed down from above or may unlock if pressed. This is vital for the safe use of two devices.

 22
Having a device that functions as both an ascender and descender is a big ask. It introduces another potential failure mode, but nevertheless, having such a feature makes escape much easier.

 23
All TRS devices should function as effective ascenders.

travel in one direction, up the rope, so unidirectional. The moment the grab attempts to reverse direction, even by one millimetre, the jaw will lock down on the rope like a Rottweiler, only letting go when either the sheath or device breaks.

This is obviously an advantage when it comes to rope climbing, as the grab can be moved up the rope effortlessly yet locks down instantly, with almost no loss of height caused by a lag or jaw creep. This makes this style of device the most efficient form of the progress capture device but also perhaps the worst for TRS if the climber wants unconstrained freedom.

An unweighted unsprung device, one that features a smooth jaw face, such as a rocker-arm device, will usually be able to move up and down a rope, making it bidirectional. But it only grabs the rope when the device is fully loaded. This makes this ascender less efficient as a progress capture device, as there is always a tiny delay in locking, but the payoff is it gives the climber greater freedom to move, as well as an ideal self-trailing device on the safety-line.

■ **Press proof** ⊠12
The device will engage or remain engaged when pressed down from above. The ideal device will grab the rope, or continue to grab when being struck or weighted by another device.

■ **Descender** ⊠13
Have the dual function of being both an ascender and a descender. Allows a climber the option of rappelling down without needing to go into self-rescue mode. Although a tough ask, some devices may achieve this functionality, but it's generally at the cost of more critical functions.

■ **Rope Ascender** ⊠14
Function as an effective ascender. Important for self-rescue, as very often it's easier to ascend the rope to the anchor rather than transfer from ascent to descent.

■ **Locked-In** ⊠15
Capture the rope fully, locking it in place so that it's impossible to escape the device accidentally. Most ascenders are designed to allow the rope to be inserted and removed easily, as this is vital for transitioning to and from a rope, especially when cleaning gear or passing re-anchors. The downside of this is that in many designs, the rope is only kept in check by the action of the sprung jaw and a safety catch. Accidents do happen in which the rope escapes the device. Some devices, notably lever arm and rocker-arm devices, tend to lock the rope in place by a jaw that is fully secured within the body of the device, meaning the rope cannot escape.

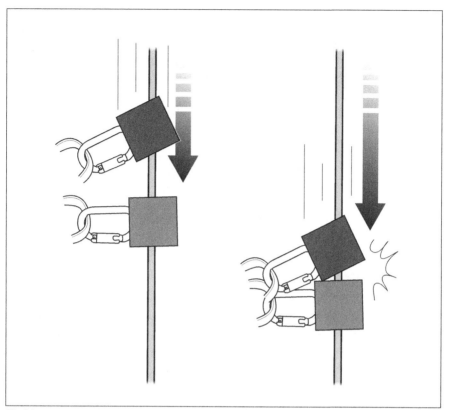

Fig.21

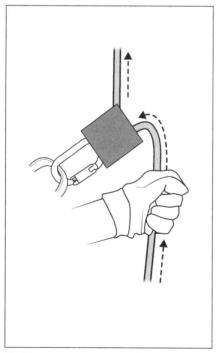

Fig.22

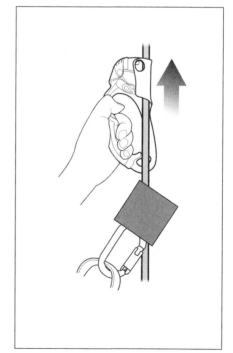

Fig.23

24
The ideal device is locked onto the rope in such a way that it's impossible for the rope to escape.

 25
It's very easy to fumble and drop a TRS device when escaping the system, so having some form of idiot loop helps to avoid this.

 26
A TRS device has a hard life, so make sure it's built to endure.

 27
A TRS device may well last a lifetime, but in that lifetime, a climber might go through a mountain of ropes, from thin to thick and from low-stretch to dynamic. It's best if a device works well on all of them.

■ Undroppable ☒ 16
The device should be able to detach from the rope with one hand while remaining attached to the climber. Another big ask, but this functionality would make escaping the system much easier, and without fear of dropping the device.

■ Multi-rope diameter compatible ☒ 17
The device should run smoothly and lock effectively on the widest range of rope types and diameters. Having a 'sweet-spot' diameter is not ideal, as even a 'perfect' rope's diameter and characteristics can change over time.

■ Robust ☒ 18
Rope running parts should resist wear, so stainless steel rather than alloy. This is important for heavy users, as worn-down parts can radically reduce the safety margins of a device.

■ Neglect-Proof
The device should have no moving parts or springs, so it requires no care or lubrication and will work under any conditions. An impossible ask, as even an ill-treated AK-47 will eventually jam.

■ Size & profile
Won't get in the way. On vertical terrain, the climber will usually keep their hips close to the rock, which can result in the TRS device scraping and scratching as they climb. Small, low-profile devices such as micro eccentric ascenders will conform much more to the climber's profile and body compared to larger, chunkier devices such as the Taz Lov3. This is one reason micro progress capture pulleys are popular, as they just interfere less with the rock.

■ Simple
Less is more. If the perfect TRS device was overly complex, then that perfection would be undermined by potential human error, and a more straightforward, lesser device, maybe more perfect for that reason. The device's mechanics, its orientation on the rope, and how it connects to the harness must all be easily understood. Devices with hard-to-translate markings, multiple clip-in points, or alien mechanics should be avoided. This is not to say that a climber expects idiot-proof devices, but rather, some devices make even the skilful into idiots.

Is there a winner?
Do any of the possible TRS devices get full marks? No. Some devices get a better score than others, but no device is perfect. The skill of the TRS climber is knowing what compromises they're willing to make.

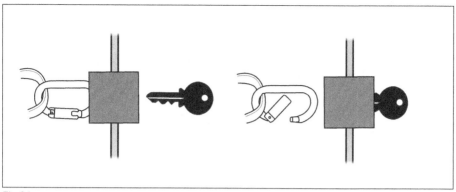

Fig.24

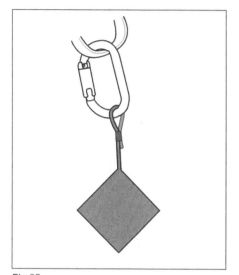

Fig.25

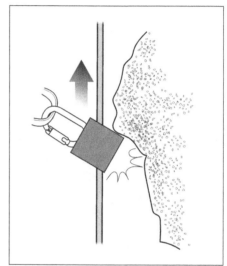

Fig.26

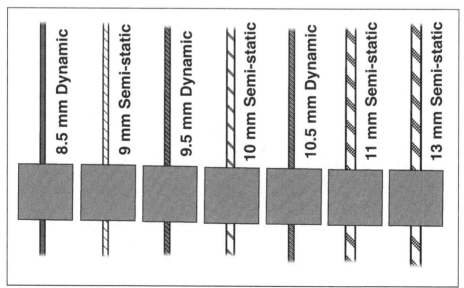

Fig.27

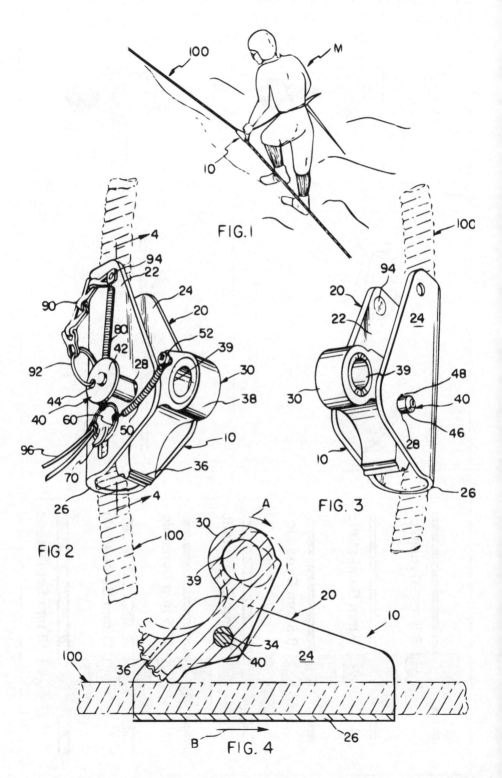

FIG.1

FIG 2

FIG. 3

FIG. 4

Fig.28

MECHANICS

 28

Peter E. Gibbs 1979 patent.

Margin Call

Although I'd climbed tens of thousands of meters of rope on 'Jumars', used progress capture pulleys to haul an equal distance, and employed various self-belay devices, I never really gave much thought to how they worked. To me, they were all the jam. However, as time passed and I faced different walls, I began to discover that some devices worked better when the rope was thick with ice, or they slipped rather than chew your rope, or moved equally smoothly both up and down the rope until you weighted them. This learning process helped me stop looking at all devices as being the same, but rather that each belonged to a subspecies of that generic 'Jumar' (Ropus Climbus); each was unique, with both strengths and weaknesses.

All devices used for TRS can be considered ascenders, but not all ascend a rope in the same way. So rather than begin with specific devices, and compare them, it's more beneficial - and the core of safe solo climbing - to understand the mechanics under the hood of the devices on offer.

Failure Points

In the following pages, I will discuss the failure point of each device mechanism, as well as specific devices, but it's vital to understand that all devices are complex mini machines, made up of moving parts; if those parts are blocked or impeded from movement, they will not work. It's also important to understand that once a device is employed outside of its intended mode of use, unforeseen failure points can often appear, and a device used for TRS is immediately voiding its warranty.

Modifications

When writing this book, I had to consider whether to include modified devices and techniques involving cutting, drilling, or altering a device to improve its performance for TRS. In the end, I decided not to explore this topic.

The first reason is that I believe there are already plenty of devices available on the market that work exceptionally well for TRS, making modifications unnecessary. While one may come across individuals on forums claiming to have drilled or cut their devices to create the ultimate TRS tool, the truth is that most climbers wouldn't trust such modified devices. They would opt for reliable, off-the-shelf options they can trust.

Secondly, climbers are already using these devices in ways that deviate from their original design, so pushing the boundaries further through modifications seems unnecessary and potentially risky. If a climber genuinely wishes to modify their device, they have the freedom to do so, and the internet is full of ideas and tutorials.

X mechanisms

Although I've covered all current mechanisms, future mechanisms, such as liquid metal nano-morphing, will no doubt appear the day after publication. Nevertheless, by careful study of the mechanisms and devices of today, a climber will better understand what comes tomorrow.

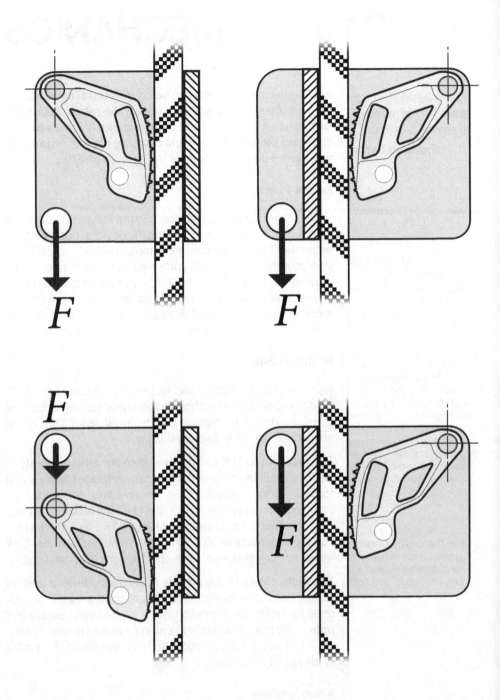

Fig.29

Eccentric

 29

An eccentric device operates using a rotating jaw, anvil, and frame. What needs to be understood is that, unlike some other mechanisms, an eccentric device can be loaded in multiple ways and the device will still lock.

Margin Call

As your brain absorbs all this technical information, with all the kiloNewtons here and safe working loads there, remember that these figures often don't align with the messy material world. Sometimes, devices will fail when they should not, or conversely, not fail when they should. I've seen people take high-factor falls on ascenders that did not damage the rope, while other times, a device will inexplicably fail to hold a rope. The numbers stamped on your gear are only a guide to potential outcomes, and only one set of numbers in a complex and multifaceted calculation that separates what breaks and could kill you, and what does not.

The eccentric mechanism represents the classic handled ascender, or jumar, used in climbing, caving, and industrial rope access. When someone thinks of an ascender, they are probably visualising one that uses an eccentric mechanism. The most widely adopted eccentric devices amongst climbers are micro or emergency ascenders, such as the **Wild Country Ropeman series, Kong Duck and Climbing Technology Rock N Lock**. They also form the rope-grabbing mechanism within progress capture pulleys, such as the **Petzl Micro and Nano Traxion**.

General Working Principle

An eccentric device works around a sprung spiked jaw that rotates on a high-strength axle fixed into a stamped or milled frame, the jaw activated through the frame. The rope is inserted in a curved channel in the frame and held in place by the jaw. When the user weights the device, the jaw, spikes, and spring combination grabs the rope. The jaw will not engage the rope when pushed upwards, only when it is reversed or weighted. The jaw spring maintains pressure on the rope so that it's always ready to grab. Without this spring, the jaw would not actively engage the rope. It would simply drop out of position, meaning the climber would have to press the jaw into place manually each time they moved. The spring keeps the jaw in contact with the rope unless a thumb or finger retracts it when reversing or cleaning a pitch.

The spring itself isn't strong enough to reliably get the jaw to fully engage the rope, so teeth, grooves or spikes in the jaw's face act as intermediaries: quickly biting into the rope before the camming action of the jaw engages. Once the jaw has engaged the rope, it will not let go. The higher the load on the device, the harder it grips.

This combination of the jaw, spring and teeth creates a very efficient rope-grabbing mechanism that eliminates slippage and instantly locks, making it a highly efficient progress capture tool.

Eccentric Frame types

Unlike most other TRS device types, eccentric devices come in many styles, each designed for a specific purpose.

30
Petzl handled ascender

31
CT Quick'Up

32
Petzl Croll S

33
CT Chest Ascender+

34
Camp Turbochest

Handled Ascender

The classic ascender, with the Petzl right and left the most widely adopted. Used either in pairs (left and right) or with a chest ascender, this style of rope climbing tool is perhaps the most efficient available.

Although a left-handed ascender can be used in a right hand, visa-versa, or as a chest ascender, when in the correct hand, it's easier to check both the rope and jaw position visually, and the thumb can be used to disengage the jaw for down climbing or operate the safety trigger to remove the device from the rope.

Examples

Petzl Ascension, Camp Turbohand, Kong Lift, Edelrid Hand Cruiser, Black Diamond Index, Grivel A1, CMI Small Ultrascender, ISC Professional, Singing Rock Lift, Trango Passport.

Chest ascender

A chest ascender operates in the same way as a handled ascender, only it lacks a handle, making it a more compact unit, able to sit comfortably between the belly button and sternum. More importantly, it has its connection points aligned to lie parallel to the body when set up correctly, whereas a handled ascender would sit perpendicularly.

A chest ascender is usually not attached via the belay loop, but rather a semi-circular connector (rapid-link or locker) clipped directly into the tie-in point, necessary for the device to lie flat against the body when weighted and unweighted.

The ascender is then connected to the upper body via a non-load-bearing chest harness, bungee cord, or sling. This keeps the device under tension, close to the body, and helps to lift the climber's centre of gravity to the sweet spot for rope climbing.

Once adjusted to suit the user, this is a very effective and efficient method of rope climbing when combined with a handled ascender, typically labelled as the 'Frog' system.

The position of the device, and its low profile, also reduce the risk of it knocking into terrain features, with the chest harness pulling the chest ascender up the rope (pulling the rope through a chest ascender is considered bad form).

If used as part of a TRS system, by having a handled ascender and foot loop ready, the climber can seamlessly switch to a 'Frog' rope climbing system anytime.

The drawback of using a chest ascender in a TRS system is that it can feel quite restrictive, mainly if one has not used a chest harness or strap before.

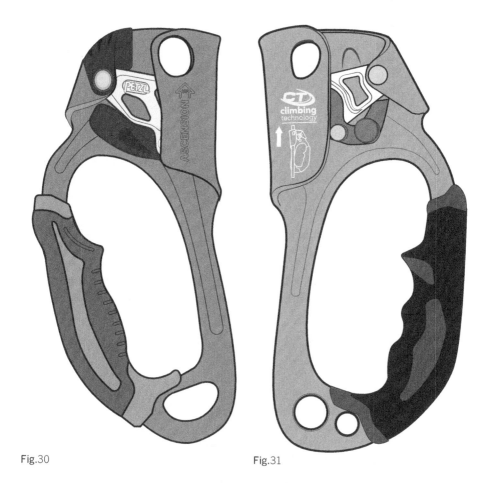

Fig.30   Fig.31

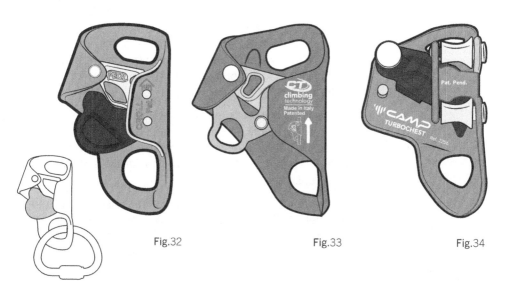

Fig.32   Fig.33   Fig.34

35
Petzl Basic

 36
Camp Solo 2

 37
CT Simple

 38
CT Roll N Lock Mk1

 39
CT Roll N Lock Mk2

 40
Kong Duck

 41
Ural-Alp Mouse

 42
Beal Tract Up

 43
WC Rope Man Mk1

 44
WC Rope Man Mk2

Examples

Petzl Croll, Camp Turbo Chest, Climbing Technology Chest Ascender +, Kong Cam Clean, Kong Futura Body, Edelrid Wind-Up, ISC Chest Ascender, Singing Rock Clean.

Non-Handled

This style of ascender is often mistaken as a chest ascender when it's just a handled ascender sans the handle. The difference between a chest ascender and a non-handled ascender is that the orientation of the attachment holes is perpendicular to the body, meaning it will not lie flat against the chest and is intended to be used by the hands.

The primary use of a non-handled ascender is a lightweight, low-bulk alternative to a handled ascender, with the hand grasping the device's body or wrapped over the top rather than a handle. These qualities make a non-handled ascender an ideal foot ascender for escaping the climbing-line.

Examples

Petzl Basic, Camp Solo 2, Climbing Technology Simple, Kong Modular.

Micro

This style of emergency ascender began with the Wild Country Ropeman, giving the climber a very compact and lightweight tool for ascending ropes, hauling, and general progress capture.

The most significant difference between the micro and most full-size eccentric devices is that they typically feature swinging side plates, meaning the rope is captured within the device and locked in place by its connector; a significant advantage in terms of safety but also a disadvantage, as it's much harder to remove from the rope; one reason why micro ascenders are best fitted with some form of a clip-in loop. Otherwise, they'll get dropped.

One issue with micro ascenders, such as the Ropeman Mk1, is that they are only designed for larger-diameter ropes (10 mm+) due to the aggressive teeth causing the device to fail minimum strength tests on thin ropes, so devices must match the correct rope.

I've also found that using large diameter round bar 12 mm karabiners, with very thick ropes, can lead to the rope interfacng with the smooth non caming part of the jaw, resulting in slipping or total failure to grab. Note, these devices are not tested using every style, shape and size of connector, meaning it's down to the climber to establish a bombproof device/connector combination they have tested and trust.

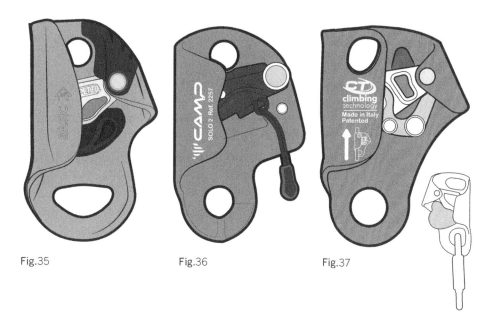

Fig.35   Fig.36   Fig.37

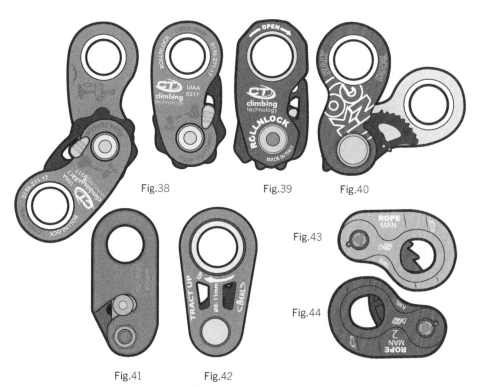

Fig.38   Fig.39   Fig.40

Fig.43

Fig.44

Fig.41   Fig.42

🖊 45
Petzl Mini Traxion

🖊 46
Petzl Micro Traxion

🖊 47
Petzl Nano Traxion

🖊 48
Ural-Alp Ti Fixing Block

🖊 49
Edelrid Spoc

🖊 50
Camp Turboblock

Margin Call

While hauling a 100+ kilo load through your progress capture pulley may make you feel as if you're going to die, in reality, I've only come close to getting killed by my micro PCP twice (that I noticed). The first instance occurred while rope soloing a run-out free pitch on El Cap's Pacific Ocean Wall, and the second happened during a life-or-death haul on the last pitch of the Nose in a winter storm. In both cases, the problem was caused by the jaw, either unlocking itself from its retaining catch or locking, so on when I wanted it off or off when I wanted it on. On both occasions, I worked it out, but each micro problem turned a high-risk situation into a near-terminal one. Was PCP to blame? Not really, as you cannot create micro-devices with all the functionality of industrial-sized devices. Instead, what you need is a higher degree of skill and experience with such a device, which, on both occasions, I probably lacked.

Examples

Wild Country Ropeman, Kong Duck, Climbing Technology Roll N Lock, Beal Tract Up.

Progress Capture Pulley (PCP)

Most progress capture pulleys work around an eccentric jaw built into the frame of the pulley and are popular amongst climbers of all types, making them a very common TRS device.

The drawback with small PCPs is that the jaw is generally tiny compared to an ascender, meaning it cannot handle large loads. It's not the limit of the pulley but the jaw.

Secondly, and more importantly, the fact that the rope is secured in place via rotating side plates means no safety trigger is included in these designs, with the Micro Traxion having a 'lock-off' catch instead, which allows the pulley to run in both directions. This feature enables the jaw to be locked off the rope via a catch, allowing the pulley to be bidirectional, which is essential when lowering. This feature can lead to a hazardous failure point in which the jaw is unintentionally locked back, meaning the climber is no longer belayed (if they fall, it won't catch them). Lock-back failure can happen in countless ways, but this is one reason I would not use just a single PCP. Perhaps due to this issue, the Nano Traxion has this feature removed.

Examples

Petzl Pro, Micro, Mini, Nano and Micro Traxion, Edelrid Spoc, Camp Turbolock.

Hybrid

The future will see an increasing number of hybrid devices that work as an ascender, pulley, rope clamp/pulley or PCP, that will sit somewhere between a handless ascender and micro ascender.

Example

Climbing Technology CRIC.

Design features

Safety Trigger

Almost all full-size eccentric devices feature some form of sprung safety trigger or catch fitted into the jaw. When the safety trigger is engaged, it only gives the jaw enough travel to progress up or down the rope. When engaged, it blocks the jaw from rotating to its full extent, which is necessary if the device has to quickly connect or disconnect from the rope.

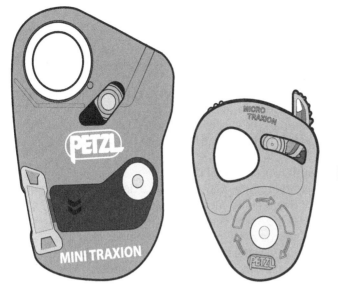

Fig.45

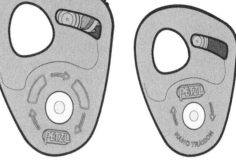

Fig.46

Fig.47

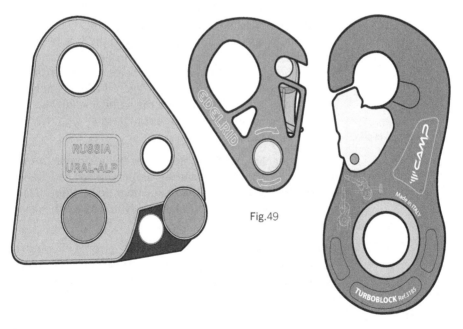

Fig.48

Fig.49

Fig.50

51

When placing a karabiner in the top hole of an ascender, it's vital to ensure the rope is captured by the karabiner. Failure to do so can easily result in the rope escaping the device.

52

The ability to use the top hole of a device as the primary connection point is vital for use in TRS, as the lower hole (standard attachment point) will not allow the device to run correctly on the rope. Rather than be lifting by the connector, the device will be levered upwards, causing the frame and jaw to jam on the rope. The problem is that it's often unclear whether a device is designed to be used in this manner (top connection point), with many manufacturers neither confirming that it's dangerous nor safe to do so. I suspect this is due to there being no CE test for this important design feature. Generally, a device that features a top clip-in point that wraps around both sides of the rope, so that the karabiner passes through two clip points either side of the rope, rather than a single point, appears to be safe to use. It should also be noted that a large diameter karabiner used in this configuration, when used with a large diameter rope (11 mm+), can lead to increased friction depending on the design of the device.

Note that the safety trigger is not designed to resist high forces, only being tested to 0.4 kN (400 kg), meaning that triggers can break if the device is misused, potentially leading to the rope escaping.

Primary Attachment point

The frames of most full-size, handless, and chest ascenders feature two clip-in points, one at the bottom and one at the top of the frame. The lower hole is the default attachment point to connect to the climber's harness or via a lanyard.

Secondary attachment point

The head or upper clip-in hole in a device has several uses and, if declared as such, can be used as the primary clip-in point for life support, placing the load above the jaw (note, this is not the case for non-eccentric devices). Manufacturers often leave the ability to load the head hole as undefined. As a rule of thumb, check that the connector passes through two clip-in holes, not just one, blocking the rope as it does so. A device with only one head clip-in point cannot guarantee balanced loading; this may result in twisting, inversion, or blocking the jaw or safety trigger from functioning correctly. If in doubt, follow the manufacturer's instructions.

This upper hole is often labelled as a safety or back-up point, with the user clipping a connector through this to secure the rope and act as a secondary back-up to the safety trigger. This back-up connector must pass through the frame and around the rope, capturing it, which helps to reduce dangerous loads on the jaw and safety trigger. If there is only one clip-in point, this cannot assure the same level of security, plus a catastrophe-knot could easily pass straight through the connector in a fall.

If the upper clip-in points can be used as the primary attachment point, the device can be employed for self-tailing, allowing the device to follow the climber up the rope. This is not the case with lower clip-in points, which cause the device to pivot and jam.

One very dangerous – let's say lethal – error is clipping the rope outside of the back-up connector, which not only reduces the smooth progress of the ascender but can also lead to the jaw and trigger failing, generally due to the trigger not locking fully when clipped back into the rope. When the climber re-weights the device, it will then pop off the rope.

The upper hole is also used to locate a positioning strap, which is best threaded directly through the hole; some models feature an oval slot for this purpose.

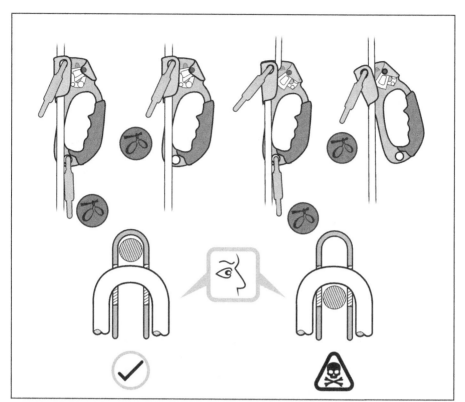

Fig.51

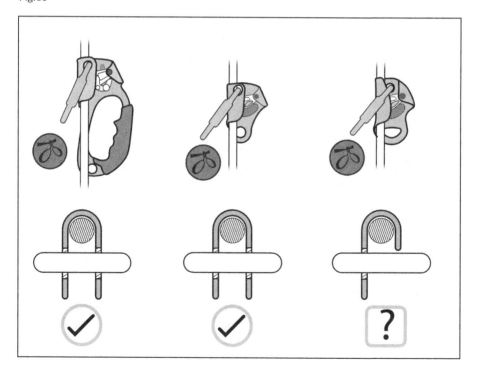

Fig.52

devices
/mechanics
/eccentric

 53
An eccentric device should not be shock-loaded because the jaw mechanics can damage the rope. This means never allowing dead loops to form above the device or getting into any position that will create a fall factor greater than 0.

✏ 54
No eccentric device should ever be extended away from the climber unless using a shock absorbing lanyard.

Margin Call
One crucial lesson learned early when using eccentric devices is to never, under any circumstances, forcefully jam the device against a knot in the rope or hard against another device. The rationale behind this caution is related to the jaw's operation, as the device requires a slight forward movement before the jaw can retract. If the device is unable to move forward, it will also be unable to move backward, making it nearly impossible to retract the jaw. You're bound to find yourself stuck in such a situation at least once in life, but at least you'll grasp the purpose of this warning and avoid repeating the mistake.

It should be noted that in extremis, it is also possible to clip directly into the handle of an ascender, giving almost unlimited clip-in room. This can be a lifesaver, but it also falls outside any strength testing and could create dangerous loads if abused.

Failure Points

The most important thing to grasp is that an eccentric jaw will not slip but will keep biting the rope until either the sheath disintegrates or the device breaks. This is not a problem if the device is used within its design parameters, which is a very conservative 100 kg or body weight, but any load over 400kg will damage the rope. Such a low safe working load may appear dangerous, but this is simply the cost of having the most efficient device possible, and the correct technique should avoid hazardous loading.

Most eccentric ascenders allow the rope to be clipped in and out quickly once the safety trigger is retracted, meaning the rope is not fully captured by the device. This is vital when passing protection or re-anchors, where the device can be removed one-handed with practice, but it can also pose a risk. One failure point is when a climber wants to gain some slack, perhaps when they're attempting to step back down, and in fiddling with the safety trigger, they allow the rope to escape the device.

There is also a risk that the jaw itself could be pulled away by a finger or foreign object at the moment of a fall, disabling it. It is also vital that the user is fully competent on the device, as many climbers have died of improper use of eccentric ascenders, generally due to failure to fully lock the device back onto a rope while passing gear.

The function of teeth or spikes is often mistaken as offering security on icy or muddy ropes, but as explained above, they are a key part of the mechanical process of rope traction. This means that mud and ice, or missing teeth, will reduce the device's security and could cause the device to slip, skip, or fail to grab. This is a warning to anyone who thinks the teeth will provide some extra safety margin for winter TRS because a jaw gummed up with ice will be more dangerous than a device that works via a smooth jaw.

The alloy frame of devices is very robust but not indestructible. Devices dropped from a great height that becomes bent or twisted or just worn out should be sent to the great rack in the sky.

Fig.53

Fig.54

55

The safest TRS system would be one that features two eccentric devices. This is not to suggest that this would be the best system, just the safest.

Margin Call

A valuable lesson in soloing big walls is realizing that when something isn't working, nine times out of ten, it's you, not the equipment, that's the issue. Getting angry and frustrated with a mechanical device, cursing its designer, the manufacturer, the shop that sold it to you, or the person who recommended it in a book is unproductive. It's more constructive to channel that negative energy, which won't solve anything, inward. Ask yourself, "Do I need to spend more time understanding how this works?" or "Maybe I'm using it incorrectly?" Often, misplaced anger signals a need to pause, take deep breaths, and shift from assigning blame to seeking solutions and perhaps finding compromises. What you're attempting isn't inherently difficult, but it's also not effortless. Achieving success requires practice, care, and attention. So, relax, reset, and try again.

Suitability for TRS

Pros

- Self-tending.
- The jaw will grab the rope when any downward movement is made or the device is weighted, establishing a high degree of dependability and confidence.
- It is hard to panic-grab an eccentric device as the jaw/rope interface is generally shrouded.
- The jaw will grab if the frame is loaded in any way, so pulled on, pressed down upon, twisted.
- Requires just a light weight on the rope for smooth running.
- Intuitive to use.
- Works safely on ropes between 8 to 13 mm.

Cons

- Aggressive to the rope, and can cause damage in a factor 1+ fall, or a force between 4 kN to 6 kN.
- The device needs to be well maintained, as the reliability of the eccentric action depends on a well-lubricated jaw and trigger, spring strength, and good teeth profile.
- The climber cannot reverse direction unless they disengage the jaw.
- Some ascenders do not fully capture the rope, meaning the rope can escape.

Conclusion & Personal Reflections

When it comes to TRS, which is fundamentally a form of rope climbing, but one where the device is not meant to be weighted, the eccentric design is the ideal starting point, being safe, reliable and effective. For the novice TR solo-ist, employing a PCP and a handled ascender or two micro ascenders would allow them safe and efficient climbing.

The primary drawback of the eccentric design is that it's uni-directional, which can feel restrictive, creating the impression of being harried or rushed by the system.

Apparent low intrinsic strength and potential rope damage if overloaded, should not be a factor if used correctly and the climber employs back-ups. The strengths of the eccentric design are its reliability, its resistance to panic-grabbing, and that it will not release when pressed down on from above. This makes the design ideal as a stand-alone TRS device, a second-ary back-up on a one-rope system, and a great starting point for the novice wishing to learn top rope soloing.

Fig.55

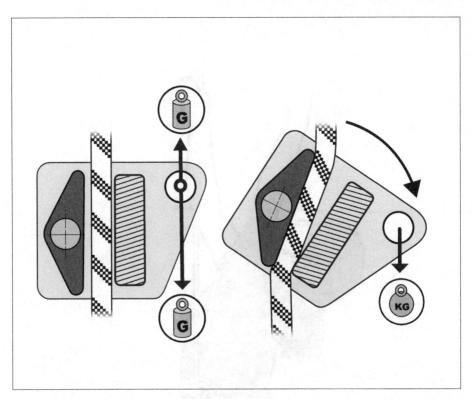

Fig.56

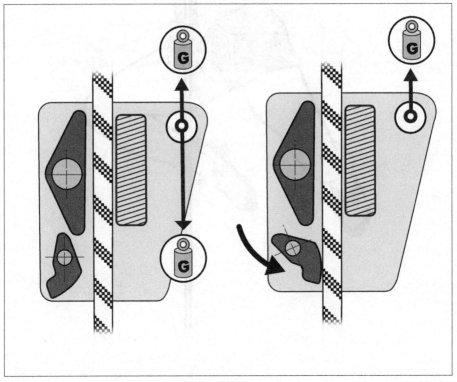

Fig.57

Rocker-Arm

 56

The rocker-arm mechanism operates using a rotating rocking jaw, a fixed anvil, and the frame they're integrated into, which encloses the rope. This creates a unique rope grabbing system that moves up and down the rope smoothly until enough force is applied for the frame to rotate and lock.

 57

Some devices feature a small catch that increases the friction on the rope, transitioning the device from free-running to fixed in place. This is essential if a rocker-arm is to be used as a rope positioning tool where the operator wants the device to maintain its position on the rope.

Invented by Russian climber Victor Kozlov in 1975, this design radically departed from Western eccentric devices established by Petzl and Jumar, offering some unique functionality for high-end users. Manufactured by Ural-Alp, these devices appeared in the West in the 90s, after the Soviet Union broke apart, with the design proving an 'inspiration' to several Western manufacturers.

The Welsh company, International Safety Components (ISC), set up by Denny Moorhouse of DMM fame, produced a version called the "Rocker" for Troll and Yates, promoting them in the industrial rope access market as a replacement for the Petzl Shunt.

General Working Principle

The rocker-arm mechanism is built around two primary components: the rocker jaw, and anvil, both milled from steel and fixed between two alloy side plates, which form the frame of the device; one plate is mobile, allowing it to be swung open to take a rope. The rocker jaw rotates around a steel axle but is blocked from full rotation by the anvil, which is fixed in place.

The rope is inserted between the rocker jaw and the anvil, the frame closed and locked shut, either via a sprung button or secured by its primary karabiner, meaning once locked shut, the rope cannot escape.

When the frame is weighted, it begins to rotate, and as it does, the rope starts to leverage the rocker jaw's top edge, which forces the lower edge to pin the rope against the anvil. But, when the rocker-arm is unweighted, the rocker jaw becomes passive, allowing the rope to pass freely within the device, making it bidirectional.

One way to visualise the rocker mechanism is like the portcullis in a castle, it allows free entry and exit, but at the first sign of danger, it slams shut. This ability to move up and down a rope without assistance is both self-trailing and bidirectional.

The rocker-arm mechanism is less affected by ice or muddy ropes, and I've used this style of ascender on icy ropes that would have been impossible to climb with eccentric ascenders.

Unlike an eccentric device, which will begin to damage the rope at between 4 kN to 6 kN, the lack of teeth or spikes, and overall mechanics of operation, result in a device that will

✎ 58
ISC Rocker Mark 1

✎ 59
ISC Rocker Mark 2

✎ 60
DMM Buddy

✎ 61
Ural-Alp Super-Droplet

✎ 62
Camp Lift

✎ 63
Grand Wall uAscend

Margin Call

Before I climbed El Cap with my 13-year-old daughter, I was asked to film at a local quarry, set up a portaledge, etc. On the day, I clipped my rope into a GriGri, clipped it onto my daughter's harness, and sat her at the bottom while I climbed halfway up the route to set up a belay for a portaledge. When it came time for her to follow me, she couldn't work out how to unclip the GriGri from her harness due to using a triple lock karabiner. A rigger came over to help her and, after a pause, asked me if I knew I'd threaded the GriGri the wrong way around. I must have threaded that GriGri a thousand times, but this time, I did it wrong. This story demonstrates both how fallible a climber can be and how easy it is to simply do something you've done countless times and should be free of error, arse-about-tit. This is why it's essential to always test a device before you trust your life to it and never become complacent.

eventually slip on the rope rather than damage or even cut it. The slippage point varies due to the diameter of the rope but will take place between 4 kN and 6 kN, with the device locking again once the load has dissipated.

Unlike an eccentric mechanism, a rocker-arm device requires an initial shock to lock, which means there is a potential for a device not to lock if a climber is falling but not fully weighting the device. This can happen on low-angled ground or if the climber has grabbed the rope.

Examples

DMM Buddy, Taz Lov2, Taz Lov3, Ural Alp Basic, Camp Lift, Camp Goblin, Kong Back-Up, Grand Wall uAscend, ISC Rocker, ISC RED, Yates Rocker, Troll Rocker, SAR Rocker, Singing Rock Locker, Vertical Kaplya.

Design features

Positioning jaw or cleat

Although there are several advantages to having a free-running bidirectional rope tool, one that only grabs the rope when weighted, there are also some drawbacks. Sometimes, a climber will want a device to hold its position on the rope to ensure it stays where they placed it, effectively converting it into a unidirectional tool. In rope access, this is done for positioning purposes, fixing the device on a rope to create an anchor point for a lanyard, much like a handhold.

Switching a rocker-arm device into positioning mode is achieved using a cleat or micro jaw. Once engaged, it grips the rope with just enough force to prevent the device from slipping. When positioning is no longer needed, the cleat can be easily disengaged from the rope.

This function also primes the device to grab and reduces the lag time before it engages with the rope. For TRS, this feature is generally only used on the safety-line, allowing the climber to raise the device level or above them. This reduces any potential fall factor if the primary device fails at a tricky spot. It also offers a psychological boost akin to top-rope confidence, perhaps when navigating around a roof, enabling the climber to move the device above the obstacle before tackling it.

When used as a primary TRS device, this feature can help build confidence in rocker-arm devices, which might be intimidating initially, making them perform more like a unidirectional eccentric device.

Fig.58

Fig.59

Fig.60

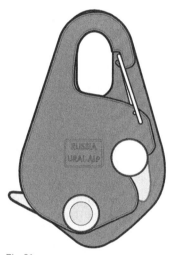

Fig.61

Fig.62

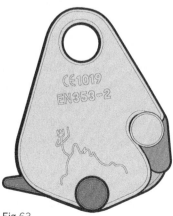

Fig.63

devices
/mechanics
/rocker-arm

✎ 64
Camp Goblin

✎ 65
Kong Back-up

✎ 66
Taz Lov3

Margin Call

I once spent a few weeks on the West Face of the Dru during winter. The weather remained harsh throughout except for the last day. Being West-facing, it received a bit more exposure to the limited sunlight. Consequently, our ropes gradually became icy, accelerated by climbing and rappelling on snow-covered ropes, causing the snow to melt and freeze. My partner used eccentric ascenders that would skitter and slip on the icy ropes, with the teeth struggling to grip. On the other hand, I had a set of Ushba-handled ascenders with a radical rocker arm mechanism. These devices flawlessly ascended any rope, no matter how icy. However, were they superior? No. On dry ropes, they were slower and less efficient than eccentric ascenders and were trickier to clip on and off when cleaning a pitch. So, they weren't better, just different, as is often the case with all devices.

Failure Points

Exotic and non-conventional designs often come with a cost, and rocker-arm devices are no exception. For every advantage over the standard eccentric mechanism, there's a significant disadvantage.

Firstly, the frame must be free to rotate and remain rotated to function. If the device is prevented from rotating or forced back to a passive position, it won't grip the rope. This can happen for a variety of reasons: panic-grabbing it before it can lock, it being trapped between the body and rock, or by a body part (such as the armpit, elbow, or between the legs).

If the rope is grabbed above the device, this may also prevent the device from gripping. It deprives the rocker jaw of the necessary primer to rotate. In such a scenario, a panicking climber might hold onto the rope and try to get the device to lock, but it won't lock as long as they're holding the rope. The worst-case scenario here is the climber grabbing the rocker-arm device in an attempt to make it lock, potentially causing it to fail to lock when fully weighted.

It's essential for the rocker-arm jaw to rotate as smoothly as possible. Some designs feature a spring-loaded rocker jaw to reduce grab lag. If the rocker jaw is clogged with dirt, causing it to be slow and stiff, or if the spring has lost its tension, failure is possible. Such failure might occur when there's not enough leverage on the top edge of the rocker jaw to engage it. This risk is compounded if using a rope thinner than recommended, specifically under 10.5 mm or 10 mm. While most rocker-arm devices are tested on 10.5 mm ropes, some are rated for 10 mm ropes. The best rope to use with a rocker-arm device is a sturdy low-stretch one, as it activates the rocker jaw more efficiently and, being low-stretch, compresses less when pinned. The least ideal rope would be a 9 mm dynamic rope, which is too thin, too smooth, and too stretchy for reliable use. If it's the only rope available, then it's better to use eccentric devices. The worst outcome in this failure scenario would be the climber falling to the rope's bottom, but often, something might jolt the rocker jaw into action. The extent of the fall, in that case, would be unpredictable.

Unlike other designs, the rocker-arm device needs a flexible and unweighted rope for optimal performance. If a substantial weight is hung from the rope, it might prevent the device from engaging. Only a light line weight is necessary for the initial few meters of climbing until the rope's dead weight is sufficient. A 1 kg (e.g., a pair of approach shoes) should suffice. The only reason to use a heavier line weight is if the device has a robust spring, which is generally best avoided!

Fig.64

Fig.65

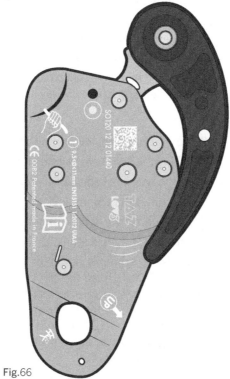

Fig.66

67

With any rocker-arm device, the connector is always positioned higher than the rocker-arm mechanism, as this allows the device to rotate when weighted. This arrangement might seem unusual to climbers accustomed to traditional ascenders, but if the connector is set in a low position, the device will not function properly.

 68

The rocker-arm mechanism will fail to function if the device is stopped from rotating. For example, if the climber is holding onto the device when they fall, the device may fall with the climber.

 69

The correct function of the rocker-arm requires its connector be free to move.

Due to its unconventional and bidirectional mechanism, a rocker-jaw device carries a heightened risk of pilot error, like the device being placed upside-down. It might seem functional, with the rocker jaw providing some grip even when inverted, but it will fail to lock under full load. Besides closely observing the stamped orientation markings, a helpful guideline is that the device's connector should be positioned high to act as leverage for the rocker-arm action. If it's at the bottom, like an eccentric device, then it's upside-down. Conducting a test hang before climbing is advised for this very reason.

When used as a back-up on the safety-line, the lanyard should be dynamic and limited to 60 cm in length to reduce the shock load on both the rocker-arm device and the climber.

Suitability for TRS

Pros

- Self tending.
- Straight rope path.
- Bidirectional.
- Locks in the rope.
- Works on both the climbing and safety-line.
- Slips rather than damages the rope.
- A minimum of moving parts.
- Less affected by icy or dirty ropes.
- Compact and low profile.
- Second and third generation models can be switched from rope positioning to free by way of a catch or cam.

Cons

- Panic-grabbing the device may disable it.
- Grabbing the live rope may stop it from functioning.
- It may be possible to disable if pressed down from above.
- Less intuitive than other devices.
- Correct function is dependent on spring strength.
- Maintenance of the spring and rocker jaw is necessary.
- Rockers are primarily made for industrial users, and so most models are been designed for, and work best with, industrial ropes. This means that most rocker-arm devices work best with 10mm or larger low-stretch ropes. Using sub 10 mm (or 10.5 mm with some models) dynamic climbing ropes may see a rocker-arm either slip under load, or fail to grab at all.

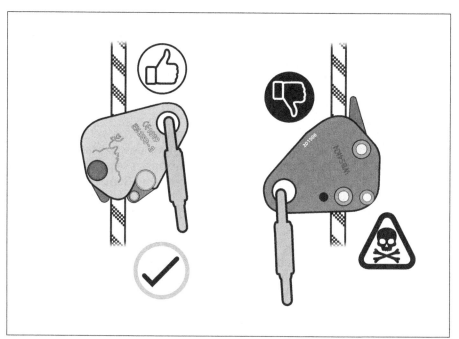

Fig.67

Fig.68

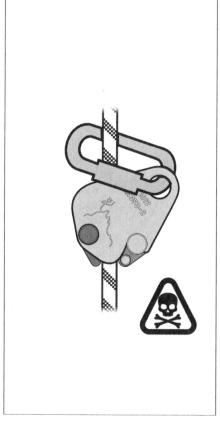

Fig.69

70

Pay close attention to how a rocker-arm device is set up the first few times it is used, and always test that it's set the correct way up and is locking.

71

One of the significant benefits of the rocker-arm mechanism is that it will slip at around 4kN rather than damage the rope. This means rocker-arm devices have become popular as fall protectors in rope access. For TRS this translates as providing a level of protection for error, mistake and f**k-up lacking in eccentric devices.

Conclusion & Personal Reflections

If one were to view the eccentric mechanism as the hardware equivalent of fish and chips, the rocker-arm mechanism would be akin to a Japanese puffer fish: a great delicacy in the hands of someone knowledgeable but potentially lethal for the uninformed.

A complication with rocker-arm devices is that individuals who have undergone their TRS apprenticeship using an eccentric device and have mastered the basics might assume the failure points of a device like the Camp Goblin are the same as a Petzl Croll. They aren't. If climbers grab the rope above the device, or the device itself, or stack it below an upper device that fails, crashing onto the Goblin, they risk device failure. This underscores the importance of discarding preconceived notions about eccentric devices and learning to use a rocker-arm device from scratch (literally).

Given their unreliability, climbers should never depend solely on a single rocker-arm device; it should always be paired with a back-up device. This could be a second rocker-arm device in a two-rope system or layered above an eccentric device (this arrangement sacrifices its bidirectional properties, but safety is paramount).

Climbers should avoid using two rocker devices on the same rope unless they are certain that neither device will interfere with the other during ascent or in a fall. If the devices collide, the upper, failing device could render the lower one ineffective.

The rocker-arm mechanism's bidirectionality allows climbers unimpeded movement, facilitating both upward and downward progression along the climbing-line. It doesn't hinder the user and will lock during a fall, making it an excellent secondary device on a safety-line. It mirrors the utility rope access workers find in fall arresters. When placed on the safety-line, the device should operate seamlessly during climbing, emergency exits, or rappelling.

The above pros and cons might suggest that the disadvantages overshadow the benefits, labelling rocker-arm devices as one of the riskiest designs for TRS. Regrettably, this is true if one assumes they can handle a rocker device like any other ascender. However, once a climber masters the rocker-arm mechanism, understanding its nuances and limitations, it arguably becomes the best design for TRS.

To reiterate, a rocker device is not recommended for novice climbers, but experienced climbers how have the skill and experience to gain the most from these innovative and robust devices.

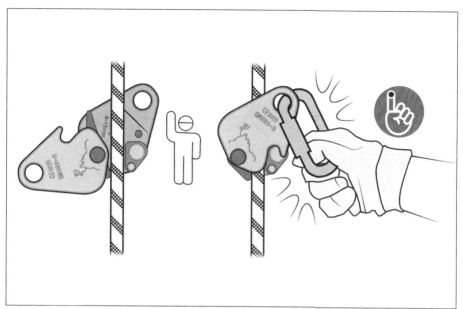

Fig.70

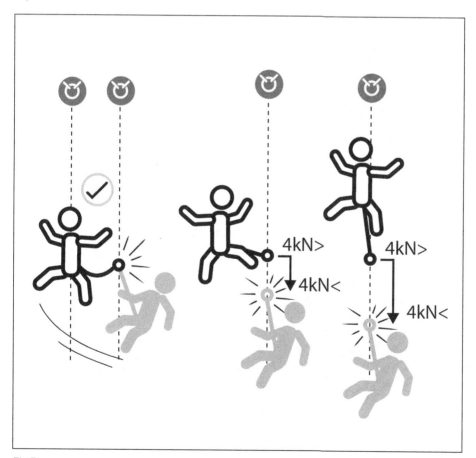

Fig.71

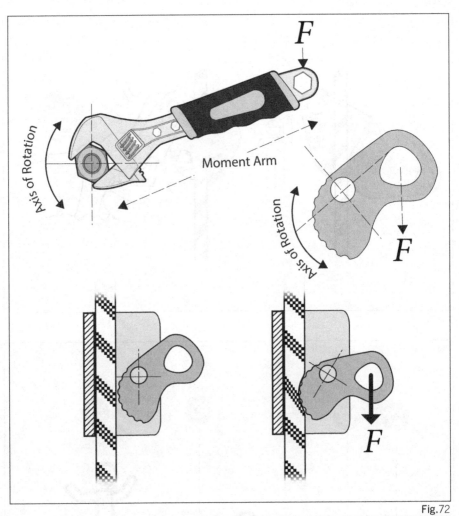

Fig.72

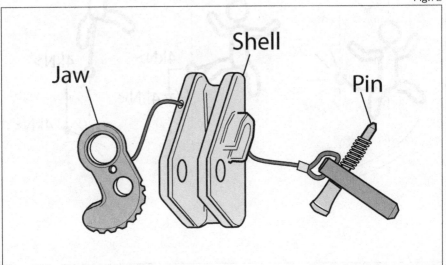

Fig.73

Lever

"Noli turbare circulos meos!"
Archimedes

 72
Levers in action.

✎ 73
A lever action device is made up of three main parts, the jaw (or cam), the axle pin, and the shell.

Margin Call
I failed my physics exam, so I've never been hot at all the technical stuff of forces, fulcrums and levers. But I've always loved how when you use a lever action device, you clip directly into this big solid piece of metal shaped into a jaw. The jaws are usually milled out of a solid lump of aluminium or steel, making an eccentric jaw appear positively fragile and puny. Best of all, the shell and pin are also equally stout, and when it comes to rope minding, I always feel happier having a lever device babysit a heavily loaded rope versus an eccentric device. As with all gear, there are pros and cons to the lever action, but the highest strength, matched to the function of slipping rather than cutting a rope, is pretty hard to beat.

Lever devices operate using a much simpler mechanism than eccentric devices. If one were to draw an engine analogy, lever devices could be compared to two-stroke engines and the eccentric devices to four-stroke engines. Both achieve the same end — progress — but the lever device does so with less engineering complexity.

General Working Principle

Unlike frame-loaded, sprung, toothy, eccentrics, lever devices function by having the load applied directly through the jaw. The frame, or shell, merely provides the jaw with a point of leverage via a removable steel axle pin, and serves as a trapping point for the rope.

Since the jaw is directly loaded, there's no need for a spring or teeth. This design offers several advantages, including enhanced overall strength, the ability to sustain shock loads, being gentler on the rope, and manual bi-directionality — it's easy to move both up and down the rope by hand.

However, there are drawbacks to this design, including its weight, cost, and a slightly steeper learning curve compared to devices like the eccentric-handled ascender. Although it was relatively popular in its early days, the design's prominence has diminished over time, now mainly seen in the rope access and rescue market. Professionals in these fields value the design's capability to handle significant loads safely, opting to slip at 4 kN rather than causing damage to the rope.

<u>Examples</u>

Gibbs Rescue, SMC Grip, Petzl Rescucender, CMI Ropewalker, Petzl Shunt, S-TEC - Duck R, CMC Ascender.

Failure Points

Like all devices, there's a risk of attaching it upside-down. Always adhere to the instructions stamped on the side and conduct a test hang before use.

If the climber panics and grabs the device before it has a chance to engage with the rope, this could lead to failure as both the device and the climber would be falling at the same rate. Similarly, if the climber grabs the rope above the device before it can lock, it reduces the weight on the jaw, potentially

🖊 74
Petzl Microcender

🖊 75
ISC Mini Rope Grab

🖊 76
Petzl Rescucender

🖊 77
SMC Grip

🖊 78
Petzl Shunt

🖊 79
Gibbs Rescue

🖊 80
S-TEC - Duck R

🖊 81
CMI Ropewalker

causing the device to not grip the rope properly. This can result in burnt hands, a long slide, or even a dangerous fall.

Another possible issue arises when another device presses down on the primary device. This can prevent the primary device from grabbing the rope or even cause it to lose its grip altogether.

If the climber presses the device against the rock with their body, this might stop the device from working, which might be a factor if sliding down slabby ground.

It's crucial to ensure that the axle pin is securely in place.

A unique failure point, discussed in more detail below, pertains to the Petzl Shunt. The rope can escape from this device, leading to complete detachment. This is mainly because the Shunt's axle pin is positioned outside the rope, which doesn't block the rope's pathway.

Suitability for TRS

Pros

- Self-tending.
- Easy to move down the rope due to the smooth jaw.
- The lack of teeth results in the device slipping before damage occurs, with a typical slip occurring around 4 kN and 6 kN. This means that if the device had to withstand a dynamic fall, it would slip rather than damage the sheath.
- Cannot be dropped, as the jaw stays connected to the climber when attaching or detaching it from the rope.
- The rope is fixed in place by the jaw and axle pin, meaning it cannot escape unless the pin is removed, resulting in a semi-permanent rope device.
- The overall strength of these devices is extremely high, with the jaw itself breaking at approximately 13 kN. Such a force would be impossible to achieve on an unknotted climbing-line.
- This overall strength comes from lever cam devices designed specifically for high industrial and rescue loads.
- Catastrophe-knots are more likely to be blocked by the device's shell than by eccentric devices.
- Less affected by dirty or icy ropes, making it a good choice for winter TRS.
- Intuitive and simple.
- Heavy-duty.

Fig.74

Fig.75

Fig.76

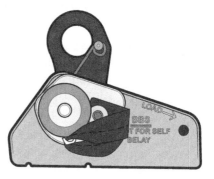

Fig.77

Fig.78

Fig.79

Fig.80

Fig.81

devices
/mechanics
/lever

 82

As the name implies, a lever-action mechanism requires the jaw to be levered against the rope. If the device is gripped, grabbed, or somehow impeded, the jaw will not lever, and the device will not lock.

 83

Rather than grab the whole device, get into the habit of pushing it up from below. This will help reduce the risk of panic grabbing.

 84

One of the major advantages of the lever mechanism is that it does not require a toothed jaw, which makes the device both rope-friendly and capable of sustaining high-factor falls. In any high-factor fall, instead of damaging the rope, the device will slip. This means a lever-action device can be safely used with a lanyard.

Cons

- There is more grab-lag with a lever device compared to an eccentric mechanism, which can be unnerving, increasing the risk of panic grabbing.

- Less ergonomic than some other devices.

- The device could be disabled if panic grabbed.

- Panic grabbing the live climbing-line can block the device from functioning.

- It can fail if weighted or depressed from above.

- Does not fit into a rope climbing system as easily (Texas style or Frog) as an eccentric device.

- Expensive and of limited use for other tasks.

- The connector needs to load the jaw in line with the shell and line, meaning it's important to eliminate any cross loading.

- Heavy for their size.

Conclusion & Personal Reflections

I've always been a big fan of lever action devices as they always feel extremely solid and sturdy, in fact one could call them industrial strength devices.

The lever action is very kind to ropes, which is why they have remained very popular in the rescue and industrial sector, where a user needs a device that is going to slip when overloaded, rather than break, or break the rope, which is also a nice thing to have in a TRS device.

Like the rocker-arm mechanism, these devices need a user who fully understands the pros and cons of the device, and understands they do not work like eccentric grabs. I view this kind of device as being a little like learning to parachute; the first time you wonder if it's going to work, "will the chute open?" or in this case, "will the device grab?", but on the hundredth jump, you don't even question it at all.

Unlike a rocker-arm, a lever device is far more intuitive.

Unfortunately, lever devices are more easily disabled due to panic grabbing or being depressed or top loaded, which makes them unsafe to use alone. They are best employed as one of the devices on a two-rope system or the upper device on a two-device, one-rope set-up. The most common set up is with a small lever action device set with a chest strap as the top device, and a small PCP set as the lower device.

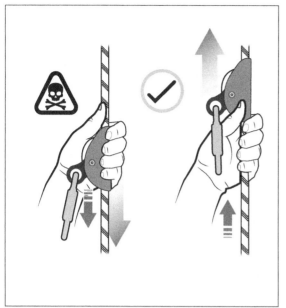

Fig.82

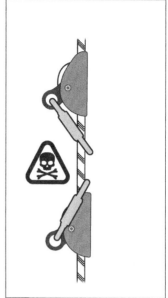

Fig.83

Fig.84

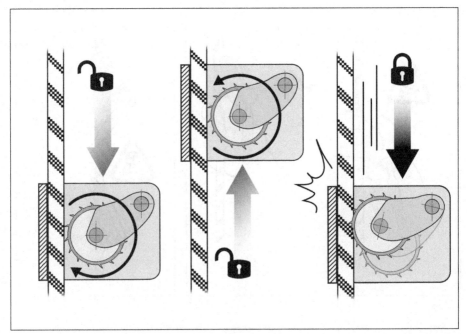

Fig.85

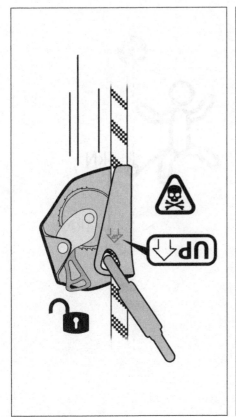

Fig.86

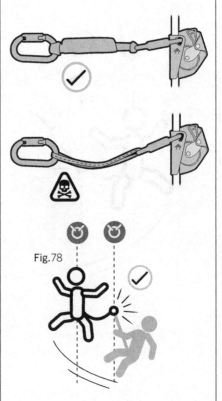

Fig.78

Fig.87

Inertia

"Nothing happens until something moves."

Albert Einstein

Although the inertia-locking brake uses a mechanism we use almost every day — the car seat belt — it has only recently become a noticeable mechanism for belay devices and fall arresters.

 85

There are multiple devices that utilize an inertial mechanism, but no two are exactly alike. The device that is of particular interest to TRS is the Petzl ASAP, which is illustrated here. Its mechanism operates as a hybrid between an eccentric action and a roller-locking inertia wheel. The device can move in both directions as long as the inertia wheel remains unlocked. However, once the specified locking speed is reached, the wheel locks, and the device then functions like an eccentric device.

General Working Principle

This style of rope tool features a bidirectional rotating drum around which the rope is passed or wrapped, allowing the rope to move freely in both directions. When the rope moves at a rapid rate, such as in a fall, the centrifugal force locks the drum, fixing it, resulting in the device turning from free flow to rope grab. How the rope is grabbed varies depending on the design, with some turning the action into something akin to an eccentric device (Petzl ASAP), cleat (Wild Country Revo), or locking knot (Rock Exotica Silent Partner).

<u>Examples</u>

Petzl ASAP, Petzl ASAP Lock, Petzl Neox, Wild Country Revo, Rock Exotica Silent Partner, Skylotec Gordon, Edelrid Fuze.

 86

One of the greatest risks associated with bidirectional devices is inadvertently attaching the device to the rope upside down. Always conduct a shock test before climbing to ensure proper orientation.

Failure Points

An inertial device is like a watch; it has many moving parts. If one part no longer functions as it should, it no longer functions. Unlike a watch, the results can be much more serious than not being able to tell the time. Reasons for a device to stop functioning include dirt and grime, ice and sub-zero temperatures, damage, and misuse or abuse. Unlike most other devices, where damage and wear are usually easy to spot, with all inertial devices, the working parts tend to be hidden, being a sealed unit.

 87

While the ASAP is considered one of the best fall protectors on the market, it must be used in conjunction with a shock-absorbing lanyard. Without it, the device won't slip when overloaded, but instead could damage the rope.

Suitability for TRS

Pros

- Bidirectional.
- Designed to eliminate panic grabbing.
- Self-tending.
- Cannot be disengaged by downward pressure from above once it grabs the rope.
- No grab lag.
- Designed as a dedicated fall arrestor on a safety-line.

devices
/mechanics
/inertia

88
Petzl ASAP.

89
Petzl ASAP LOCK.

90
Wild Country Revo.

91
Petzl Neox.

92
Edelrid Fuse.

93
Wren Silent Partner.

Cons

- Some models require manual feeding, like an ABD.
- May fail to grab the rope in slow, low shock falls, such as falls down slabs.
- May fail to lock if the live rope is grabbed before the device can engage.
- Being a non-standard design means it requires a greater level of skill to use safely.
- Most devices are not designed for high-impact forces (apart from Silent Partner) and suffer the same issues as eccentric devices.
- Require a shock absorbing sling or lanyard if a fall factor greater than 0 is expected.
- Bulky and expensive.
- May be affected by sub-zero temperatures.
- The device needs to be well-maintained, and retired if it shows signs of wear.

Conclusion & Personal Reflections

Inertial devices are innovative but complex, and no two devices are alike, mostly because they're designed for different uses. For example, the Wild Country Revo and Petzl Neox are designed as assisted breaking belay devices, while the Silent Partner is a dedicated lead solo device.

The Edelrid Fuse and Petzl ASAP would appear as ideal TRS devices, as they've been designed from scratch as fall protection devices for setting on a safety rope. But they are not primary rope devices, but back-ups. If used as intended on a safety-line, they make ideal secondary TRS devices.

In the industrial sector, the ASAP is not recommended for hard repetitive loading or constant falling, the reason being these devices are fundamentally eccentric mechanisms in sheep's clothing. In the industrial sector, if you keep falling onto your fall arrestor, you're doing something wrong, and this is the case also with TRS, and doing so will eventually wreck both the device and the ropes, but the ropes first. As a secondary device, it's best to view this style of device as a reserve parachute, a piece of ass-saving safety equipment not intended for heavy, day after day, jumping.

But what about as primary devices on the climbing-line?

Personally, so far, none of these devices have proven to be better overall than small, cheaper, and more functional device.

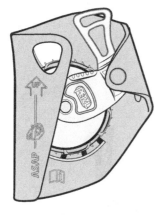

Fig.88

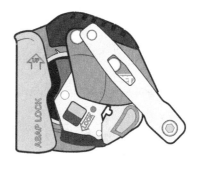

Fig.89

Fig.90

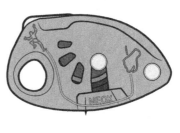

Fig.91

Fig.92

Fig.93

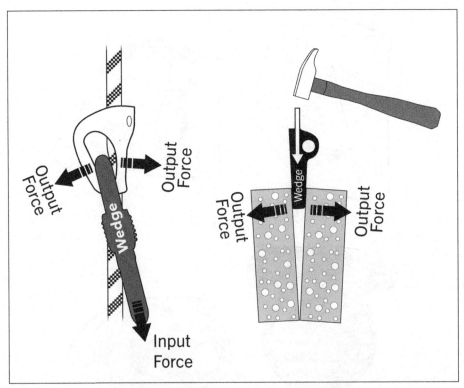

Fig.94

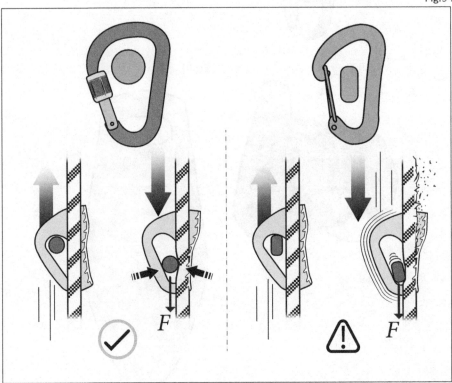

Fig.95

Wedge

 94

Many of man's earliest simple machines revolved around the mechanics of the wedge, with the best example being the axe. The wedge allows an input force to be redirected. In this context, a downward force compresses the rope.

 95

The size and profile of a Tibloc's karabiner are vital for smooth operation, especially when using the Tibloc Mark 1. As a guideline, the ideal karabiner has a large diameter (12 mm) with a round section. The most troublesome karabiners are the small, I-frame snap gates.

The only device in this category is the original Petzl Tibloc and the much-improved Tibloc 2, an inventive design constructed from stainless steel, with the original version having no moving parts. The Tibloc was intended as a featherweight metal Prusik, primarily for self-rescue, especially for crevasses, where one can function like a progress capture pulley, or as a straight rope ascender.

General Working Principle

The rope is inserted into the U-shaped body of the device, and then a karabiner is clipped into two tapering slots. When the karabiner is loaded, it slips down into the bottom of the slots, pinching the rope between the karabiner and the Tibloc's frame, creating a very effective rope locking wedge.

The original Tibloc relied on the weight of the karabiner to keep it in position on the rope, meaning it was common for the device to fall down the rope when unweighted. This can lead to the loss of the Tibloc if the device is not attached to the climber at the time. There is also a scenario in which the karabiner and Tibloc fall at the same speed, meaning the Tibloc did not grab the rope, leading to climber having to manually press the Tibloc onto the rope each time. The Tibloc 2 overcomes this problem by adding a sprung plastic sleeve that keeps tension on the karabiner at all times, keeping the device constantly on guard to grab.

The Tibloc features a handy hole for tying in a retention loop or lanyard, which reduces the risk of dropping it.

The Tibloc works on all diameter ropes, and even though the device is a featherweight design, it passes the minimum strength test of 4 kN before rope damage; the Tibloc itself is tested to 12 kN.

Examples

Petzl Tibloc, Petzl Tibloc 2.

Failure Points

Often, the simpler something becomes, the more onus there is on the user's skill to use it properly, and the Tibloc is firmly in that camp. In the hands of a novice, the first-generation Tibloc proved unpredictable, which is not welcome in an ascender. When the Tibloc first appeared, climbers would often employ featherweight I-beam style offset D karabiners, the result leading to the device skidding and skipping down the rope and destroying the sheath, as well as the climber's nerves.

The spring on the Tibloc 2, although increasing reliability in traction, still works best if a karabiner is used that has a uniform contact with the rope and Tibloc frame, a large cir-cumference (between 10 mm and 12 mm), and is oval or circular. Typically, these features are found in HMS or Oval karabiner either made from 12 mm round bar, or constructed to handle moving ropes, so without hard edges or cut-outs.

Petzl has also made a Tibloc-specific karabiner in the form of the Petzl Sm'D, with the Twist-lock being the ideal choice as the movement on a rope will generally open up most screw-gate collars. My own preferred combination is the Petzl OK.

As with all micro devices, it's best to stick to a well-tried and tested Tibloc/locker combination rather than just going with the karabiner at hand.

Suitability for TRS

Pros

- Self tending.
- Works on 8 mm to 11 mm ropes.
- Very Small.
- Lightweight.
- Inexpensive.
- High likelihood that a climber will own a Tibloc.

Cons

- Unpredictable.
- The Tibloc mark 1 should not be used as it's far from reliable, while the Tibloc 2 could be used as a secondary device, but never alone, if a climber had no other option.
- They can be very aggressive on the rope.
- Unidirectional.
- Requires correct karabiner to work.

Conclusion & Personal Reflections

The Tibloc 1 is only useful for escaping the system, as its action requires input from the climber in order to reliably lock. The Tibloc 2 is a little more reliable — a little — but if matched with the correct karabiner, and used with care, could work as a secondary TRS device, but never as a primary device.

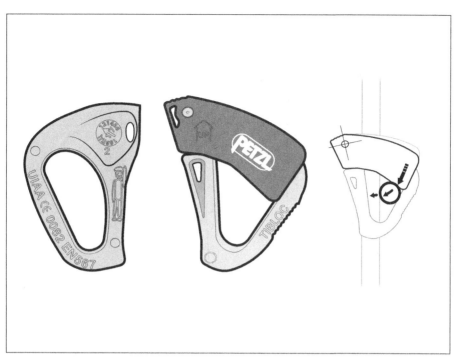

Fig.96

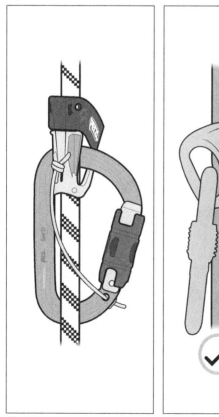

Fig.97

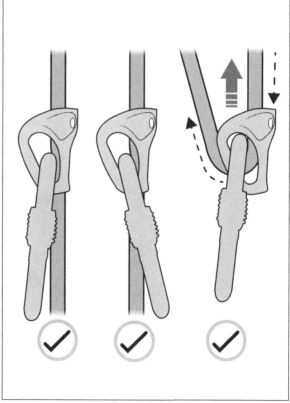

Fig.98

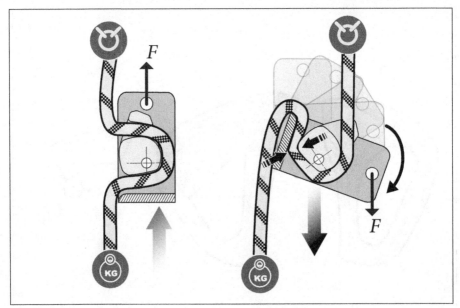

Fig.99

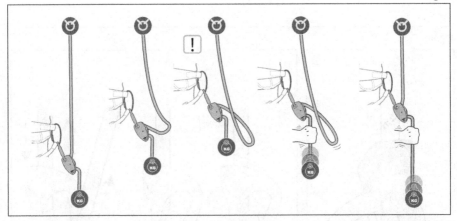

Fig.100

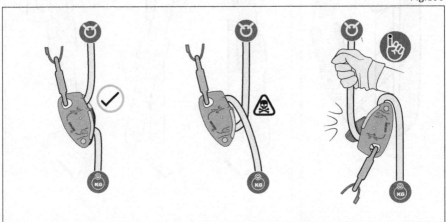

Fig.101

99
The first commercially successful ABD was the Petzl GriGri, and as a result, most ABDs operate using the same mechanics of a spring-loaded pivoting cam. Note that for TRS, an ABD is set with the live 'climber' rope going to the anchor.

 100
The biggest drawback with almost all ABDs is that the friction introduced by the spring and cam means the user must pull the rope through the device as they climb.

✏ 101
Using an ABD unconventionally exposes the user to the risk of setting the rope in the wrong direction. The climber should carry out a test of the device, such as a test hang, before climbing.

The locking assist function and mechanics of modern assisted braking belay devices (ABDs), such as the highly popular Petzl GriGri series, enable most models to double as highly effective and rope-friendly devices.

When used as ascenders, these devices are typically set up with the ABD clipped into the belay loop (similar to their configuration for belaying another climber) but with an additional device installed above to function as a foot ascender. The climber steps up on the ascender, pulls in the rope with the ABD, rests, advances the foot ascender, and repeats the process.

ABDs also serve as auto-locking descenders, becoming the go-to device with which some climbers become deeply familiar, performing most technical climbing tasks with their ABD. It's no surprise, then, that climbers who have a comprehensive understanding of and proficiency with these devices, and who are well-versed in both their strengths and limitations, often adopt them for top-rope soloing (TRS), despite several drawbacks compared to other devices.

General Working Principle

The majority of ABDs function using a spring-loaded, pivoting cam contained within a robust frame. The spring is calibrated to provide balanced resistance between the cam and the rope's movement during slack feeding. A more robust spring results in the device resisting locking up, whereas a weaker spring—or its absence—renders the device more susceptible to locking. An excessively strong spring might hinder the device from securing the rope under low loads, such as when a climber's weight is distributed across multiple quickdraws. Without a spring, the device becomes hypersensitive, locking incessantly, necessitating the belayer to manually override the cam, potentially leading to device failure and a falling climber. It takes merely 3.5 seconds for a climber to fall 60 meters, often the same time it takes for a belayer to realize they're obstructing their ABD. The tension of the spring is a frequently underestimated aspect of ABDs. Many devices "break in" over time as their springs lose some tension, and users become familiar with the level of resistance.

Manufacturers technically stress that ABDs are not "hands-free" or "auto-locking" devices because, even if they function as such 99% of the time, the remaining 1% poses a fatal

devices
/mechanics
/abd

✏ 102
Edelrid Eddy.

✏ 103
Camp Matik.

✏ 104
Petzl GriGri Mark 1.

✏ 105
Trango Vergo.

✏ 106
Petzl Neox.

✏ 107
Beal Birdie.

✏ 108
Petzl GriGri 2.

✏ 109
Mad Rock Lifegaurd.

✏ 110
Petzl GriGri+.

✏ 111
Mad Rock Safegaurd.

risk. Encasing the mechanism within a frame minimizes the chances of the mechanism becoming jammed but doesn't completely eliminate it. Once locked, the rope is firmly held in place by a karabiner.

When subjected to the force of a fall, the cam's lever action rotates, securing the rope between the steel cam and anvil plate. If the force is too great, the cam will slip at around 4kN, similar to rocker-arm or lever action devices, instead of damaging the rope. Unlike an ascender, an ABD is designed to absorb high dynamic forces, such as a 100kg climber experiencing a factor 2 fall onto a belay.

The loaded rope can be released either by removing the load, allowing the spring to retract the mechanism, or by engaging a handle that operates counter to the locking rotation.

For TRS, the device is typically used in the same manner as it is for belaying, except the anchor substitutes for the climber. With most devices, the rope passing through creates excessive friction, preventing auto-feeding and requiring manual intervention. This pattern—executing a move or two, drawing in slack, then repeating—creates a specific risk of high-factor falls onto the rope. Experienced climbers seem undeterred by such falls, even if caution would be advisable. Usually, climbers will either grab the rope before a fall or endure the fall, resulting in a shock load on the system. Many climbers value the ability of an ABD to facilitate rapid rappelling to reattempt moves. Generally, ABDs are utilized as specialized TRS tools, predominantly to refine a specific set of movements.

ABDs that provide some level of auto-feeding help prevent the formation of dangerous loops, making them suitable for use with a secondary TRS device and appropriate line-ballast .

Examples

Petzl Grigri series, Camp Matik, Trango Vergo, Wild Country Revo, Mad Rock Lifeguard, Mad Rock Safegaurd (Lifegard sans spring), Edelrid Eddy, Edelrid Megawatt, Climbing Technology ClickUp +, Beal Birdie, Syklotec Lory Pro.

Failure Points

In addition to the challenges of manual feeding, a significant concern with using a device that also functions as a descender is the inherent contradiction between these two roles. It's far too easy for the required action to be unintentionally reversed or bypassed. Comparable to an accidental firearm discharge, such failures can manifest in numerous ways, both rare and alarmingly common. If a device can fail, it will eventually. Even when failure seems improbable, it can still transpire.

Fig. 102

Fig. 103

Fig. 104

Fig. 105

Fig. 106

Fig. 107

Fig. 108

Fig. 109

Fig. 100

Fig. 111

✎ 112

A typical image of an experienced climber head pointing a route using an ABD. This set-up would be used to practice a few moves at a time, with the climber using the ABD to rappel back to their starting point each time. I cannot condone this set-up, as it lacks any real redundancy.

Margin Call

There is no 'High Table' in climbing that will pursue you if you violate the unwritten rules of the climbing community. Indeed, there are codes woven throughout all aspects of climbing, primarily focused on safety and respect for the climber, fellow climbers, and the environment in which they climb. but no one enforces them. You are free to take risks and make your own choices, cut your own corners, and no will stop you. If you want to TRS with a single device or climb on a rope that's too thin for safety, it's your prerogative. Books like this are here to suggest what you could do, not dictate what you should do. Just make sure you're informed enough to know what the rules are, and why there are rules before you go about breaking them.

The most common failure occurs when a climber, panicking, seizes the device and presses the handle. Less frequent issues may arise if the handle is accidentally engaged by a sling, karabiner, or clothing. Devices with an 'anti-panic' feature can partially counteract this, but a climber holding the device too tightly can override it long enough to fall.

The strength of the spring within the ABD, which opposes the device's engagement with the rope, can create an illusion of malfunction if the climber lacks full trust in the device. For example, a climber might lean back on the ABD tentatively, without applying sufficient weight to counteract the springs resistance, leading them to believe the device won't lock. This misconception could prompt the climber to grab the rope above the device, inhibiting its engagement, and causing the climber to clutch the rope even more firmly. This negative feedback loop can culminate with the climber sliding down the rope, sustaining burns on their hands, while mistakenly attributing the failure to the device (when, in fact, it was due to improper use).

ABDs are often optimized for specific rope diameters, and the ideal thickness tends to decrease with each new model. For example, the GriGri 1 worked well with 10.5 or 11 mm ropes, but 10 mm was ideal. More recent GriGri models struggle with thicker ropes, excelling with diameters between 9 and 9.5 mm. This specificity is vital for TRS, as climbers need to match the right device with the rope—a consideration that should already be second nature when using the device for belaying. Proficiency with an ABD, along with an understanding of its distinct traits, is crucial for its safe and effective use.

Suitability for TRS

Pros

- Instantly convertible to a descender.
- Rope-friendly.
- Engineered to withstand shock loads.
- Designed to slip before causing rope damage.
- Rope is securely held within the device.
- Users often develop robust familiarity and skill over time.
- If combined with a secondary device, it facilitates easy system escape or rappelling for a reset when practicing specific moves.
- The mechanism is more likely to be activated by a catastrophe-knot.

Fig.112

113

The ideal way to use an ABD is as part of a two-device system, with the ABD high on the body and an eccentric device as a secondary. This should allow the user to have the ABD take their weight, and then allow them to rappel once they've disengaged their secondary. For this to work, you need to find an ABD that will self-feed.

Margin Call

One device or two — that is the question. I'd say that at this moment, in late 2023, the majority of people on this planet who are practising TRS are doing so with only one device, that device probably being a Petzl Micro Traxion or some micro ascender or PCP. Are they dropping like flies? No, but then I grew up in an age when most buildings, especially schools, were stuffed full of asbestos, and that didn't do us any harm (apart from those it did). But the thing is, if there's a better way that's twice as safe as your way and for only the cost of another low-cost TRS device, then why not take it? A two-device system is a little like wearing a car seat belt. A first, it was a pain in the ass. It was a hassle and inconvenient. You, and most everyone else, had gone all their lives without dying for lack of a seatbelt (apart from those who did die). But the law compelled you to the new 'way', so you did it, and very soon, that was the only way, the right way, and only a fool or crazy person would do it the way it was once done.

Cons

- High friction unless thinner, suboptimal ropes are used.
- Generally necessitates manual feeding.
- Prone to being grabbed in panic.
- Mechanism can become jammed.
- Rope-specific.
- Unidirectional.
- Can be easily mounted upside down.
- Requires expertise for safe usage.

Conclusion & Personal Reflections

The most significant drawback of ABDs for TRS is that many require manual feeding, necessitating the climber to pull the rope through the device as they ascend. This can result in a "dead loop" of slack forming when the climber is unable to release their grip on the rock to feed the rope, potentially causing a shock load to the device, the climber, and the entire system in the event of a fall. Furthermore, the psychological strain on the climber intensifies when they become conscious of the forming loop that needs addressing with every move. This awareness can range from being a mere distraction to sheer terror, depending on the loop's size.

One advantage — and simultaneously, a disadvantage — of an ABD is its dual function as a descender. This allows climbers to quickly rappel to the ground if they fall, eliminating the need to escape the system. This feature explains its popularity for working on short sections of a climb. However, constantly pulling through the rope for longer pitches can become tedious.

To some degree, it's possible to enable the device to self-feed, especially if the ABD has a very light, or no spring, and the thinnest ropes are used. However, this characteristic renders it unsuitable for TRS, where thicker ropes are generally preferred.

The heightened risk of the device failing to lock, being inadvertently gripped in panic, or becoming entangled with other equipment means an ABD shouldn't be operated without a secondary device.

While ABDs present various challenges for TRS, some climbers seem willing to navigate these difficulties until they transition to a more efficient system or find this system worth the drawbacks when used for a specific task, like working on just a few moves. If used in this way, I'd advise that the climber tie into the rope below the ABD, rather than just using a catastrophe-knot, as this would act as an effective safeguard if everything went wrong.

Fig.113

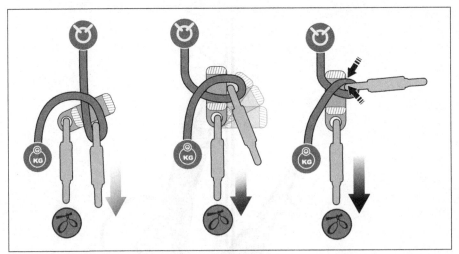

Fig.114

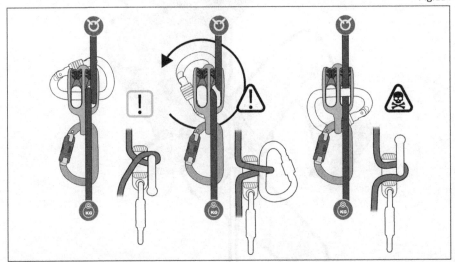

Fig.115

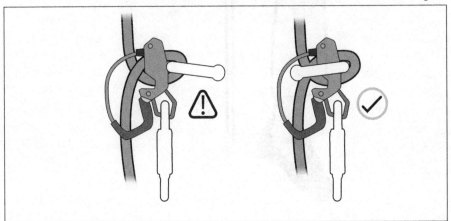

Fig.116

GMD

 114
A GMD only works if the ropes, blocking locker, and device all remain aligned and in their optimum position. If they shift out of alignment, the rope can switch from belay-assisted to free.

 115
When using a single rope, especially a small diameter rope, one failure mode can be triggered by the blocking karabiner twisting, which will cause the belay assist mode to disengage.

 116
One way to maintain the orientation of the ropes and blocking karabiner is to enclose the body of the device within the karabiner. This is not always possible, but is vital with old school 'magic plate' style models.

A GMD (Guide Mode Device) is a belay tube or plaquette that features an assisted braking function (like the Petzl Reverso or BD Guide, for example). It's designed for direct belaying of the following climber(s) by creating a simple progress capture system. The locking function of such a device also means they are often used as makeshift ascenders, typically for self-rescue, as well as a potential - albeit marginal - TRS device. Although I wouldn't recommend any GMD for TRS, I'll address it here since omitting it might be misconstrued as an oversight.

General Working Principle

In direct belay mode, a GMD is connected directly to the anchor via a direct connection point either milled or forged into the body of the device. The primary locker used for standard belaying, which connects the device to the climber's belay loop, is unclipped from the harness and serves as a blocking karabiner. If the rope(s) are positioned correctly, the ropes will run in only one direction and will block if reversed. A GMD is designed to belay one or two following climbers, meaning the live ropes will run through the device but lock if one or both climbers fall. When climbing a rope, the device is set so the live rope, leading to the anchor, locks, allowing the device to function as a progress capture device.

As with all devices that climbers might classify as 'auto-locking', manufacturers caution that the GMD mode is not hands-free, even if that's how most climbers, including professional guides, tend to use them.

Examples

Petzl Reverso, Black Diamond ATC Guide, DMM Pivot, Wild Country Pro Guide, Edelrid Giga Jul, Grivel Master Pro, Mammut Nordwand, Camp PIÙ.

Failure Points

No GMD is self-tending. This means they encounter the same problems as an ABD, but with additional hazards. A GMD is not designed for shock-loading falls but rather for maintaining constant, vigilant tension over the ropes.

The capability to pull a climbing rope (or ropes) through a GMD with one hand varies widely, ranging from super smooth to arm-pumpingly stiff, to downright impossible. This ease

🖉 117

Margin Call

Most books like this are very Western-focused, as if everyone reading it lives a cushy Yankee-Euro-style reality, where money is cheap, even if you're a dirtbag, and anything you want is just a mouse click away. Sure, climbers might grumble about the price of a pair of handmade Italian rock boots while spending an equivalent on a coffee within the same week, but things are not quite so at the new frontiers of climbing. I've met climbers all over the planet climbing on a shoestring, sometimes literally! There are more and more climbers in countries where Western gear is far too costly to buy and almost impossible to order, even if it could be afforded. For such climbers, ideal solutions are often not an option, leaving only less than perfect. For a young, keen climber wanting to practice on the granite crags in the North of Kenya or an Omani who wants to work the limestone crags near his house, using a GMD or friction hitches might be their only option. It's not for us to deny them knowledge of how that might be done (even if we deem it unsafe).

of use depends on numerous factors: device design, rope diameter, rope age, sheath construction, and the shape, profile, and size of the blocking karabiner. If you manage to get a well-matched system, using the thinnest certified soft dynamic rope and a round-bar oval karabiner, it can work efficiently. However, pair it with a thick, rigid low-stretch rope and a micro I-beam karabiner, and you'll find yourself struggling. The necessity for small-diameter ropes should raise concerns, especially for TRS.

Another complication with small-diameter ropes is that when used on their own, there's a point at which a free-floating blocking karabiner can twist, transitioning the device from a blocking mode to a free one. The most reliable way to mitigate this risk is to use two ropes and/or ensure the blocking karabiner can't rotate.

Like with ABDs, any obstacle in taking in slack will lead to an accumulation of excess rope, which can result in high-impact falls. Unlike an ABD, neither the GMD device nor the blocking karabiner is designed to withstand such forces. In such a fall, the device could potentially be loaded in a manner that disables the blocking karabiner, rendering the device useless.

Different from a direct belay scenario, when self-belaying, nothing remains under tension, making it easier for components to shift into hazardous alignments.

Lastly, if a climber were to experience an inverted fall, for example, getting flipped by a ledge, a GMD would not block the rope but instead would release the slack. Moreover, it's worth noting that it's not a "hands-free" device.

Conclusion & Personal Reflections

This style of device would only ever be chosen by a climber who feels they have no other option, such as climber who lives in a country where it's impossible to purchase better devices. But, in reality, free soloing might be safer, or employing a friction hitch system, or a combination of hitch and GMD.

Opting for a GMD could also suggest a lack of general experience and a misunderstanding of the difficulty and risks associated with using such a device.

If one decides to use a GMD, it should only be on easy terrain where both hands can be used to take in slack. This might be combined with a back-up friction hitch and consistently clipping into catastrophe-knots. However, my advice would be to forgo the illusion of protection that a GMD offers. Instead, just tie loops into the climbing-line and clip into these as you ascend.

Fig.117

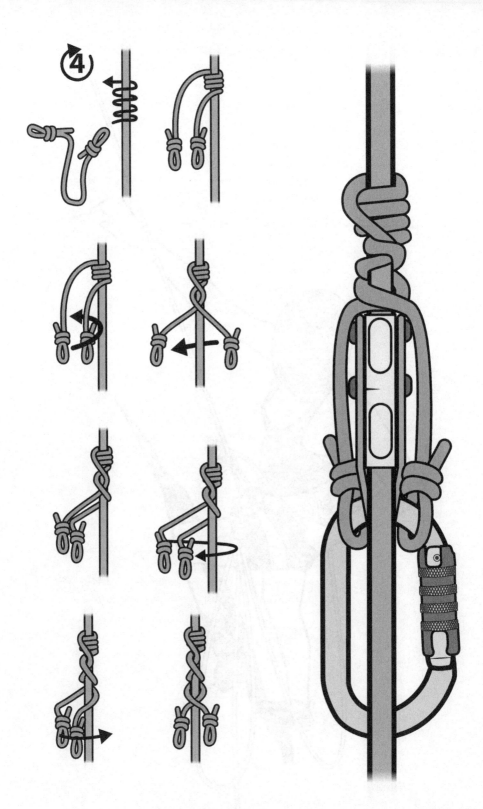

Fig.118

Hitches

 118
The XT is an advanced friction hitch that moves very well on the rope.

Margin Call

In the Second World War, bombers were fitted with crew escape axes, little tomahawks designed to hack through the thin aluminium skin of a crashed aircraft. When you were all out of options, you reached for the axe. Perhaps it's a stretch, but the humble length of cord on the back of a climber's harness carries out the same duty in that it can get a climber out of all sorts of desperate situations. It might only be a metre and a bit of 5 mm cord, but with that cord, you can climb a rope, create a third hand, a fixed link to a device, and a releasable escape knot. If you carry a longer rescue cord' (2.5 metres of 7 mm), you can do even more, including a Purcell Prusik, rescue spider, docking cord, for example, all from a couple of cord lengths. So, what I am trying to say here is that you should never leave the ground, be it a single-pitch sport climb or the South West face of Everest, without at least one hitch cord on your harness, even if it's holding on your chalk bag. And for TRS, always carry two, as they will save your ass.

It's uncommon to use soft friction hitches, such as Prusik loops (e.g., the French Prusik or Autoblock), for TRS. This is because they tend to have low intrinsic strength, mainly when made from accessory cords like Perlon. Moreover, they are not as consistently reliable as mechanical devices. For instance, a friction hitch might fail once in a hundred falls, whereas a mechanical device might only fail once in a hundred thousand falls. Nevertheless, these hitches do have their place as back-ups to mechanical devices and are indispensable for self-rescue and escaping from a system.

General Working Principle

A cord or sling is attached to the rope using a specific type of binding friction hitch. The hitch can either be moved up the rope manually by hand or by running the rope through a hitch minding tool, such as a small pulley or quick-link. However, the most efficient way to advance the friction hitch is for it to ride on top of a mechanical device, allowing for hands-free operation and a back-up for the device.

Why use a back-up? A back-up is best employed when a climber has only a single mechanical device, such as a PCP, but wants to avoid putting all their trust in one solution. The back-up can be clipped into the device's karabiner or through a separate karabiner for complete independence. Although the specific type of friction hitch a climber chooses is not critically important as long as it's tidy (a sloppy back-up might interfere with the device), using a cord instead of a loop tends to be neater and less likely to be dropped.

Examples

Auto-block, Distel, Klemheist, Schwabisch, XT, FB (Franz Bachmann) sling hitch.

Failure Points

Friction cords are less dependable than mechanical devices. While they operate based on a consistent action sequence—weight, unweight, move—cordage and slings have many variables that affect their consistent function, many of which are outside the climber's control.

Failures can manifest in several ways: slipping due to an incorrect knot or inappropriate cord diameter, partial or total failure to grip, or material failure leading to the cord snapping. This

🖉 119
Schwabisch friction hitch, an easy one to learn. It can be combined with a pulley, or hitch minding device, in order to allow it to be operated with one hand.

🖉 120
FB friction hitch, an important knot to learn for climbers who wish to build a friction hitch from a sling.

can result from age, insufficient base strength, or melting due to slippage from shock loading. Even a short fall could create a cord-breaking shock load.

If a friction cord is used as a back-up, care must be taken to ensure the back-up doesn't interfere with the primary device. Common issues include the fabric of the friction cord getting snagged on the teeth or spikes of the device, which in a fall can disable the device. Ideally, the back-up would then engage even if it caused the primary device's failure. However, there's a risk that the hitch could fail to lock and be dragged down the rope. Another possible failure is if a long knot tail feeds into the device, which can reduce its grabbing force. This is one reason why commercially sewn hitch cords are preferable to self-tied loops. Moreover, commercial cords are generally four times stronger (20kN vs. 5kN). The bottom line is that climbers should be aware of these potential issues, ensuring that back-ups are neat, tidy, and of the appropriate length.

Suitability for TRS

Pros

- Featherweight, low cost, and low bulk.
- Hitches are manually bidirectional.
- Multiple friction hitches can be used.
- Vital for self-rescue.
- Inexpensive.

Cons

- Not 100% reliable and should not be used singularly, but rather as an extra back-up layer.
- Can be panic-grabbed.
- Requires manual feeding unless riding on top of a device
- Low strength unless an aramid or Dyneema cord is used.
- Can foul mechanical devices when used as a back-up.
- Extra faff when transitioning.

Conclusion & Personal Reflections

All climbers should carry friction cord for both rappelling (as a back-up) and self-rescue. Therefore, it's worthwhile to understand how to use such cord or slings as a TRS tool. In practice, a climber might only use a friction cord for TRS during a self-rescue or to back-up a mechanical device that isn't fully trusted. Learn how to use a friction hitch effectively, then store that knowledge for emergency situations, akin to 'break glass in case of emergency.'

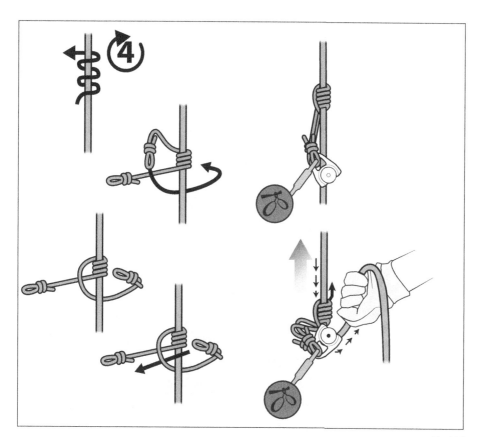

Fig.119

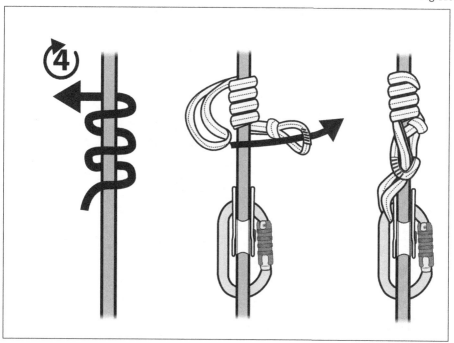

Fig.120

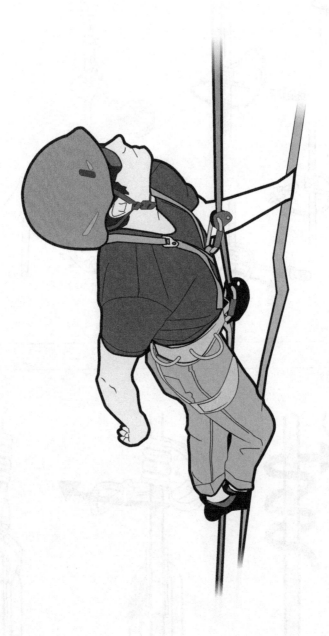

Fig.121

DEVICE FOCUS

 121

The ideal device is like the ideal relationship, a bond based on unconditional trust.

In this chapter, I will focus on a select number of devices: some that are ideal for TRS and others that aren't. By examining the latter, I can highlight key reasons why certain devices are suitable for TRS while others are not.

This is not an exhaustive list of the best devices on the market, but simply further nudge to help the reader work out what device they might — or might not — be.

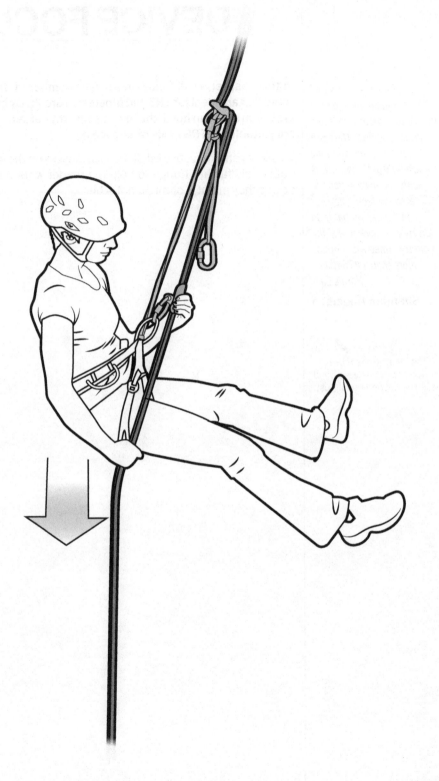

Fig.122

Petzl Shunt

Technical details
Type: Lever
Weight: 188 g
Min. rope:
8 mm (double),
10 mm (single)
Max. rope:
11 mm

Typical TRS set-up

The Shunt is attached to the belay loop using a locking karabiner. Some climbers use a short lanyard or quickdraw to provide a bit of flexibility and make it less restrictive.

 122

The Petzl Shunt as shown in the 2012 Petzl instruction manual, being used for its intended purpose, which is as rappel back-up.

One of Monsieur Petzl's first designs, the Shunt was the go-to TRS tool for decades and remains one of the most misused and misunderstood devices ever made for climbing.

Fernand Petzl's original idea was to design a rappel back-up device that would work on dry, wet, icy or muddy ropes. Like a well-conducted science experiment, what Petzl wanted were repeatable results, namely, a device that would not let a climber plummet to the end of their rope.

The Shunt was designed to attach to the belay loop below the descender or be extended above by a lanyard or quickdraw, with the climber depressing the jaw as the descended. It could accommodate both one or two ropes, which remains a very unusual feature.

Petzl employed a variation of the lever action mechanism that allowed two ropes to be grabbed and was also extremely rope-friendly. The Shunt's flexibility and adaptability were both a boon, but also led to its later misuse and abuse, often in ways that Fernand could never have imagined. Initially, these new ways of using a Shunt were documented by Petzl, such as for belaying, releasable abseil anchors, and TRS. However, over the decades, these unconventional methods were gradually retracted, redacted, and reconsidered. Now, the Shunt is limited to the sole purpose Fernand originally envisaged: as an abseil back-up tool.

Cavers also used Shunts in a manner very similar to a TR system, as a back-up when free climbing wire caving ladders, a method of ascent that was eventually — and thankfully — replaced by ascenders and Single Rope Technique (SRT).

Although climbers and cavers developed early industrial rope access, cavers contributed the lion's share of technical know-how. Thus, the Shunt was employed in its designated role for abseil protection, essential when much of the work required hands-free. It was also the obvious choice when there was a need for a second back-up rope or safety-line, just in case the working line got damaged.

In this role, the Shunt was usually connected to the worker via a dynamic rope lanyard, or 'cow's-tail,' shadowing the climber as they moved up and down the rope.

This technique of two lines and a self-trailing fall arrester soon became standard practice worldwide. The only issue was that the Shunt was never designed for this job.

✎ 123
Detachment Failure: It's important to note that the connector is not shown, but it can play a role in this mode of failure.

✎ 124
The ideal connectors for all TRS devices also apply to the Shunt. It's vital to avoid cross-loading and to use an oval karabiner for balanced loading.

✎ 125
There are several ways a Shunt can fail to engage, many of which are related to the incorrect use of the connector or unsafe loading.

Although the Shunt provided excellent service, it was not without accidents. While most incidents are common to all such devices, such as panic-grabbing or shock-loading, it also suffered from unique issues: slipping under relatively low loads or failure to release the tow line when falling (the tow line is a little piece of cord that disables the device when descending).

The Shunt was never designed to be shock loaded but rather to be fixed above or below a descender. So, placing it on a one-meter rope lanyard meant it could be exposed to short, hard factor 1 or 2 falls. The device was solid, with a forged jaw and heavy-duty alloy frame, but this was not what it was intended for.

The Shunt was also designed to hold the weight of just one person and would slip if overloaded—a problem during pick-off rescues, as the Shunt could slide down the rope if the weight of both climbers was transferred too quickly.

Although rare, these failure points, considering the tens of thousands of rope access workers using them every day for decades, led to several accidents.

Petzl began expressing concerns about the misuse of the device and how its warranty was being voided. Around the same time, there was a move towards greater professionalization of the sector. Rope access had long been relatively laissez-faire, but with increased regulations concerning health and safety, a search for better, dedicated devices for fall protection commenced, with a primary focus on addressing the Shunt's failure points. These devices included the Petzl Asap and IMC Rocker.

During this period, the Shunt also established itself as the number one tool for TRS, most often using only a single weighted climbing-line.

Accidents involving the Shunt for TRS mirrored those in rope access, and although they were rare, tales of near misses became part of climbing lore. Overhanging climbs were often a factor, caused by climbers grabbing the rope, the device, or both during a fall. A heavy line-ballast on overhanging terrain could also lead to the jaw being pressed against the body, impeding its action, and leading to panic grabbing.

Detachment failure marked a resurgence in the Shunt's use for TRS, highlighting a new and deadly failure mode. The Shunt had a design flaw. Unlike a standard lever-action device where the rope is captured by the jaw's axle pin, the Shunt features a fixed axle. This means if the Shunt were to invert in just the wrong way during loading and the rope looped into the gap between the jaw and frame, then shock-loaded, the rope could escape the device entirely.

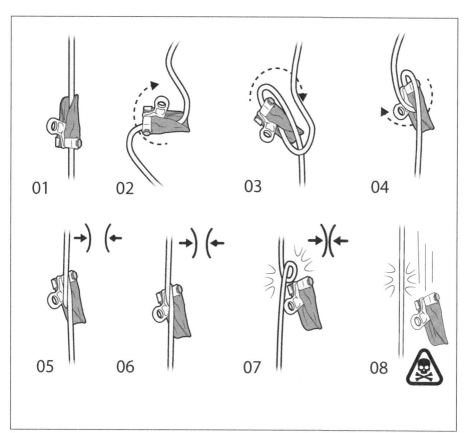

Fig.123

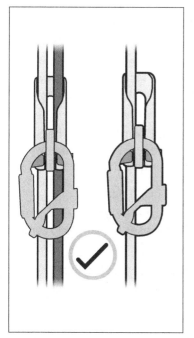

Fig.124

Fig.125

devices
/device_focus
/petzl_shunt

 126

A Shunt is typically racked with the lever retracted within the frame, held in position by its connector. This configuration allows for the rope(s) to be inserted while the Shunt is still racked on the harness or belay loop. Once the rope is secured, the connector is removed, and the lever springs into position. The method can also be applied in reverse.

 127

Like all lever action devices, panic grabbing of the Shunt can easily result in its failure to grip the rope.

 128

The Shunt's tow line allows the user to prevent the lever from activating while descending, which should be a very valuable feature. Unfortunately, this short length of cord has led to several accidents when operators, in panic, failed to release it, causing the device to malfunction.

The risk of such failure increased with smaller diameter ropes, as did the use of highly dynamic ropes, which become thinner when elongated under load, allowing them to fit through tiny gaps.

Where climbers once used Shunts with 11 and 10.5 mm ropes, now they were using 9.5 mm or smaller. Several other factors also affected the outcome, including the length of the lanyard, the karabiners used, and line-ballast, which could cause the Shunt to invert (most accidents are multi-factorial).

The most dangerous aspect of such failure was that it rendered any catastrophe-knots on the climbing-line redundant. If the rope escapes the Shunt, you're going to hit the ground.

Beyond reducing the likelihood of such a failure through the correct choice of ropes and karabiners, the best way to avoid the issue is to employ a two-line system, or take the view that the days of the Shunt were over, and that there are better options available.

Suitability for TRS

Although the Shunt has served climbers, cavers and rope access technicians well over decades, and is a credit to Fernand Petzl's skill it's had it has probably had its day. After appearing on the market in the 70s, it rapidly became a do-it-all device, which was fine in the risk tolerant 20th century, but not the 21st. It's understandable why Petzl have now attempted to restrict its purpose, or drop it completely, and make it a does-not-do-it-all device, and solely to a rappel back-up.

As a rappel back-up it stands alone, even if few would ever employ it for that task, with auto-locking rappel devices, ABDs, and better friction knots and materials now being more commonly employed.

When compared to other lever modern devices, the Shunt has a number of drawbacks, some serous if a climber wants to use it for life support, rather than as part of a system. Chief amongst these, and often overlooked, is that its variation on the lever mechanism is just not high strength compared to other lever action devices, such as the Rescuecender, and that what makes it unique also exposes the device to serous safety issues.

So, even as a life long Shunt user (in fact the first device I bought as a climber was Shunt) the days of the Shunt seem to be pretty much over.

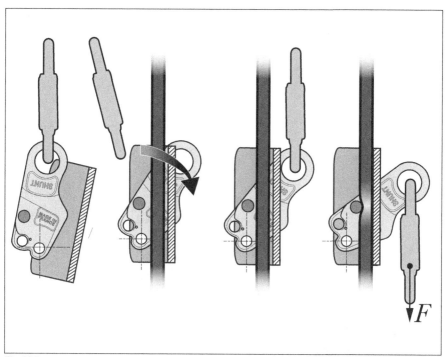

Fig.126

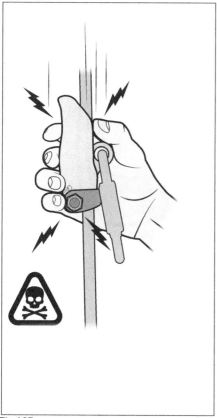

Fig.127

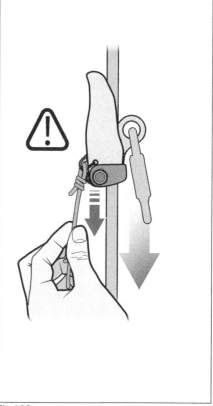

Fig.128

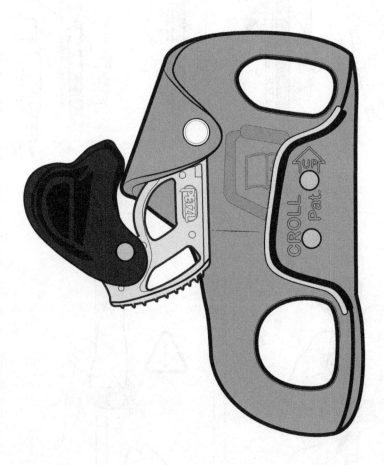

Fig.129

Petzl Croll S

Technical details

Type: Eccentric

Weight: 85 g

Min. rope: 8 mm

Max. rope: 11 mm

Typical TRS set-up

The Croll is typically positioned on the chest area in order to slide up the rope as you ascend.

 129
Petzl Croll S

Although numerous chest ascenders are available on the market, the most common is the Petzl Croll. Petzl now produces both a small (S) and large (L) version. The larger design is intended for industrial users, while the smaller one is for sport and is more suitable for TRS because it is a compact unit and less likely to catch on the rock.

The Croll features both an upper and lower clip-in point. The lower hole is designed to attach to a vertical connector (either a D-shaped quick-link or locker), clipped through the legs and waist of a harness (bypassing the belay loop). The upper point is used to connect the Croll to some form of a chest strap, most commonly the Petzl Torse.

Although this top clip-hole can be clipped into, either by a locker or quick-link, the chest strap is usually threaded through it and tightened, resulting in a streamlined package.

This two-point system ensures the Croll remains taut and close to the body.

A small plastic safety trigger prevents the jaw from disengaging from the rope. However, as the rope is not fully secured within the device, there is a potential risk, perhaps when climbing a squeeze chimney, that the trigger could be pressed, allowing the jaw to detach from the rope, which could then escape the device.

One of the biggest disadvantages of the Croll is that it cannot be attached via its top hole, which means it cannot be dragged as a secondary device on the belay loop.

Suitability for TRS

When set correctly as a chest ascender, with a secondary device on the belay loop, this is an ideal foolproof TRS tool, as its position is low on the chest and its eccentric design means there is almost zero lag in grabbing the rope. If one was a novice, this would be a good system to begin with, plus it would also allow rope climbing to be practiced.

The downside, of course, is that this can also feel restrictive, as a chest ascender works best when under some tension from its chest strap, and can be hard to and can be a tough device to use on routes that move left or right, making this system sub-optimal for more experienced climbers.

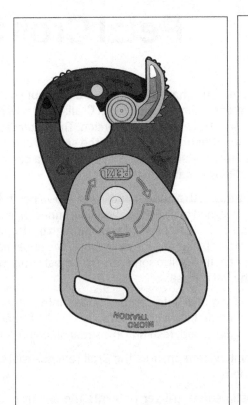

Fig.130

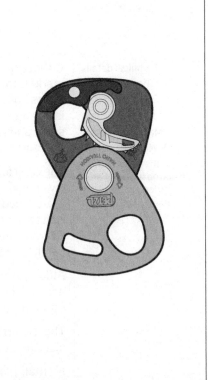

Fig.131

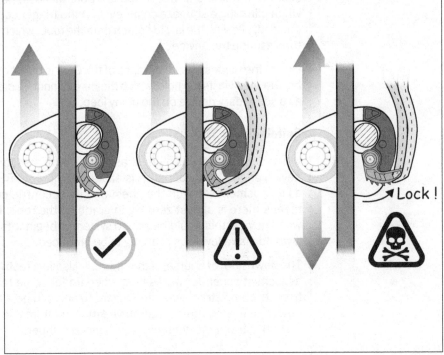

Lock !

Fig.132

Petzl Micro/Nano Traxion

Technical details

Micro Traxion

Type: Eccentric

Weight: 85 g

Min. rope: 8 mm

Max. rope: 11 mm

Nano Traxion

Type: Eccentric

Weight: 53 g

Min. rope: 7 mm

Max. rope: 11 mm

Typical TRS set-up

The traxion series of progress capture devices are generally attached direct to the harness belay loop. In order for the Traxion to balance on the karabiner, a locking oval karabiner works best.

130
Petzl Traxion.

131
Petzl Nano Traxion.

132
Demonstration of how it's possible for the jaw to lock open while using the Petzl Nano Traxion.

The Micro Traxion, and earlier Mini Traxion, quickly overtook the Petzl Shunt as the most widely adopted TRS device, due to it being a far more adaptable and multi-functional climbing tool than the Shunt, and a go-to device for rock climbers, alpinists, instructors, and guides.

The primary role of the device was as a small rescue PCP pulley, with an eccentric jaw built into the frame, meaning that as the load was hauled via the pulley, its weight is held by the jaw during each reset. This makes the device ideal for bag hauling, rescue, running belays, and all sorts of rigging techniques, both sanctioned and unsanctioned.

The Micro's jaw featured a small catch, that allowed the jaw to be locked off the rope, allowing the pulley to become two way, or when a held load had to be released and lowered,

The small jaw also made the Micro a very effective micro ascender, and sometimes belay device, for bringing up a second climber at speed, a technique outside of the device's design parameters but employed by many anyway (this requires a high level of skill and awareness of the dangers involved, as a shock-load could damage, or sever the seconder's rope).

The low weight and cost of the device resulted in the PCP evolving from a tool for big wallers and industrial users to the climbing mainstream, first with guides, alpinists, and skiers, then to multi-pitch rock climbers.

The widespread adoption of such a tool, to climbers who had probably never used an ascender, meant that it was easy for this to become the tool of choice for climbers looking for TRS functionality.

For TRS, in most cases, the Micro was used singly, clipped into the climber's belay loop with a locker, the jaw catching the climber if they fell. This would prove to be a high-risk set-up. The set-up was further improved by lifting the device with a chest strap, and eventually climbers began to adopt a two device system, with two Micros, or some other back-up.

Although popular, the device had two major failure points for TRS.

First, the larger the rope's diameter, the more the tooth jaw is exposed, the teeth being very aggressive. Therefore, it was possible for the teeth to snag on anything that came close,

devices
/device_focus
/petzl_traxion

✎ 133
Both the Nano and the Micro Traxion can accommodate both a 'no-drop' clip loop, as well as a retraction loop or pull knotted pull strand. The benefit of linking the jaw to the rear clip loop hole is this reduces the risk of the cord fouling the mechanism.

be it rope, slings, or clothing. Invariably when something becomes hooked onto the teeth, the jaw could be pulled away from the rope; this could be dangerous in itself but can happen with most eccentric devices. The issue with the Micro was that once pulled back; the jaw would easily be caught by the lock-off latch, disabling the jaw, and resulting in a rope-grabbing device being instantly transformed into a pulley.

I experienced this while soloing, when the tail of the belay loop retention strap snagged on the jaw teeth and locked it off the rope. Not good when fifty feet off the deck and clinging on for life, and I soon learnt that others had experienced the same issue.

If this were to happen, the climber would fall to the end of the rope, or catastrophe-knot, if one had been tied.

To overcome this issue, some climbers began modifying their Micros, removing the lock-off feature and voiding the device's warranty.

A less drastic way to overcome this point of failure was to double up on the Micro, having both devices clipped to the belay loop, either free or with the top device held on the chest by a retaining strap or cord. This system worked well, as the eccentric action is not disabled by a downward pressure from above, which could happen if the upper device failed but struck the lower device.

Enter the Nano

Perhaps Petzl was listening as the follow-on PCP from them, the Nano, was not only smaller and lighter but also did away with the lock-off feature; this does not mean that the device was failure-proof, as the teeth can still catch and the jaw pulled away from the rope, but at least it won't lock off.

Suitability for TRS

Although popular, neither the Micro nor Nano can be considered safe for TRS if used singularly (even though this is common practice). Doubling up devices or using one as a secondary to a more suitable device is a safer option, but being both unidirectional and not being designed to hold a heavy fall without damaging the rope remains a significant issue.

In the real world, as long as climbers rig correctly and can guarantee no heavy, dynamic loading on the rope, and ideally use a double rope system, then the Nano is an adequate option, but not ideal, but will probably be a go-to device for many.

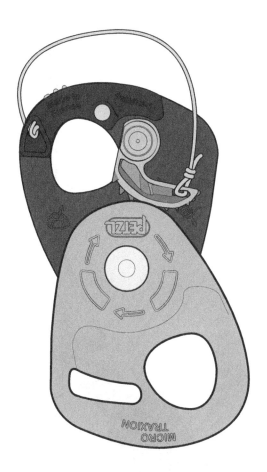

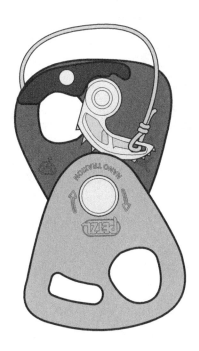

Fig.133

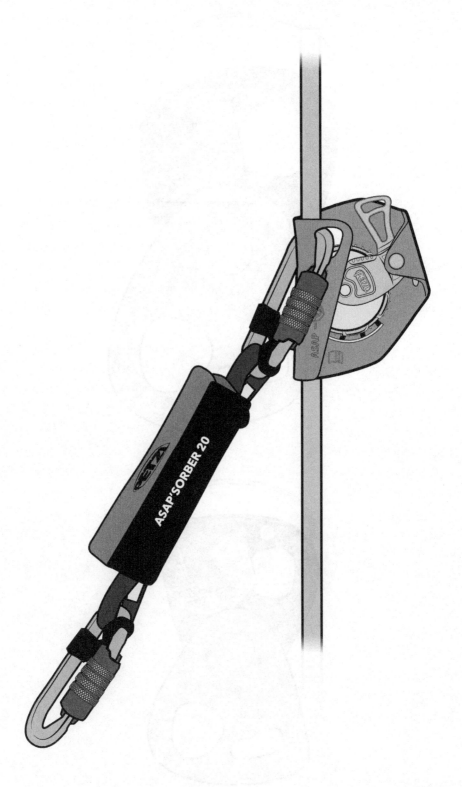

Fig.134

Petzl ASAP

Technical details
Type: Inertia
Weight: 295 g
Min. rope: 10 mm
Max. rope: 13 mm
Typical TRS set-up
The ASAP is connected
to the harness via a
short shock absorbing
extender or lanyard.

 134

Petzl ASAP fitted with short
ASAP'SORBER extender.

Seeing that the Petzl Shunt was the number one rope access fall arrestor for decades, even though Petzl disowned it, it was fitting that Petzl would produce a dedicated replacement in the form of the ASAP.

Unlike the Shunt, which – like any device – could be employed in multiple ways: rope climbing, progress capture, fall-arrest, and rappel back-up, the ASAP was designed from scratch solely as a fall-arrestor. Although this may appear to be a negative, what is gained from such a dedicated design is the elimination of several failure points suffered by standard rope grabs in the industrial sector.

Unlike a regular rope grab, the ASAP works by way of an inertial wheel system, which in this case, is a little like a circular-toothed eccentric jaw. The drum/jaw is free moving during standard movements, such as moving up and down a rope, making it bidirectional and self-trailing, but locks and grabs the rope in a fall. Once the device is unweighted, the wheel/jaw returns to free-running mode.

This system allows a back-up to run smoothly in ascent and descent, which is ideal for free climbing.

The ASAP was also designed to make it virtually impossible for the device to be panic-grabbed, unlike the Shunt, or disengaged by downward pressure, making this an ideal fall arrestor.

Suitability for TRS

It seems like a no-brainier that the ASAP is ideal for TRS, but there are no perfect devices. The biggest problem with the ASAP is it's too bulky to be a primary device, clipped direct to the harness, but also requires a shock absorbing lanyard if used as a secondary, as it functions like an eccentric device when loaded, i.e. it won't slip, but would destroy the rope without a shock absorbing link. Most climbers will not own, or wish to buy expensive industrial shock absorbing lanyards.

The ASAP is also not recommended for hard repetitive loading or constant falling, as this would eventually damage the complex mechanism. I view it more like a reserve parachute, a piece of ass-saving safety equipment not intended for heavy, day after day, jumping. The ASAP excels at doing what it was designed to do, but that was not TRS.

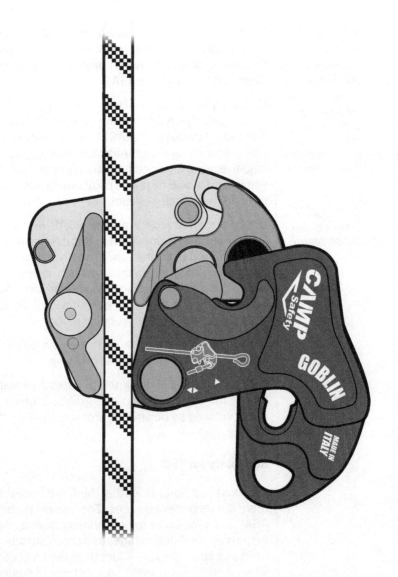

Fig.135

Camp Goblin

Technical details

Type: Rocker-arm

Weight: 280 g

Min. rope: 10 mm

Max. rope: 11 mm

Typical TRS set-up

The Goblin requires an oval karabiner, and is connected to the belay loop. It can be set high or low on the belay loop, with the high position reducing lag time in a fall. It can also be attached via a short static extender, or longer (sub 60cm) dynamic lanyard.

Notes

It's important to take note of the minimum rope diameter, as anything less than 10 mm will slip. The device works best with low-stretch ropes.

As with all rocker-arm devices, I recommend that the user invests time in fully testing out the mechanism before committing their life to it.

 135
Camp Goblin in the open position.

Among the various rocker-arm style devices available on the market, the Camp Goblin stands out for its advanced design, offering extra functionality compared to earlier models. I would view this as a third generation rocker-arm device.

The device boasts several strengths, including bidirectional capability, the ability to slip under heavy load, rope friendliness, and a compact size.

The Goblin differs from other rocker-arm devices due to having a two part opening mechanism, which means the rope is held very securely within the device.

One notable feature of the Goblin is its option to switch from free moving to rope positioning, uni-directional to bi-directional. This is done via a small retractable jaw and catch, that allows users to quickly go from a free, to a positioning device, being able to be moved anywhere on the rope without risking it slipping back down. This is a great feature once the user understand how best - and when - to employ it.

Lastly, the Goblin features a hole into which a small loop of cord can be tied in order to create a 'no-drop' loop.

Suitability for TRS

The effective rocker-arm design makes the Camp Goblin an ideal choice as a primary TRS device, set above a secondary device (not below), or used alone with a secondary device on a safety-line. The Goblin is also ideal as a secondary fall arrest device on the safety-line, as this is what it was designed to do.

Like all rocker-arm style devices, the main failure point of the Goblin is depression, which is why it should not be used as the secondary device on a one-rope system. It is crucial to ensure the Goblin is correctly oriented before use.

When paired with another rocker-arm device or the Petzl ASAP on a safety-line, a climber can achieve significant freedom of movement, making the Camp Goblin an exceptional choice.

The primary negatives are - like all rocker-arm devices - the risk of panic grabbing, and being disabled by downward pressure from another device. The Goblin is also not a device one can be free and easy with when it comes to rope sizes, and will only work safely, and consistently, on ropes of 10 mm and above.

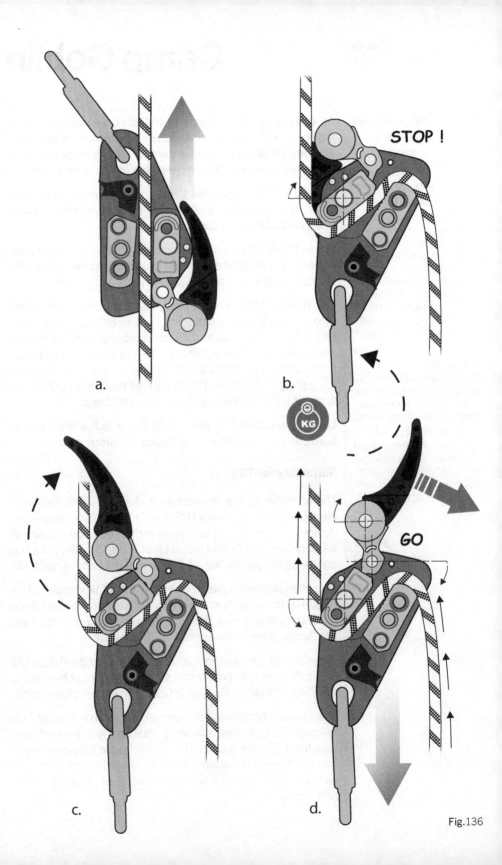

STOP !

GO

a.

b.

c.

d.

Fig.136

Taz Lov3

Technical details

Type: Rocker-arm

Weight: 380 g

Min. rope: 9.5 mm

Max. rope: 11 mm

Typical TRS set-up

A connector attaches the device to the climber's belay loop, or hard link on the harness (industrial harness). For TRS, the Lov3 is often lifted up by a chest sling in order to reduce lag.

 136

The Taz Lov3 could be viewed as a third-generation rocker-arm device, as the designers have added an ingenious mechanism that allows the weighted grab to release its grasp of the rope. In the diagram, you can see the device able to move freely up (and down) the climbing-line (a), then lock when weighted. This happens by the device inverting, with the passage of the rope trapping itself between the jaw and the anvil (b). The handle is then rotated (c), and leverage is used to release the jaw (d).

If a climber were to create a TRS device wish list, it would include bidirectionality, rope friendliness during shock loading, self-tending capability, and the ability to function as both an ascender and descender, and belay device. Such a device was merely a dream until 2015, when Pascal Ollivier, in trying to come up with a rope access device that could work with tensioned ropes, came up with the Lov2, and later the improved Taz 3, ground breaking devices that changed the paradigm of what a device could do.

The Lov3 is a cutting-edge rocker-arm device that combines the excellent rope friendly and bi-directional rocker-arm mechanism, ideal for TR soloists, with the added capability of rappelling like an ABD. It successfully passes CE tests for ascending, fall arresting, and descending devices. Moreover, the Lov3 comes with a body that can be opened when connected, via a button, allowing for easy insertion or removal of the rope without detaching it from its connector, making it virtually impossible to drop.

Initially designed for rope access and arborists, the Lov3 has quickly emerged as the top device in the market. However, it is not without its flaws; being bulky, heavy, and the most expensive device of its type.

Suitability for TRS

The Lov3 can function as the top device in a one-rope system or as the primary or back-up device in a two-rope system. As it is longer than a standard rocker-arm device, if clipped into the belay loop, there will be a noticeable lag and drop before it rotates into position and grips the rope, far greater than a smaller frame rocker-arm device. This delay could tempt inexperienced users to panic-grab the rope or device. To minimise this lag, it is recommended to use the device with a chest strap connected through the clip-in point. Although there is a small hole in the frame designed for a keeper cord, for the best lift, it's best to fix a small loop directly into the main clip point. This loop needs to be as small as possible so as not to interfere with the rocker-arm mechanism.

As with all rocker-arm devices, it works unlike other climbing devices, so I would advise a climber to invest time in using it in ascender and rappel modes first, so as to fully understand how it works before using it for TRS.

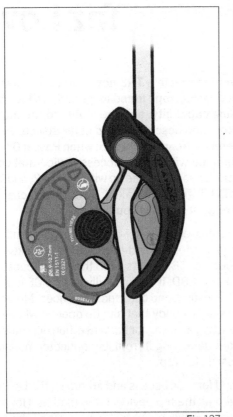

Fig.137

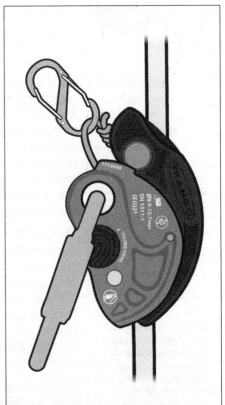

Fig.138

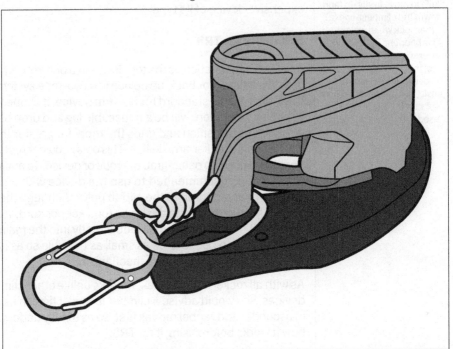

Fig.139

Trango Vergo

Technical details
Type: Rocker-arm
Weight: 195 g
Min. rope: 8.9 mm
Max. rope: 10.7 mm

Typical TRS set-up

Standard ABD configuration, with locking karabiner attaching the Vergo to the belay loop. As device is designed for belaying, not TRS or rope climbing, care must be taken so that the device does not shift on it's connector. For example, if the connector rolls over the top of the Vergo it could disable the mechanism, leading to failure to grab.

137
Rope path through the Trango Vergo.

138
Trango Vergo set up when attached between belay loop and chest sling.

139
Location of lifting cord.

The ideal device for TRS is a device like an ABD, that can be used to both climb the rope and then rappel once the climbing is done, or has hit an impasse. Unfortunately, almost all ABD designs incur too much friction as they move up the rope, making self-tending either impossible, or only working with a very heavy weight on the end of the rope, making climbing as fun as doing a tracker pull with your gonads.

The Trango Vergo stands out as one of the only ABDs that have an acceptable level self-tending for TRS. It's not as good as other devices, but by adding a little extra weight and using soft, sub 10 mm dynamic ropes (9.5 mm to 10 mm), the Vergo moves up the rope very well.

This functionality is achieved by an unusual design of action, that allows the rope to pass through the device with only marginal deviations of friction. Whereas a rope passing through a Petzl GriGri will take a 360 degree turn (it comes in and out the same side of the device), the Vergo has the rope pretty much pass straight through the device, with only a slight dog leg to help it catch.

As with all non-standard mechanisms, the Vergo is a device that requires practice and experience to use, and is best employed as a general rope tool first, for belaying, rappel and rope climbing, before using it for TRS. It may appear to function like the Petzl GriGri, but it does not work like a GriGri.

Suitability for TRS

The Vergo is an ideal device for any climber who wants an easy escape, but without all the hazards and hard work of using a more traditional ABD, i.e. having to pull the rope through the device as they climb (or not).

The Vergo, like all TRS devices, should not be used alone, but in partnership with a second device. In a one rope system, the Vergo should be set at the top of the device stack, as the primary with secondary device, ideally a eccentric device should set on the belay loop.

On a two rope system the secondary device can be a non eccentric one, and due to the requirement for a thinner diameter rope, a two rope system, with the safety-line being a low-stretch, may well be the safest option for a ABD set-up.

The Vergo is best high using a chest sling connected to device via a loop tied into the device.

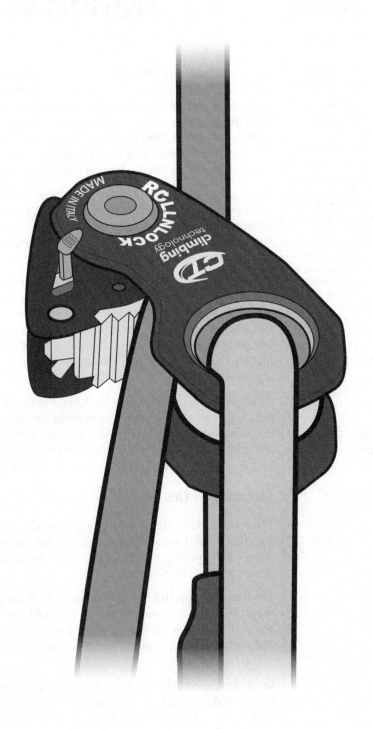

Fig.140

CT RollNLock

Technical details

Type: Eccentric

Weight: 85 g

Min. rope: 8 mm

Max. rope: 13 mm

Typical TRS set-up

Standard TRS set-up using an oval anti-rotation karabiner. The RollNlock can be set both in high or low position on the belay loop.

 140
MT RollNlock in rope climbing mode.

The RollNlock appeared with little fan fair in 2012, around the same time as the Petzl Micro Traxion, and on the back of earlier devices such as the Wild Country Ropeman series, Kong Duck and Petzl Tibloc. Like the Traxion, the RollNlock could be considered as a second generation micro ascender, designed to full fill the same duties of these earlier devices, but with the added utility of a bushing, making it an ascender, pulley and PCT.

The take up of the RollNlock was much slower then with the Petzl devices, and for a long time it was a culty piece of hardware; those who owned one loved it, but few had ever seen or heard of one. The only real discussion of the RollNlock came about when people discussed alternatives to the Micro Traxion.

Although the Petzl Micro Traxion seems to have become the de facto - but flawed - TRS device of choice in the last ten years, primarily due to its availability, the RollNlock is perhaps a more deserving device due to lacking two flaws with the Traxion.

First, the jaw lacks spikes meaning there is nothing to snag the rope, or anything snaggable that might come close to the jaw. Rather then having sharp spikes, the RockNlock has five Z shaped, grooved teeth. This reduces the potential for terminal lock-off of the jaw, but also the inadvertent lock-on when rappelling (the traxion must be removed for this reason). Although such teeth would give the impression the RollNlock would have a reduced capacity to hold a loaded rope before damage occurs, as such tooth designs usually chop a rope at less that 2 kN, the RollNlock maintains a working load of 4 kN.

Second, the locking mechanism that locks the jaw off the rope, in order to switch the device to a two way pulley, is more resistant to accidental lock off.

Suitability for TRS

As with all TRS devices, the RollNlock should not be used alone, and works as both a primary or secondary device on a one rope system. The RollNlock can be used in partnership with a second RollNlock, or as a secondary, lower, device to a lever or rocker-arm device. If used with a Traxion device, pay close attention to the rope path from one device to another, which is effected by how the devices are stacked, and the size of connectors, in order to create the lowest drag.

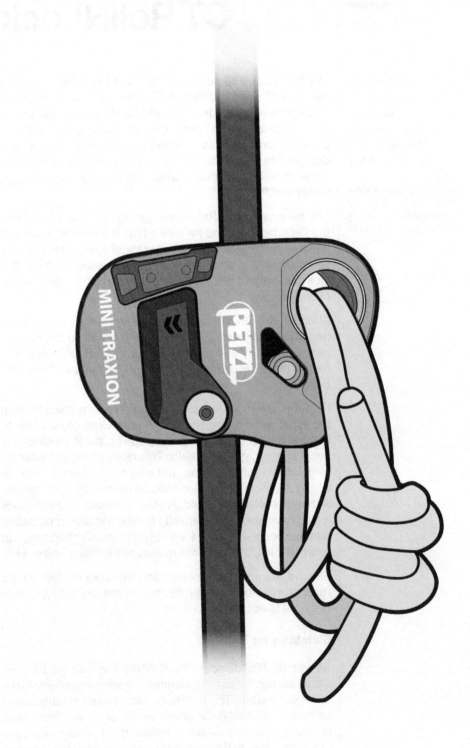

Fig.141

Petzl Mini Traxion

Technical details
Type: Eccentric
Weight: 150 g
Min. rope: 7 mm
Max. rope: 11 mm
Typical TRS set-up

Standard TRS set-up using an oval anti-rotation kara-biner. The Mini Traxion can be set both in high or low position on the belay loop.

 141
Petzl Mini Traxion

The Mini Traxion sits between Petzl's two micro PCPs – the Micro and the Nano – and the full-sized, industry-focused Pro Traxion. Compared to the Nano, the Mini's pulley is nearly twice as big, giving a marginal hauling advantage but at the cost of three times the weight and double the size. Unlike the Nano and Micro, the Mini is not the kind of device one would carry as part of a standard rack but rather a dedicated hauler.

The reason the Mini makes this list is the simple fact that it features an improved method of closure compared to its near-peer devices. Unlike other small/medium-sized PCPs, which require the connector to be removed and the side plates to be rotated to remove them from the rope – always a drop risk for the clumsy – the Micro can remain attached to the connector at all times. This means a climber can attach the Mini to their belay loop at the beginning of the day and stay there until the climbing is finished. This could also be done with larger Pro styles of PCP, but the Micro, although larger than smaller PCPs, remains small and compact enough not to get in the way when climbing.

A three-step process opens the Micro: (1) rotate the cover on the locking button downwards, (2) rotate the plate unlocking button upwards, (3) slide open the side plate to expose the sheave and jaw. It's worth noting that unlike a standard PCP, which will be locked once the connector is inserted, there will always be a risk of the Mini not being fully closed, with the only indicator that it's not locked being a visible sheave (red to indicate danger). Pay attention to the all-important 'click' when it locks closed, and keep the locking mechanism clean and lubricated. The Micro also features a catch that will not accidentally lock off the jaw and requires the catch to be depressed.

Suitability for TRS

One of the best ways to employ a Micro is to tie it directly into the harness using a 1-meter length of 7 mm cord or 5.5 mm Dyneema, creating a double loop through the leg and waist. This knot can be tied off with a double Fisherman's knot (Dyneema requires a triple), two Overhands, or a rethreaded Overhand. Knots are best tied/untied before putting on the harness. Ensure all tails are neither dangerously short nor too long and could interfere with the device (tail length should be approximately the cord diameter x 5), so 3 cm – when the knot is tight - for a 6 mm Perlon and 5.5 mm Dyneema.

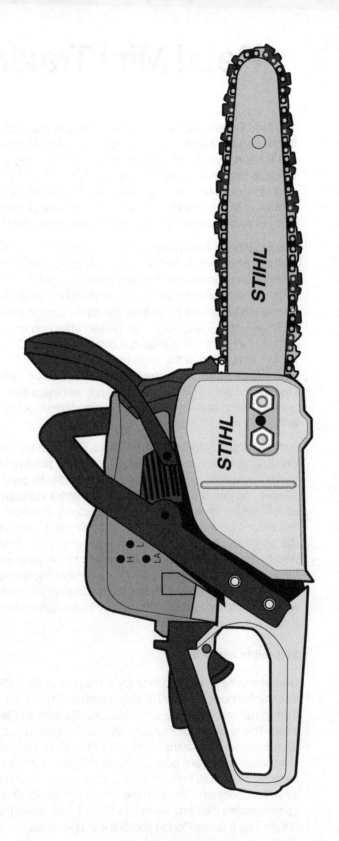

Fig.142

Equipment

In this section I will break down all the hardware and software, the extra bits, a climber needs in order to create a safe and functional TRS system.

✏ 142
Stihl Chainsaw

Margin Call
Ever since the first man-ape-thing smashed another man-ape-thing over the head with a giraffe jaw bone, we've been master tool makers and users. First, we did it to survive, then to make life easier, and finally, we had to make things to spend our money on. We invented the pulley to make it easier to lift a sail, the hand cannon so zero-rank serfs could bring down high-rank knights in their armour, and air fryers so we could make chips without burning down the house or our faces off. People not interested in equipment, how it works, and why it works that way, should probably avoid TRS and stick to free soloing or mine.

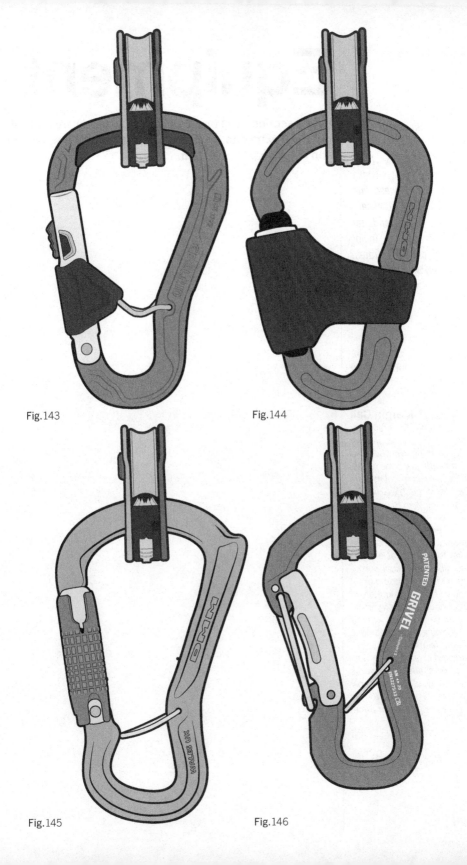

Fig. 143

Fig. 144

Fig. 145

Fig. 146

Karabiners

✏ 143
Edelrid HMS Bulletproof.

✏ 144
DMM Belay Master.

✏ 145
DMM Ceros Locksafe.

✏ 146
Grivel Clepsydra L K10G

Margin Call
Something many climbers ignore is that karabiners, like any piece of life supporting equipment, needs to be looked after if they're to work reliably. No matter how much thought and high tech manufacturing prowess went into a triple locking karabiner, if it's gummed up with salt, sand and general rock gunge, it's ability to do what it's designed to do, which is save your ass, is going to be compromised. To clean, wash with warm water, scrubbing with a tooth brush, allow to dry, the apply 3-in-One oil or Cam Lube on all moving parts. Wipe some oil over the body to stop surface corrosion.

The climber must establish a link between their harness and the devices they use, and in this book, I've used the catch-all term "connector" to refer to these links, but in most cases it will be a locking karabiner. The type of karabiner used depends on the climber's preference and could include a manual screw-gate, twist-lock, twin gate, or even a plain gate. Karabiners will also be utilised with lanyards and extenders, used to create some distance between the climber and their device.

The karabiner a climber uses can either form a reliable link that can be trusted without worry or become a potential hazard that might lead to a failure. Therefore, careful thought is required when choosing the right ones. The weakest link in all lockers is human, so in TRS it's best to use as few connectors as possible and keep the set-up simple.

Anti-Rotation

The most significant hazard with karabiners in a system is cross-loading, which occurs when the karabiner sustains an extreme load it wasn't designed for. Extreme cross-loading, such as a factor 2 fall onto a misaligned karabiner, can cause even a sturdy locking karabiner to fail as easily as a smaller snap-gate. Even though a karabiner might have a high kN rating along its major axis, the rating does not include the gate's axle pin or the hooked nose, which could cause failure if broken.

It's essential to remember that a failing karabiner doesn't necessarily have to snap; it might simply lose the rope or device. Such failures might not require extreme loading; I've witnessed karabiners bending and breaking under bodyweight loads, which can be surprising but not entirely unexpected.

In addition to cross-loading, mobile TRS devices and karabiners moving around each other can lead to unforeseen failures, such as the karabiner getting caught on a device, disabling or limiting the mechanism.

To avoid these issues, climbers have several options:

Harness/Karabiner Capture
There are several locking karabiners that can capture the belay loop, fixing the karabiner in place via a small wire gate set into the body, a pin, or a removable nylon clip. Once locked in position, the connection cannot rotate from its major, opti-

🖉 147
Petzl OK with Captiv karabiner positioning bar.

🖉 148
Petzl Attache SL fitted
with Petzl Tanga.

🖉 149
Rock Exotica rockO
with elastic band.

🖉 150
DMM PerfectO Lock-
safe with captive bar and
Configuration Aids.

Margin Call

In my climbing life, a common cause of karabiner failure has been the issue of sticky gates, either due to a gummed-up hinge or weakened spring, resulting in the gate failing to close fully. A sticky gate on a connection between a harness and a device can be a killer if unnoticed. This terminal failure can be compounded by the climber blindly screwing down a locking barrel, locking the karabiner open. When such a karabiner is continually weighted and unweighted, the karabiner will eventually detach from either the harness or device. Apart from keeping your karabiners clean and lubricated, the best way to avoid this failure mode is to pay attention whenever you close and lock your karabiners. One advantage of twist lock designs is that they will generally only rotate on a closed gate, offset by the fact that this locking mechanism is also prone to becoming gummed up.

mal loading axis, eliminating the risk of cross-loading or gate leverage. It's advisable to use an anti-rotation karabiner on all devices since many accidents occur due to karabiners shifting into sub-optimal orientations. This feature is most commonly found in locking karabiners, but some models of quick-links, like the Salewa Maillon Twist Lock and Petzl Delta, also incorporate this feature.

Device/Karabiner Capture

The second point where alignment and shifting need to be addressed is where the karabiner clips into the device. Several solutions can help:

- **Rubber band**: Placing a heavy-duty rubber band on the karabiner before attaching the device and adding a second elastic band can help keep the device in place. Most climbers will soon tire of adding the second band, but using a fixed band to reduce misalignment.

- **Stow Bands**: A progression from rubber bands, these heavy duty silicone bands, designed for parachute packing, operate in the same manner but simply appear tidier.

- **Petzl Tanga**: These small rubber bumpers can be slipped onto a karabiner, creating a rubber stop or bumper against the device. While practical, they can be prone to loss since they need to be removed each time the device is removed. A DIY version can be made by cutting up small sections of thick-walled 10 mm rubber hose.

- **Petzl Captiv**: This accessory captures the device instead of the belay loop, similar to anti-rotation karabiners. It works well with devices that feature a safety gate, allowing the karabiner to be permanently fixed to the device.

- **DMM Wallis**: A durable yet flexible high-grade polymer bridge can be inserted into the clip-in point on most devices, preventing the device from freely moving on its locker.

- **Hump**: Some karabiners feature a hump on the spine designed to stop a device from sliding off the major axis, with the gate mechanism providing additional support in the other direction. Twist-locking karabiners, in particular, have a larger locking barrel that acts as an effective bump.

- **Radius**: Smaller karabiners have a tighter bend radius that helps to orientate the device.

Nose

Karabiners with a keylock are always superior to old style hooked nose designs, but this is especially true when trying to smoothly escape the system or transitioning to descent, as they are less likely to snag on slings, devices, or belay loops.

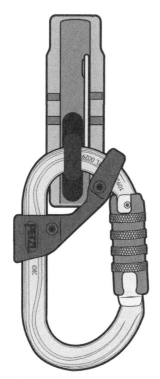

Fig.147

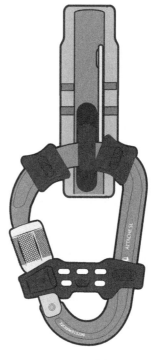

Fig.148

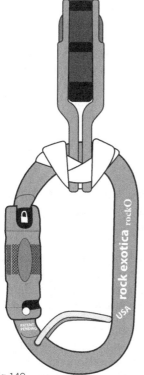

Fig.149

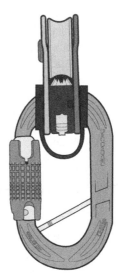

Fig.150

equipment
/karabiners

 151

A device on a free-roving locking karabiner, when repeatedly weighted and unweighted, will eventually shift out of position.

Margin Call

All TRS climbers should understand the issue of jammed lockers and how this can be caused by old versus new-style screwgate collars. The old style had screw gate collars that could be screwed up tight against the nose of the karabiner. If the karabiner was then weighted, the frame would flex enough to allow another fraction of a turn on the collar, something a climber might do when their life depended on the locker. The problem was that the collar would be almost impossible to unscrew once unweighted, feeling as if it had been welded shut. This problem could prove life-threatening and has led to climbers cutting themselves free or breaking the gate of the karabiner in order to escape when all that's needed is to weigh the locker again. Luckily, modern designs feature a 'stop' inside the collar, making it impossible to over-tighten. To check if you have an old or new style locker, test by tightening the screw collar as tight as possible, and if you still have a little play between the nose and the gate, it must feature a 'stop'. Any old locker that can be overtightened should not be used as a primary locker but saved instead for lesser duties.

Size

The size and length of a karabiner require consideration. A very large HMS locker can increase the drop compared to smaller karabiners. While experienced climbers might not notice much of a difference, novices might experience a noticeable drop, leading to potential panic grabbing. On the other hand, large karabiners can act somewhat like a short extender, providing more room to move, which can be useful with unidirectional devices.

Shape

Symmetrical karabiners generally create a well-aligned system, while offset D or pear-shaped karabiners, though excellent for general use, can lead to misalignment and cross-loading. Climbers might be drawn to large-volume HMS lockers, but it's important to note that these are not designed as general high-strength karabiners, but for rope bearing and belaying applications. For TRS, the ideal choice is a smaller-volume, focused karabiner specifically designed for security.

Material

Most climbers utilise alloy climbing karabiners; however, those who subject their equipment to heavy-duty use and abuse might contemplate using steel karabiners for devices. Repeated falls onto a device can result in battered, notched, and worn karabiners, diminishing their strength over time and becoming potentially dangerous if used with ropes. Steel karabiners are more robust and resistant to abuse, encompassing cross-loading situations. For instance, the alloy Petzl OK has a major axis strength of 25kN, while the steel Petzl Oxan boasts a major axis strength of 38kN.

Locking Mechanism

There is a variety of locking mechanisms available, ranging from traditional screw collars to twist locks and multi-action locks. The priority should be to choose a locking system that provides the utmost security and remains locked at all times, without the need for constant checks or reliance on luck in the event of a fall. This rules out screw gate karabiners unless the screw collar is secured in place by a secondary element, such as in the DMM Belay Master or Petzl Attache SL.

Single Twist lock karabiners should also be avoided as they're also prone to failure, and only double or triple twist locks should be employed. These will require some muscle memory need more care and cleaning, as dirt or ice can gum them up.

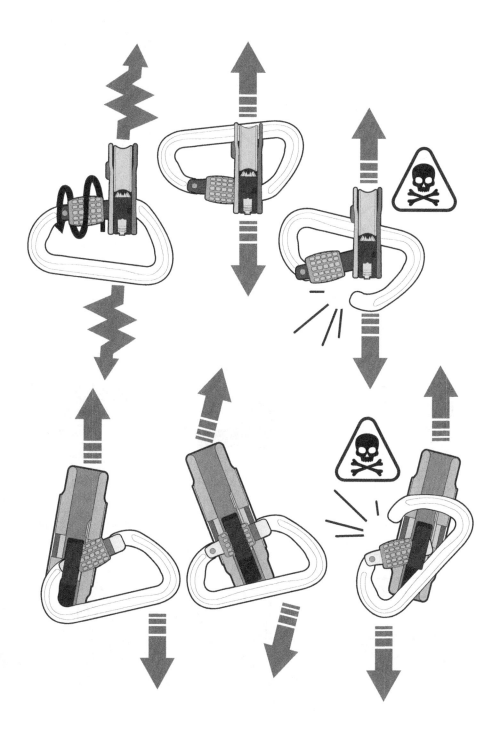

Fig.151

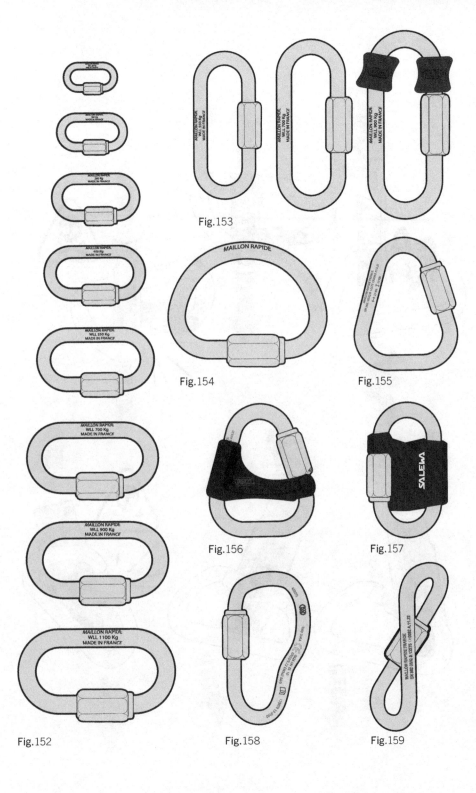

Fig.153

Fig.154

Fig.155

Fig.156

Fig.157

Fig.152

Fig.158

Fig.159

Quick-Links

🖊 152
Peguet Quick-Links
3 mm to 10 mm .

🖊 153
Large Opening Quick-Links
7 mm, 8 mm and 9 mm
fitted with Petzl Tanga.

🖊 154
11 mm D Quick-Link.

🖊 155
10 mm Delta Quick-Link.

🖊 156
Petzl 10 mm Delta with
positioning bar.

🖊 157
Salewa 8 mm Mail-
lon Twist Lock.

🖊 158
Kong 7 mm Asymmetric.

🖊 159
8 mm Normal Twist
Maillon rapide.

Invented 80 years ago as a way of joining chains together for agricultural use rather than welding a new link, the quick-link (or Maillon-Rapide, French for 'fast link'), soon became indispensable for any job that required high strength and semi-permanent security.

Although an industrial solution, the quick-link was adopted by French cavers as a low-cost, stronger, and more robust alternative to alloy karabiners, as the sport often required hundreds of karabiners to be left in situ in a cave system. These karabiners would also be subjected to repeated loading, generally when clipped into sharp bolt hangers, something alloy karabiners are not ideal for, as they soon become damaged, which in turn can damage ropes.

The early days of sport climbing and industrial rope access techniques, which were based on the caving single rope technique (SRT), introduced the quick-link to the broader, less subterranean world, with their low cost but high security, especially when fixed in place, establishing them as a core component in climbing rigging, primarily as low-cost lower-offs on sports climbs.

Quick-links are also very low cost, not that cost is important, but their industrial heritage means they can stand up to far more heavy abuse and neglect than a climbing karabiner; one is like a sports car, the other a tractor.

Construction

Unlike a karabiner, a quick-link has no hinged spring-loaded gate, and rather than being constructed from several parts (frame, gate, spring, rivets, locking sleeve, etc.), it's constructed from just two: the frame and the locking collar.

The frame, or body, is constructed by cutting steel wire to the correct length, then milling a thread on each end, and then it's cold pressed into the desired shape, which is generally an oval (more accurately, a disco-rectangle).

The hexagonal collar locks the quick-link closed, and it's worth noting that as with an oval karabiner, it's vital that the quick-link is a closed loop so that the load is passed along both spines, rather than one, to achieve maximum strength.

Open quick-links should never be loaded as this makes them significantly weaker and can lead to distortion in the smaller diameter sizes, making it impossible to close them again.

The collar is hexagonal to allow it to be secured by a spanner for maximum strength, with a 12 mm spanner needed for a 7 mm quick-link and a 16 mm spanner for a 10 mm link.

Finger tightening and untightening can be made easier by adding a few wraps of finger tape to the collar.

If the collar becomes jammed for some reason, or it needs to be locked tightly without a spanner, then a wide-opening 7 mm quick-link can be used like an adjustable spanner, making it well worth including in any rigging kit.

The lack of a hinged gate means quick-links have much smaller gate openings, but this is also an aspect of their greater security, as there is no hinged gate to be depressed by terrain features, the rope, or the climber's body. This comes at the cost of much more limited space for inserting ropes or slings, which is why wide-opening designs are recommended, especially when used with thick ropes.

In my experience, unlike a screwgate collar, which can often be found open when it's supposed to be locked, and vice versa, quick-links tend to be far more reliable.

Materials

Quick-links come in various materials, including alloy and plastic, but for life support, use zinc-plated steel or stainless steel. Stainless is considerably stronger but far more expensive and designed for maritime use or by those who want maximum strength and quality.

Strength

The strength of a steel quick-link is considerably greater than most locking karabiners size for size due to both shape and material, as steel is far stronger and more robust than aluminium; there is also minimal risk of a gate open failure, which is how most karabiners fail. This increased strength, as well as the use of steel, means a quick-link is also resistant to unnatural or dangerous abnormal loading, such as cross-loading, twisting, bending, or rock impacts, making them ideal connectors for TRS, attaching rope soloing devices to the climber's harness, where such forces can easily take place.

Security

Although a piece of safety equipment can be trusted 100% and so needs to be monitored, a quick-link that has been securely fastened shut can almost be considered as a closed link in the system, not that it cannot be opened accidentally

– because it can – but because of its ability to hold up to abnormal loads.

Nevertheless, before climbing, all quick-links should be checked (screw down, not up).

Quick-links are much smaller in size but with an equivalent or greater strength than a karabiner, making them less likely to catch on terrain, snag, and become misaligned. The size difference is offset by the fact the quick-link will generally be heavier than an equivalent karabiner, although the minimal number required for top rope soloing makes this a moot point.

Shape & Size

Unlike a modern karabiner, which can be hot or cold forged into all sorts of shapes, a standard quick-link is like an old-style karabiner, it's simply a bent length of bar stock. This means the available shapes are more limited, the primary shapes being a symmetrical oval, both standard and long (wide opening), delta (D-shaped), triangular, trapezoid, and twisted.

One new shape on the market is Kong's asymmetric model, which is shaped more like a modern hybrid D HMS karabiner, giving it a larger volume at the working end, making it more suitable for micro eccentric devices, such as the Kong Duck.

In terms of TRS, the smaller symmetrical quick-link gives a device less room in which to twist and hang up or cause the connector to become cross-loaded.

Quick-links as TRS connectors

Although heavy, a standard steel 9 mm or 10 mm quick-link can make an increasingly strong connector between the device and the harness, and removes any fears about cross-loading due to that strength. A rapid-link also shortens the lag and fall distance, especially if a 7 mm or 8 mm quick-link is used.

It's important to avoid smaller diameter options, which, although strong enough for the job, will not stabilize the device, as well as a larger, more karabiner thickness, quick-link.

The quick-link can also be improved by using anti-rotational add ons.

These advantages are offset by the fact that a quick-link is more fiddly to use, and it's down to the climber to decide if this option is better or worse than using a locking karabiner.

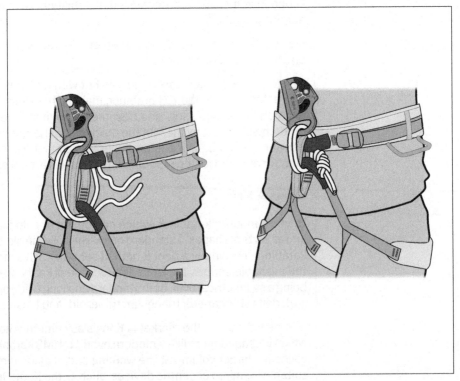

Fig. 160

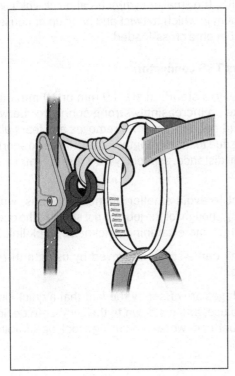

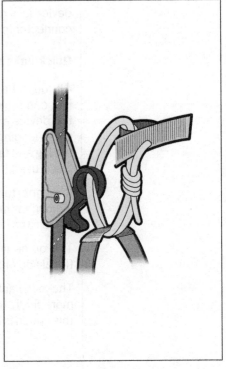

Fig. 161

Fig. 162

Rope & Cord

 160

Petzl Basic tied directly into the harness with a double loop length of 7 mm cord, tied off with two overhand knots. Note that the Basic would also be connected to a chest sling (not shown).

 161

Lever action device tied directly into the belay loop.

 162

Lever action device tied directly the leg and waist loop.

The most secure connector, although the least common, is to tie your device directly into your harness with a double loop of cord, either via the belay loop or the tie-in point. This uncommon method was first adopted by the Rock Exotica Soloist and Soloaid with the aim of eliminating the risks and hazards associated with rigid connectors, and it has several advantages. This should be regarded as an advanced technique, as failing to execute it correctly could result in a flawed and dangerous connector.

Tying in

A 1-metre length of 5.5 mm climbing Dyneema or 6 mm Perlon/Nylon cord is double-looped through the device's clip-in point and tie-in points on the harness. This loop can either be left the same size as the belay loop (10cm) or cinched down tight, pinching the tie-in points as if suspended.

This cinched method reduces grab lag to a minimum but places the TRS device closer to your body than any other method, offering both advantages and disadvantages. The cord is then closed with either Fisherman's knots or an overhand knot (ensure each part is tight), backed up by a second overhand knot. The result is a connection that won't come undone and isn't affected by the hazardous forces or failure points of a rigid link.

Generally, a karabiner connects horizontally to the vertical clip-in point on most devices, which theoretically could be a problem, as the tie-in loop creates a vertical connection. This would lead to the device sitting at 90 degrees off-axis. In reality, unless the loop is tied extremely tight, there's always a bit of play and twist in the loop, allowing the device to orient itself correctly on the climbing-line.

The obvious question is: why not use thicker cord, like 7 mm or 8 mm, to gain greater strength? The limiting factor is the diameter of the clip-in hole, making it challenging to insert two strands of thicker cord easily. A single thick strand, such as 8 mm cord, could be used, but then you're faced with a much bulkier knot. Remember, a 6 mm strand of Perlon is rated at approximately 7kN, 11kN when looped (160%), and 22kN when double-looped. So, don't worry.

Note that Perlon, although weaker than Dyneema, creates more stable knots, and all knots require both monitoring and adequate tails (5 times the width of the cord).

🖉 163
Soft-shackle parts
and how they work.

🖉 164
Small Dyneema 6 mm
soft-shackle, rated at
3500 kg breaking strain.

🖉 165
5 mm Dyneema soft-
shackle, rated at 2120 kg.

🖉 166
3 mm Dyneema soft-
shackle, rated at 1270kg.
This is an ideal size for
using as a tension keeper.

Margin Call

*Although soft-shackles have
never been a part of climbing
equipment, where tradition
has consistently called for
rugged aluminium or steel
karabiners, the same is not
true in sky diving, sailing or
slacklining, sports that also
feature dangerously high
loads and tragic outcomes
if failure occurs. In these
sports, soft -shackles
have been appreciated for
decades for their strength,
low weight and profile,
resistance to snags, hang-
ups or cross-loading, and
the ability to be custom-
made by anyone willing to
learn the simple art of rope
splicing. Once you know
how to splice and have some
essential tools, like a splicing
fid, there is no end to the
valuable things you can do
with high-strength Dyneema
and a bit of splicing, stuff
you'd only be able to make
with an industrial bar-tacking
machine or bulky knots.*

Soft-shackle

An alternative to cord is the soft-shackle, crafted from high-strength hollow-core 12-strand Dyneema. This obviates the need to tie and untie knots. Soft-shackles are designed to be easily secured or opened by using an eye spliced into the Dyneema and inserting a button knot spliced at the other end. Once the eye is closed, the button knot cannot pass, creating a robust closed loop.

The strength of a typical 9 mm soft-shackle is around 130 kN, unequivocally making it the strongest piece of equipment in any system. A 9 mm shackle might be too cumbersome for TRS; however, a 6 mm shackle, boasting a breaking strain of over 4000 kg, would be more suitable. When double-looped, its actual strength exceeds 8000 kg. There are various styles of soft-shackle, but a self-closing soft-shackle offers the highest security.

The most significant advantage, and disadvantage, of a soft-shackle is that the loop size is fixed. It's ideal if you discover the perfect length but less so if not. Ideally, you should learn how to tie and splice your shackles, creating a custom shackle for TRS — a skill handy for various gear-related issues. A soft-shackle should be regarded as specialist equipment and must be thoroughly understood before being utilised for life support.

Device Suitability

This method is most practical when using a device that can be attached and detached from the climbing-line without having to remove it from the harness. Such devices include most lever-action devices, like the Petzl Rescuecender, and full frame eccentric devices, specific pro models of PCPs, and the Taz3. With these devices, you tie them to your harness at the start of the day and simply remove them at the end.

Once you master tying in and out, it's feasible to use this technique with any device. Soon, the use of bulky rigid metal karabiners will seem suboptimal compared to a soft connection.

The only devices that should not be used are those where the climbing-line touches or runs close to the tie-in cord, such as on a Petzl Traxion device, as this will result in melting and connector failure.

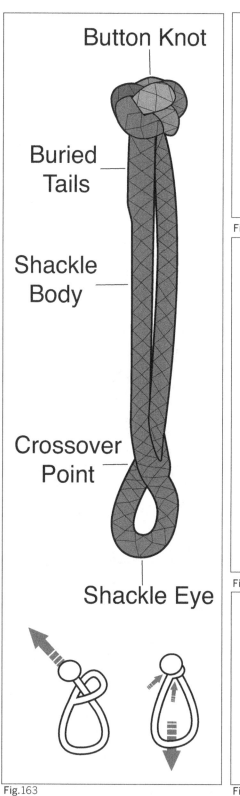

Button Knot

Buried Tails

Shackle Body

Crossover Point

Shackle Eye

Fig.163

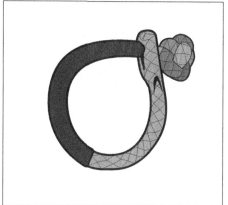

Fig.164

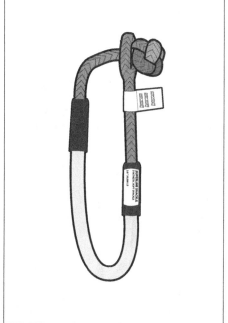

Fig.165

Fig.166

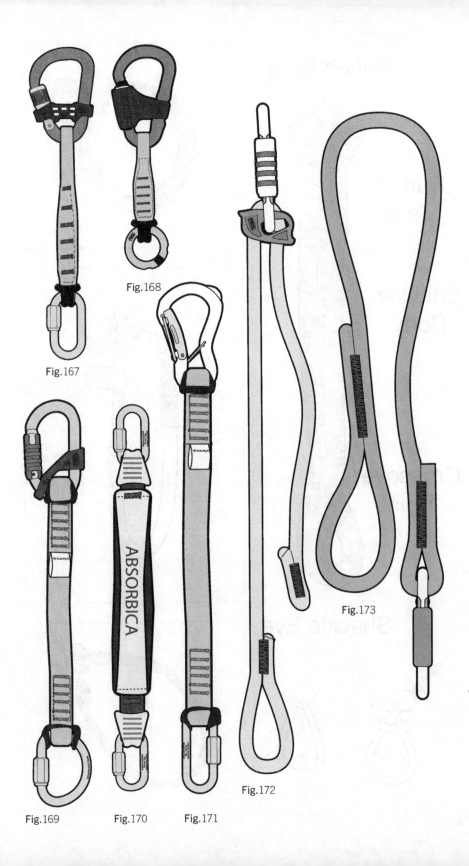

Fig.167

Fig.168

Fig.169

Fig.170

Fig.171

Fig.172

Fig.173

Lanyards

 167
22 cm Express quickdraw fitted with 7 mm quick-link and Petzl Petzl Attache SL.

 168
11 cm Express quickdraw fitted with DMM Belay Master and Petzl Ring Open.

 169
Camp 26 cm Goblin Lanyard fitted with a Petzl OK (with Connector bar) and 11 mm delta quick-link.

170
Petzl 40 cm ASAP'SORBER.

171
Camp 40 cm Goblin Lanyard fitted with a Grivel Clepsydra L K10G and 9 mm wide opening quick-link.

172
Petzl Adjust.

173
Beal Dynaclip.

Margin Call
Make it a rule that whenever you use a non-shock-absorbing lanyard, never allow your belay loop to go higher than the clip-in point on your lanyard. The factor-2 forces generated if you fall could be enough to break karabiners, lanyards, devices, or you!

There are several reasons why a climber might want to create some distance between themselves and their TRS device.

These include:

- Reduce the risk of panic-grabbing the device.
- Move a secondary away from the primary device.
- Extend the distance between the climber and the secondary device attached to the safety-line so that the line stays out of the climber's way.
- Allow the higher secondary device on a 2:1 system some distance to grab the rope without striking a non-functioning primary device.
- Clip in and out of anchors.
- Clip in and out of re-belays and re-achors.

Basics

An extension or lanyard, whether made from webbing or rope, needs to be extremely high strength, dynamic — so shock absorbing — and kept to a length that does its job but will not increase the fall factor to a dangerous degree.

As a rule of thumb, an extension should be less than 60 cm in length (without connectors).

Although some climbers may look to employ climbing slings in this role, these are not suitable in terms of strength or ability to withstand a hard factor-2 fall. For example, if an 80-kilo climber were to fall onto their secondary device close to the anchor, with almost no stretch in the rope, the secondary device 60 cm+ below them, a 60 cm Dyneema sling could easily break.

Instead, the climber should use either a dedicated industrial shock-absorbing extension sling, a short (10 cm to 30 cm) 'dog-bone' or express quickdraw, a rope lanyard, such as the Petzl Adjust, or a self-tied cow's-tail made from a single rated rope. All of these should be able to hold a hard factor-2 fall without breaking.

I would use a short extender if using any eccentric device or any device that will damage the rope rather than slip, as this shorter extension will reduce the risk of a high-factor fall, being more of a swing.

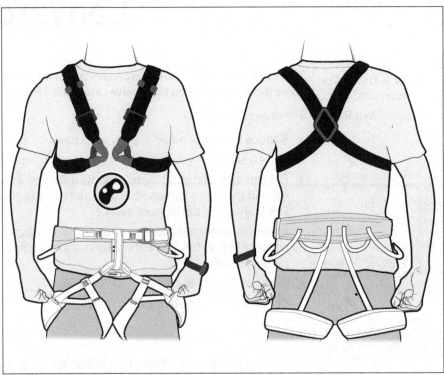

Fig.174

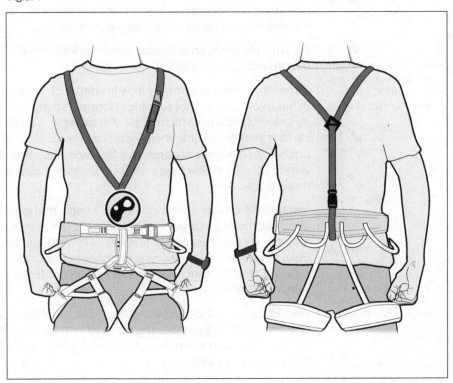

Fig.175

Chest Slings

 174
Full weight chest sling, designed to work with either a delta quick-link or delta karabiner.

✎ 175
Petzl Torse positioning sling.

Margin Call
When I was about 16, I was rappelling back down a climb and discovered the rope didn't quite reach the ground, necessitating some down-climbing. It seemed better to jump down the last bit at some point, which I did, but only to come to a yanking hard stop before my feet hit the ground. It took me a second to understand why I was hanging there, and then I realised a sling I'd been carrying over my shoulder had hung up on a tiny spike as I jumped. This story was very instructive because if I'd had the sling around my neck, I'd either have broken it (my neck, not the sling) or strangled myself. Ever since that day, I've been very weary of putting anything around my neck or even over my shoulder, as there are countless ways to get hung up when climbing. You can also note that people who operate heavy machinery don't wear lanyards for the same reason.

Many TRS devices work best if lifted above the waist, positioning them between the sternum and the belly button. This higher suspension point is also vital when running two TRS devices on the climbing-line, as it stops them from clashing. There are several ways to elevate a device, each having its own pros and cons.

Full Strength Chest Harness

This is a heavy-duty webbing harness that fits across the shoulders and is secured at the front, most often by a delta quick-link or d shaped locker, such as the Petzl Omni Tri-act-Lock. The primary users for such a harness are industrial rope access workers and cavers, and the chest harness is a key component of the 'frog' rope climbing system, used to lift the chest ascender as the climber pumps their foot-loop.

Although such a harness is an excellent way to support the upper body and works great with chest ascenders, it can also be heavy, sweaty, and uncomfortable. To be effective, and move the chest ascender up most efficiently for rope climbing, a chest harness is usually fitted in such a way that the user is hunched over when standing.

Although good for rope climbing, for TRS, a full-weight chest harness is overkill as it's more of an industrial solution, and has even fallen out of favour for caving.

If you own a full strength chest ascender then try it, as you might like it. Otherwise, move on to the other better alternatives.

Positioning sling

This is a lightweight webbing sling that attaches to the back of the harness, runs over both shoulders, and is usually threaded into the device rather than using a hard link. A metal buckle on the front of the sling allows tension to be increased and decreased, a vital feature when using a chest ascender, which requires tension to work effectively.

This style of sling is lightweight, low cost, and can be sewn up by the climber if they don't want to buy a commercial version.

For TRS, this style of sling avoids most of the issues found with a full-weight chest harness but does require a certain amount of getting used to.

Parisienne Baudrier Harness: put your arm through the sling and wrap it around your back. Tie the two loops with a Sheet Bend. Don't put the sling's end through the shoulder loop, or it could create a dangerous knot that gets tighter under pressure and could kill you. Use the leftover loop from the knot to attach more gear.

There are several ways to use either a single 120 cm sling, or two 60 cm slings to form a chest sling. In this version a 120 cm sling is twisted at the back, and each end tied with a larks foot into a locking karabiner. If the sling is too long, then knots will need to be tied to shorten.

Chest sling constructed from two 60 cm slings with knots added to achieve a good fit.

Neck elastic. Effective, but could lead to strangulation!

178

Bungee sash: neck elastic over the shoulder, safer, but can slip off the shoulder unless there is enough tension.

X Chest sling

This style of sling is made by crossing over a 120 cm sling or linking two 60 cm slings and putting arms through each loop, with knots used to fine-tune.

This system is simple and uses standard gear all climbers will own, and yet is very high strength. The downsides are it needs fine adjustment to work effectively and will often be either too baggy or too restrictive.

Making your own webbing X sling with off a roll is also an option if you want to get the perfect fit, but the best X slings can be made out of a medium-weight bungee cord (5 mm or 8 mm), which makes getting the correct fit easier, as the loop is tied to fit the user.

Neck Elastic

Wearing a loop of 3 mm bungee around your neck, like a lanyard, appears to be a popular choice for TRS, being cheap, simple, and unobtrusive. The obvious flaw with this approach is that anything that wraps around the neck, even if one end is attached to a device, poses a risk of strangulation and asphyxiation, and climbing has many stories of climbers who were strangled by ropes, slings, and even scarves.

If using this method, it's vital that the neck elastic is connected to the device in such a way that it cannot detach in a fall and leave the climber literally hanging high. As an aside, when not in use, either take off the neck elastic, or put one arm through it, as you can also strangle oneself when coming down from a climb as easily as going up one.

Climbers should also not be under the false assumption that using thin 3 mm bungee, as it would break if fully loaded, is safe; this is false, as a loop of 3 mm bungee can still hold body weight, so strangulation is possible.

Some may also believe that as long as the neck elastic remains connected to the TRS device that they are safe, but if one is knocked unconscious, it's still possible to sag upside down in a harness and for the cord to strangle the climber.

Bungee Sash

And alternative to a neck elastic is to use a bungee loop that runs over one shoulder. As long as tension is maintained, it should stay in place, but still requires careful adjustment for the user.

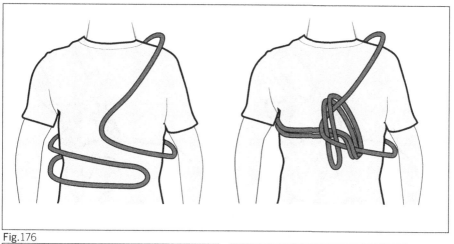

Fig.176

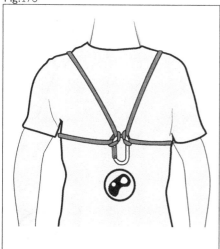

Fig.177

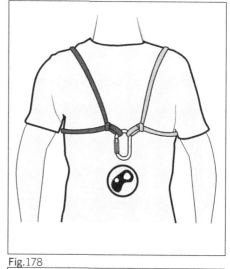

Fig.178

Fig.179

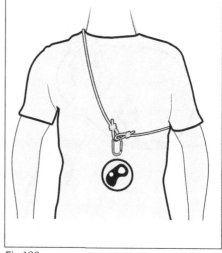

Fig.180

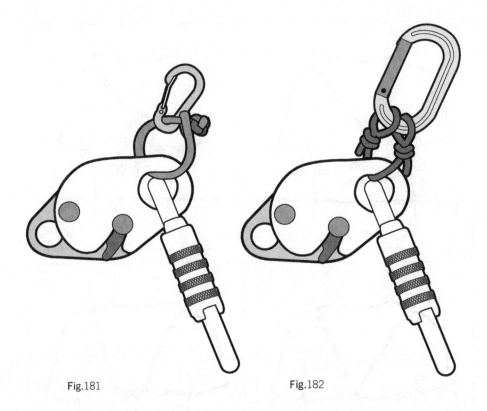

Fig.181   Fig.182

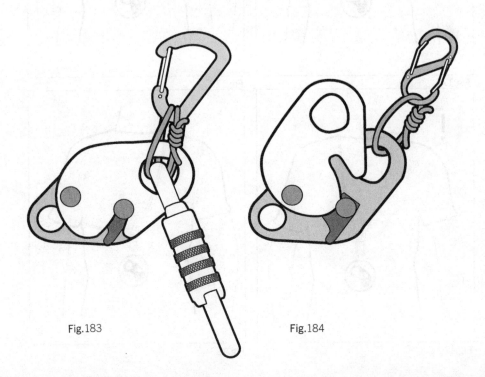

Fig.183   Fig.184

Link Cord

🖋 181
Soft link tension link through one side of the TRS plate.

🖋 182
Small diameter cord with clip in loops at each end, passed through device clip in point.

🖋 183
Cord loop looped on either side of the connector.

🖋 184
Loop tied directly into clip in point with micro connector.

While it's ideal to maintain a tension between the chest sling and harness that's just on the edge of being uncomfortable for rope climbing, this kind of set-up isn't optimal for TRS climbing. However, the right tension is crucial; every centimetre of slack equates to an additional two centimetres of potential drop onto the rope as the device rotates to meet the load. Also, it's vital that devices are kept in an optimal feed orientation, which can require the kind of micro adjustment in pull that a full size chest strap cannot provide. To harmonize these conflicting needs, climbers can introduce a small elastic or cord link into their set-up.

This link can be a simple loop made from a thin bungee cord, which can be attached in various ways. The primary concern is low strength. If it fails, it can pose a strangulation risk if used in combination with positioning straps or neck cords.

One method to enhance the strength is by crafting a full-strength tension loop: feed heavy-duty elastic through a short piece of tubular webbing and sew it into a loop while the elastic is taut. Alternatively, one could adapt one of the robust elastic lanyards available in the market, typically designed for holding tools like chainsaws, by cutting and tying or sewing.

For TRS set-ups, a traditional chest harness connects to a chest ascender using an upper clip-in point located on the ascender's frame. However, most TRS devices lack a secondary clip-in point, and the primary one is often occupied by the main connector. To navigate this, climbers can employ a small-diameter cord to elevate the device and attach it to the chest harness. Here are some methods:

- **Strop**: Use a short cord with loops tied on both ends. Feed this through the clip-in point before attaching the primary connector. Then, secure it to the chest harness using an accessory karabiner.

- **Shackle**: Utilize a 3mm Dyneema shackle. Loop it through the device, lock it in place, and then connect either directly or with a compact connector.

- **Loop**: A 20cm 3mm Dyneema loop can be set on either side of the primary connector. It can be threaded directly into the chest harness or attached with a smaller connector. While a non-Dyneema loop can serve the purpose, it usually has a knot that might interfere with the TRS device.

- **Fixed Loop**: Tie a fixed loop of cord into one side of the device plate.

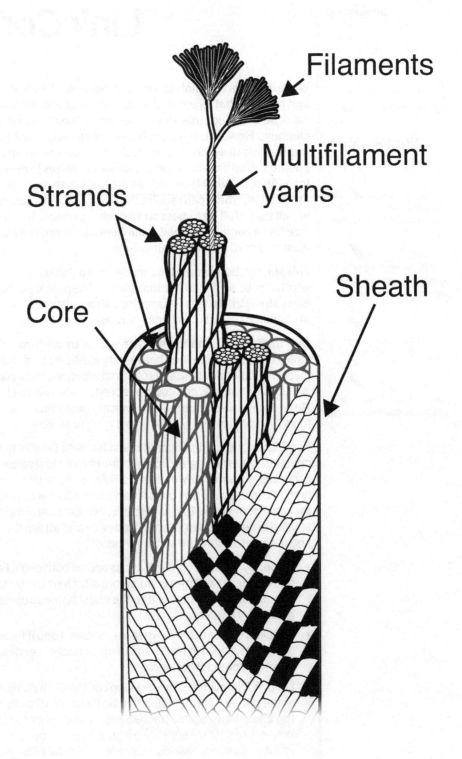

Filaments

Multifilament yarns

Strands

Sheath

Core

Fig.185

TRS Ropes

"Every guilty person is his own hangman."

Seneca

✎ 185
Rope construction.

Climbing ropes never seem to get the kudos they deserve in being the glue that connects everything together, the climber to their life most of all. Instead, they're used and abused, torn up and abraded, dunked in the sea and frozen solid, then thawed out in the boot of a car. TRS ropes are no different, but it's worth noting that TRS ropes are typically not used the same as climbing ropes but rather as rigging ropes, which are different.

A climbing rope is designed to balance weight, strength, and dynamic catch, as well as robustness and cost; they're for moving over stone, ice, and snow. A fixed rope does not really move, and its primary role is one of security and strength. Many of the TRS accidents can be traced to confusion over climbing versus rigging ropes, and studying caving or rope access manuals is far more productive for the novice TR soloist than books on climbing technique.

TRS Rope Types
There are two types of ropes that can be used for TRS, the climbing-line and the safety-line. The climbing-line is the rope that will carry the climber's primary TRS device(s), accept catastrophe-knots, and be rappelled down once they have finished. This acts like the climber's primary parachute, and traditionally, climbers have only employed a climbing-line.

The safety-line is the reserve parachute and hangs in line with the climbing-line, although often offset by a meter so as not to interfere with the climbing-line. This rope carries a secondary TRS device that self-trails up (and ideally down) the line as the climber moves. No catastrophe-knots are tied into this rope, and the rope will only catch the climber if their climbing-line, or primary device, fails.

Diameter
If ropes are rigged correctly and the necessary skill level in TRS is developed, ropes should never be taxed by sharp edges or be asked to withstand high dynamic forces, such as high factor falls. Instead, they will be used more as rigging ropes, fixed in place, employing the same methodology as caving or industrial rope access.

Although climbers will use a wide range of ropes for TRS, including their everyday lead climbing dynamic ropes, the ideal climbing-line is a medium (10 mm) to large (11 mm) diameter, low-stretch, single-rated rope. This will give the

Margin Call

A good quality low-stretch rope is not something a beginner will want to invest in, as one needs many other bits of equipment and kit first. But once you're fully in the game of climbing, owning a thick and stout static, ideally a 70 metre x 1 1 mm (or 60 metre 10 mm if you want a lighter weight option), will give you a decade of good service. Such a rope can be used for TRS, top roping (ignore anyone who says you shouldn't), and fixed rappels for access and retreat, such as on sea cliffs, plus the odd big wall. If it's looked after and well stored, you'll reap a big safety dividend and have a better tool for specific jobs than using your fancy dynamic climbing rope.

climber a very solid and dependable rope for years of solo climbing and general rigging. A low-stretch rope is also built for rigging, with a sheath and core construction able to best handle rope tools, such as ascenders and rappel devices, and tough enough to handle intensive rope climbing and descent.

A safety-line can also make use of the same type of rope, but due to its role as a back-up, it may be worth considering a medium diameter, workhorse, dynamic rope between 10 mm and 10.5 mm. Many of the ropes designated for climbing wall use are ideal for this purpose, as they are very robust but have a higher degree of shock absorbency over a low-stretch rope.

In terms of safety, low-stretch ropes that weave the core and sheath together are highly advisable, as they offer much higher protection from abrasion.

Weight

One issue worth considering for the TR soloist is that they have to carry all of the rack, ropes, rigging kit, and assorted climbing junk. On a roadside crag, this isn't a big deal, but a climber will not have to go far for it to suddenly weigh them down. This is one reason why medium-weight ropes are often ideal and why doubling up a single rope for a two-rope system makes sense if the crag is the appropriate height.

Rope Length

Most solo climbers will have a certain crag where they practice TRS, so they can customize a rope system for that crag. For example, the standard rope length is 60 meters, but if used to top rope 20-meter outcrops, that's a lot of wasted rope, doubly so if a two-rope system is used. Instead, shorter static ropes or offcuts or simply using a single rope doubled can produce two 30-meter strands.

The opposite is also true, and some climbers who want to TRS much bigger cliffs might choose to use extra-long ropes, allowing them to anchor the rope at the top of the cliff and perhaps span two or more pitches in one rope length. It is also possible to tie multiple ropes together, but these require re-anchors; otherwise, a fall low down could see the climber crater due to rope stretch, even with low-stretch ropes. It's also important to know how to pass knots along the way.

Device Matching

It's vital that TRS devices are used with the correct diameter rope and understand that even if a device says it will work with 8 mm ropes, this would be considered an expedition rope, not a rigging rope. Also, note that several modern belay devices are designed for the current standard sport climbing ropes, say between 9 mm and 9.5 mm, which, again, are not rigging rope diameters.

As a rule of thumb, most industrial devices are rated for 10.5 mm low-stretch ropes and above.

In my experience, all devices tend to work well on a 10 mm low-stretch, apart from specialized small diameter sport belay devices that some might use for TRS, such as the mark II GriGri.

Can a static rope take a dynamic fall?

The longest expected fall on a well-rigged system will be less than two meters: this being a fall onto a secondary device on a 60 cm lanyard attached to the safety-line. But generally, in the ideal set-up, the climbing-line should not have to hold a force greater than a climber simply sagging down on their TRS device, a distance of less than 60 cm.

There are several ways that a catastrophic failure could take place, in which the rope would be asked to hold a high-impact force. These include:

- The device fails, and the climber falls down the rope to a catastrophe-knot.

- The rope does not feed through the device, and so a 'live loop' builds below the climber, increasing the fall if they then fall.

- The climber climbs above the belay, re-direct, or re-anchor without noticing, and then falls.

- The live rope becomes jammed above the climber, and the climber climbs beyond the jam, creating another type of death loop, and then falls.

- On a high wind day, with an inadequately weighted rope, the live rope may act like a sail and drag itself through the device, magnifying any fall, even creating a ground fall outcome.

Suboptimal Ropes

Many climbers will not have access to ideal ropes and will use the ropes they have. I would strongly advise against using half ropes (8 mm - 9 mm), as they're just not designed for rigging.

If a climber owns just a very thin single 'sport' rope (9 mm - 9.8 mm), then this style of rope should be used with extreme caution, both in terms of checking they're compatible with the TRS device and their lack of robustness. The only safe way to use such ropes is to rely heavily on re-anchors and re-directs to minimize the yo-yo action of the rope. Pay close attention to any wear points, as a brand-new sporty rope can be rendered bin-ready in only a few minutes of swinging about.

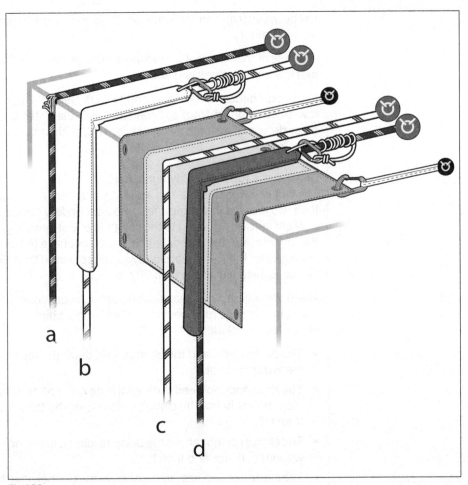

a

b

c

d

Fig.186

Fig.187

Rope Protection

 186
Unprotected rope (a), rope with rope sleeve (b), rope set on rope pad (c), and rope protected by both a rope sleeve and rope pad.

 187
A friction hitch on a rope sleeve or pad will only have to hold a tiny load, and so a climber can use a very basic friction hitch to set the protector in place.

Margin Call
I've experienced a lot of damaged ropes in my time, and apart from rock fall (rocks you pull off while leading or rocks trundled by the mountain Gods, just for fun), most damage was caused by carelessness, complacency, or a misplaced confidence in how much damage the sheath of a rope could endure. The first time I ever stripped a sheath was when top rope soloing on a rope far too skinny for the job. Every time I fell, the rope would saw across a cheese grater gritstone edge – until the fateful last fall – when I didn't stop but zipped down the rope on a now mobile sheath. What saved me was the sheath bunching up on my catastrophe-knot. Lesson learnt – in fact, several lessons.

Edge protection is a key component of rope rigging and should be standard practice, no matter how benign edges appear. If you take the time to rig your ropes properly and set robust edge protection, it sets a precedent for others to follow. Thus, it is not an extra step in the process of building a TRS system but an integral part of it.

Edge protection ensures the security and integrity of your ropes, reducing the likelihood of your climbing-line being abraded or cut. Full separation is typically caused by cycles of lateral movement, such as multiple swinging falls, leading to the edge sawing at the rope. Repeated direct loading and unloading can also cause damage, especially with ropes that have high static elongation. In either scenario, the presence of flint, crystals, or broken pebbles in the rock can exacerbate potential damage. Beyond safeguarding your ropes, edge protection also helps to maximise a rope's lifespan and minimises impact on the rock, ensuring no visible trace of climbers' activities.

Edge protection is available in both hard and soft forms, such as metal edge rollers versus canvas rope wraps. Hard protection is designed for moving lines, suitable for rope rescues, while soft protection is ideal for static lines.

Historically, the best materials for rope protection have been natural fibres like canvas. Traditional heavy-duty fabrics made from Nylon or Polyester tend to wear and melt rapidly under rope friction, which is evident when a rucksack or fleece is used as padding. However, materials like Kevlar and ballistic Nylon are becoming more prevalent, with top commercial products often blending different fabrics.

Commercial edge protection for TRS is categorised into:

Rope Sleeves

These are popular edge protectors. They're essentially fabric rectangles that wrap around the rope, secured with Velcro to form a tube. The sleeve stays in place with a hitch loop attached via an eyelet or tab. While you can tie the rope sleeve into a knot in the rope, it introduces another potential wear point, and such knots might be challenging to untie unless the rope is unloaded. I'd recommend replacing the typical 3 mm cord with a single 5 mm strand with a small karabiner at the end. This arrangement is more manageable one-handed and allows quick setting and resetting of a friction hitch by wrap-

🖊 188
Rope Sleeve.

🖊 189
Rope pad.

🖊 190
How to use a rope pad.

Margin Call
*The brilliant dry tooling tip
of imagining you have a cup
of coffee balanced on the
head of your axe, once it's
set on a rock edge, can also
be applied to rope climbing.
What destroys rope sheaths
is jerky, violent, hard stop-
start movements. Imagining
a cup of coffee, or tea (not
Earl Grey), balanced on
your ascenders should help
to maintain a smoother
transition from weighted to
unweighted. Also, smaller
movements are kinder to
both the body and rope,
and will usually see you
to the anchor faster than
big strokes with your top
ascender and crazy rock
overs into your foot-loop.
Fundamentally, the best way
to avoid damaging, or even
cutting, your rope, is to learn
how to climb ropes properly,
which simply takes a little
time and practice.*

ping the cord around the rope and clipping the end back into itself. Do note that a full-strength friction hitch isn't necessary; it's merely for positioning.

The Spiroll protector deserves a special mention, as it is a length of Polyurethane that wraps itself around a rope without the need for friction hitches.

Using rope sleeves mid-pitch can be cumbersome, but they're convenient near the anchor. Regardless, each time a climber wishes to scale the same line, the rope sleeve needs resetting.

Rope sleeves vary in length, but opt for longer ones (60+ cm) for maximum protection. As ropes move when loaded and unloaded, it's prudent to set a rope sleeve while descending, allowing for optimal positioning. If the line is unweighted, climbers must ensure the protector will be correctly positioned when the rope is under tension.

Rope Pad
Larger than sleeves, these are rectangles of durable, sometimes padded, robust fabric - generally natural fibres that will not melt - sewn with multiple clip-off points. Unlike sleeves, pads are attached to the rock edge itself and give a broader coverage of edge protection. While ropes might shift slightly upon loading and unloading, the pad remains stationary.

They can be secured using karabiners, friction hitches or by wrapping them within the pad, creating a large rope sleeve.

Impromptu rope pads can be fashioned from carpet remnants, doormats, or rubber matting (add clip in loops).

One advantage of rope pads is that they protect both knots and individual strands of rope, making them ideal for bulky masterpoints, plus they give you somewhere to sit while drinking tea, contemplating your place in climbing, and universe.

Choosing between a sleeve and a pad isn't an either/or decision. Layering protection is advisable, especially on jagged, abrasive rock types or on delicate rock.

Why bother?

Ropes might appear fickle: most of the time, they can handle sustained abuse without damage or complaint, and then — in the blink of an eye — they rub and abrade down to shoelace thickness. In reality, the mechanics of rope damage are straightforward; it's the motion of a loaded rope across a static edge or protrusion. Eliminating all motion could save your ropes, but this is often impossible, so using something to absorb and soak up that motion — like a sleeve or pad — is the best way to save your ropes and your life.

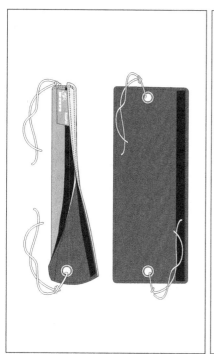

Fig.188

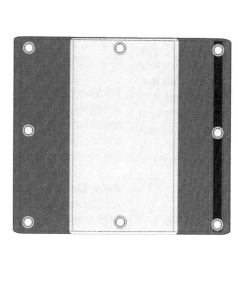

Fig.189

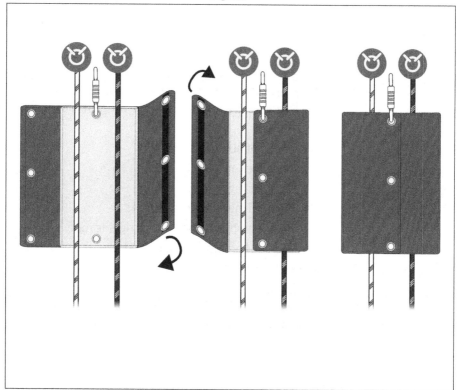

Fig.190

Other Gear

"The rifle is the first weapon you learn how to use, because it lets you keep your distance from the client. The closer you get to being a pro, the closer you can get to the client. The knife, for example, is the last thing you learn."

Leon

Harness
Any climbing harness with a standard tie-in point and belay loop works great for TRS.

Friction Hitches
It's vital that the climber can escape the system alone, so they should always carry a short (1.3 metres) and long (2.5 metres) friction cord (5 mm or 6 mm). These should be carried even if the climber has mechanical ascenders.

Belay Device
A climber who cannot carry on will climb the rope using their TRS device or rappel, meaning a belay device is vital. If the climber is a clumsy idiot, then consider carrying two.

ABD (Assisted Breaking Belay Device)
Having an assisted breaking belay device can be very handy when escaping the system or setting re-anchors, but never put all trust in its locking abilities when undertaking complex escapes, as the word is "assisted" or "automatic". Learn how to do both a soft and hard lock on your ABD.

Rigging Equipment
Anyone reading this book should know how to set up an anchor, but a top rope belay is a little different and might require some extra gear. Here's the run-down of a typical rigging kit:

- 2 x sets of climbing nuts (1-10).
- 1 x set of 'Hex' style nuts (7-11).
- 3 x 120 cm slings.
- 2 x 7 mm x 5 metres cordelettes.
- 1 x 20 metres 10 mm low-stretch rigging rope.
- 10 x locking karabiners (small and large).
- Edge protection.

A rigging rope can be used for slinging very large objects, extending far-off pieces, or used as a super cordelette. If it hangs down over an edge, in order to protect the climbing-line, don't forget to protect it.

Micro Ascender

If you own one, carry it, as it will make getting off your TRS device far easier, and with less hassle. If you don't own one, buy one.

Knife Stack

When all else fails, a knife always comes in handy (practice on a loaded rope to see how dangerously easy it cuts). Carry it on your harness in a position that allows it to be unclipped by either hand. I carry mine on a loop of cord that includes a 5 mm quick-link, whistle, and small role of Mueller tape. The tape can come in handy for everything from running rope repairs, taping up plain gate karabiners when you've run out of lockers, to emergency first aid. If you find yourself needing to cut a rope or sling without a knife, use a friction hitch like a wire saw, using the heat generated to melt through the material.

Helmet

When TR soloing, the rope is always above and has the capacity to dislodge 'stuff', which is just one reason why wearing a helmet is a no-brainer, while not wearing one could lead to no brain at all.

First Aid Kit

A solo climber has no one to call on but themselves, so a small first aid kit should always be carried. Yes, the amount of first aid you can do on yourself is limited, but having something to keep the blood out of your eyes is handy while you stagger for help. All my first aid kits, no matter how small, always contain a small micro LED torch, the style that uses a flat battery. This will save your bacon one day, guaranteed.

Emergency Communication

Always have a phone and tell someone where you're going. If you're going somewhere remote and may need someone to come and find you, consider taking a modern emergency contact device, such as the Garmin inReach Mini or Spot. Perhaps the best low-tech emergency communication come in the form of a whistle on your harness, attached to your knife, as this can alert other climbers if you find yourself stuck on the rope.

Light

If there's a one-in-a-hundred chance that darkness might catch you on the rope, carry a micro headlamp on your harness or helmet. If it's one-in-a-million, have one in your pack. If you don't have a light, use your phone light.

Flask of tea

Not Earl Grey.

Fig.191

SYSTEM

Having studied all the equipment needed for safe TR soloing, let's start piecing the various rope systems that can be employed. For clarity, the terms 'single rope' and 'double rope' will be avoided and replaced by 'one rope' or 'two ropes' to avoid a mix-up with CE/UIAA rope labelling.

 191

A two line system, with one climbing and one safety-line, is based on standard working practice in industrial rope access. It further expands a systems overall redundancy.

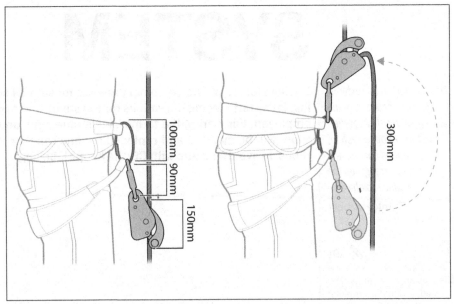

Fig.192

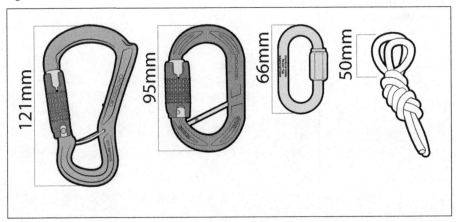

Fig.193

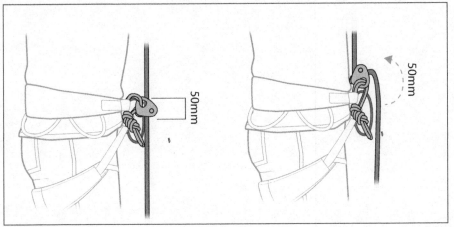

Fig.194

Attachment

Now that I've covered the devices, connectors, ropes, and rope systems, let's look at linking them together and how to attach a device or devices to their ropes.

1:1 - 1 Device/1 Rope

🖉 192
Lag times are cumulative.

The climber attaches one TRS device to the climbing-line.

🖉 193

The size of your connectors can matter, unless a little fall is no big thing.

Set-ups
I will set out four methods below, and it should be noted that one of these will form the core set-up of multiple device systems as well.

🖉 194

A micro device, tied directly into a harness gives the smallest degree of drag, like a fall factor of 0.1.

In the descriptions below, the starting point is that the TRS device is attached to the climbing-line in the correct orientation.

BELAY LOOP SET-UP
Clip a connector into the TRS device, ideally a connector that limits cross-loading or twisting, then clip this into the belay loop. That's it.

Margin Call
Some climbers have an irrational fear of their belay loop snapping. They must wake up at night, screaming while clutching their crotch. When you compare the safety chain a climber uses, from ropes to karabiners, cams to belay devices, be assured the last thing that will break is the belay loop. I've seen harness pull tests where they stick a harness on a metal torso, invert it, and start pulling as if the climber weighed fifty tons or were holding a fifty-ton leader in a fall. In every test I've witnessed, it was stopped before the belay loop failed, as it looked like the testing machine would break first. The only time to be afraid of a belay loop is when it's gone bad, is worn out, or damaged. Now it's time to get the heebie jeebies (bin it and buy a new one).

As the climber climbs, the connector slides down to the bottom of their belay loop, generally placing the device between their groin and knees, depending on the size of the connector, device, and groin. As the climber moves up, the device is uplifted by the belay loop.

If a device has poor self-tending properties or is a low-diameter device used on a high-diameter rope, there will be some harness drag, where the harness is pulled down, creating the same effect as rope drag. This needs to be avoided, and ideal devices will move with so little friction that it will go unnoticed until the climber weights it.

If the climber falls or sits back onto the device, they will experience what feels like a significant drop as the device connector travels to the top of the belay loop, rotates 180 degrees, and then fully loads the device. The drop distance will be approximately the height of the belay loop plus the height of the connector times two, roughly between 30 cm to 60 cm. Although this might sound like a short drop, this can still be jarring and does put a strain on all links in the chain. The momentary weightlessness, waiting for the device to catch, can also be scary for those who have yet to establish confidence in their system and could lead to panic-grabbing of the rope or device, which could partly or fully disable it.

195
TRS device clipped
into belay loop.

196
TRS device clipped
into lift loop.

197
Lift loop tied direct into
the harness belt. Although
this would be danger-
ous in a dynamic fall, as
the transfer of fall energy
to the legs is vital, for a
static hang it feels OK.

The size of the connector is a double-edged sword in that the longer it is, the greater the drop, but the greater the drop, the greater the wiggle room before the device locks if the climber wants to move down a little. A quick-link can create a very short drop but will result in the climber fighting the rope more. For example, a DMM Boa locker creates a drop of 244 cm, while a 7 mm quick-link is only 148 cm.

There is also the issue of the instability of a low device, increasing the risk of flipping upside down when the device is below the belly button, this risk increasing the steeper the climb.

Some climbers stress about the strength of their belay loop, but in a break test of every link of the climbing chain, the belay loop would be the last to break.

The thing to worry about is a free-floating connector in the belay loop, as the connector has to be in the correct orientation when force is applied, which is why anti-rotation is vital.

There is also the risk that the device might get trapped between the climber's thighs, which could disable it, although having a device go between a climber's legs can stop it from scraping or catching on the rock.

The pros of this set-up are simplicity and that extra degree of freedom; the cons are that the device and its connectors are free to move around, plus there's a slight jarring fall.

BELAY LOOP / LIFT-LOOP SET-UP

This works as above but lifts the connector from the bottom of the belay loop to the top, holding it in position by way of an extra mini loop that passes through the harness's waist belt, clipping the connector through both this mini-loop and belay loop.

This loop can be formed in several ways:

- 1m x 5mm double loop of Perlon, tied with a Fisherman's knot or two overhand knots. Ensure tails are tucked away so they cannot interfere with the device.

- Delta Quick Link. This method attaches a medium-sized quick-link to the tie-in point, creating a low-profile hard point.

- Soft Shackle. This is easy to remove and is very strong (go with around 4 mm Dyneema), and is both body, harness, and connector-friendly.

By clipping the connector into the mini-loop and belay loop, the climber removes the travel distance up the belay loop in a fall and also lifts the device just below the groin. This reduction can reduce both panic-grabbing as well as interference from the climber's thighs.

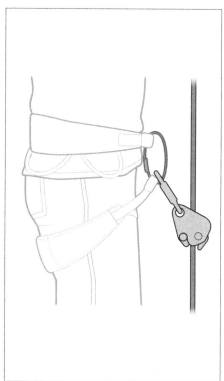

Fig.195

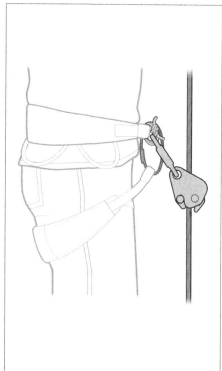

Fig.196

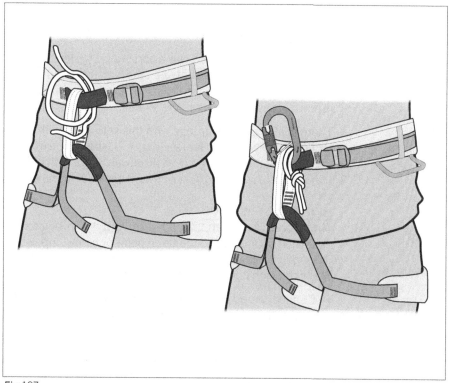

Fig.197

198

TRS device set at belly button.

199

Laggy TRS device set at belly button.

200

Chest ascender set at belly button.

201

Front view of belly button position.

The evident risk with this arrangement is that a climber might fail to clip into the belay loop and instead only be attached to a slender loop of cord. The pull on the harness is now directed solely to the harness's waist, which can be uncomfortable with a high-drag device and could be hazardous for dynamic falls or prolonged suspension.

The other issue is that such an approach would appear to shift the load solely to the waist belt, rather than distributing it between the waist and legs. Although this shift would be dangerous in dynamic falls, in expected TRS load, such loading will feel normal as the waist belt will lift and engage the leg loops.

BELLY BUTTON SET-UP

This follows the belay loop method but then adds in some form of chest positioning strap that lifts the connector to the top of the belay loop (and can also work in partnership with a mini-loop).

The device is held under tension between the positioning strap, connector, and belay loop. The moment the climber falls or sags onto the rope, the device should grab with minimal lag.

By lifting the device, the centre of gravity also rises, making the climber more stable. The device is also under tension between the chest and waist, resulting in less chance of cross-loading while also removing the risk of the device getting trapped by the thighs.

Lifting the device can also play a part in a 2:1 system, as it can provide enough distance between the high (primary) and low (secondary) devices to stop them from clashing, although this is down to several other factors as well.

There is also a disadvantage with this set-up, as with unidirectional devices, it will feel restrictive, as the device will grab the moment the climber moves downwards, but with bidirectional devices, such as rocker-arms, it can be an ideal match.

HIGH CHEST METHOD

The climber lifts the attachment point further by using a short extension connected to the tie-in point or belay loop, with a chest positioning sling holding the TRS device at the sternum. This extension can be made in several ways:

- Connect an open Dyneema or Aramid sling via the belay loop or through the leg and waist tie-in points. This can be looped, with both ends clipped into the device connector, larks footed, or tied, in order to fine-tune the distance. The obvious failure point when using an open sling is neglecting to clip in both ends, leading to failure. For this reason, it's

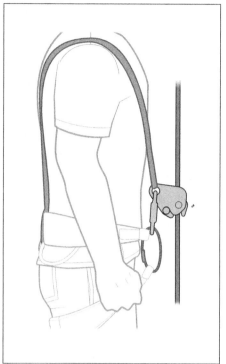

Fig.198

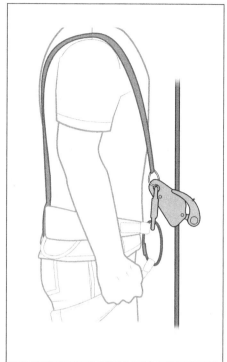

Fig.199

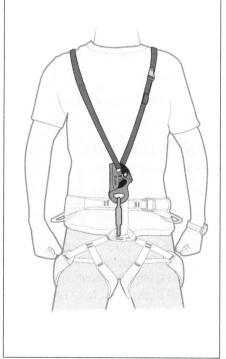

Fig.200

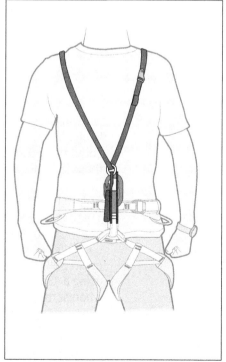

Fig.201

🖉 202

TRS device set in high chest position.

🖉 203

TRS device set at high position, with secondary set on belay loop. Note the distance if the secondary device locks.

🖉 204

Looped sling used to create distance for high chest position.

🖉 205

Dog bone and wide opening quick-link used to extend clip in point.

🖉 206

Petzl Ring used as a connection between a dog bone and the belay loop, with 7 mm Kong asymmetric quick-link used as connector to device.

🖉 207

Larks footed 30 cm open sling, connected into belay loop.

best to connect both ends into the connector using a Petzl String or equivalent at the start of climbing, or knotting the sling.

- Tie a loop of 5.5 mm Dyneema through the legs and waist tie-in points, fine-tuning it to the correct length. This removes the risk of mis-clipping a looped sling, but requires tying and untying. To reduce wear, it's also worth making it a double loop.

- Use a 7 mm large opening quick-link and a 10 cm 'dog-bone' quickdraw. The quick-link goes through the tie-in points on the harness and is then connected to the quickdraw. This is a very neat system. You could also use a Petzl Ring in place of a quick-link, but this will require a hex key for installation.

- Utilise a twisted 7 mm quick-link. This is attached to the belay loop and creates a 72 mm extension, with the twist allowing the device to be attached in the correct orientation. This is a very simple and robust solution, but I recommend that the quick-link is secured with a spanner.

The advantages of a higher attachment point include all those associated with the low chest method, plus a higher centre of gravity and less bulk around the waist, which can be important on hard climbs. This method also creates further space between primary and secondary devices, but it comes with the risk of the device striking the climber in the face, which is why any high system requires very careful consideration and testing.

Back-up
With no secondary device, the only option for a back-up comes from tying 'stopper' knots below the device into the climbing-line, but such a back-up should be viewed as unreliable. If a manual feeding device is used, then the climber could tie catastrophe-knots into the climbing-line and clip these into their belay loop.

Failure Points
There is very little room for error with a single device, and one must study the failure points of each part of the system carefully because catastrophe-knots are not that reliable and could well be simply illusionary. This means that the climber using a 1:1 system needs to be ultra thorough and paranoid when setting up each part of the system, from route choice to anchor, device choice, and connection.

Conclusion
In the past, most climbers used a 1:1 system, with the belay loop method being the most widely adopted, with catastro-

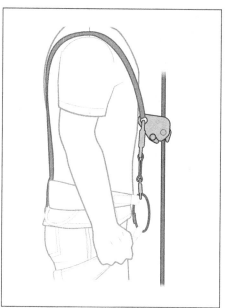

Fig.202

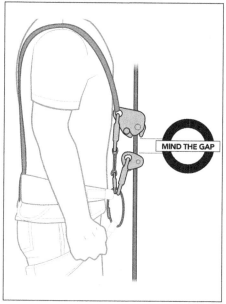

MIND THE GAP

Fig.203

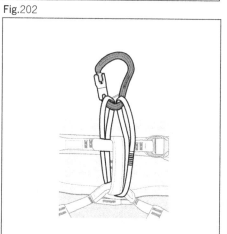

Fig.204

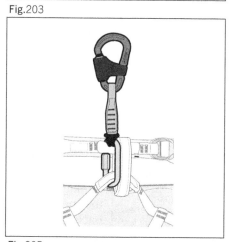

Fig.205

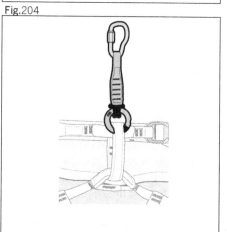

Fig.206

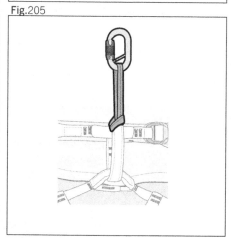

Fig.207

🖉 208
Primary and secondary devoices clipped into belay loop, with secondary device extended.

🖉 209
Primary and secondary devoices clipped into belay loop, with primary device connected to lift-loop.

🖉 210
Primary and secondary devices, with top device becoming the secondary device, as it's being pushed by the lower, primary device.

🖉 211
Primary set at belly button, with secondary on belay loop.

Margin Call
There are two keys to finding your perfect TRS set-up. The first is like buying a new pair of rock shoes: you must try as many shoes as possible to get the best shoe for you; you don't just go for the shoe someone on a forum tells you is the best. In this context, you try as many devices, systems and set-ups as possible. Try the state-of-the-art and old-school ways, but feel free to find your way. This process allows you to discover what works and what does not, and what you ultimately stick with can either be a hybrid of 'the way', 'the old way', and 'your way'. The second key is understanding it's the best system for you and no one else (so beware of telling everyone else it's the best).

phe-knots tied along the way. In retrospect, there are a lot of things that could go wrong, especially as there was limited concern about cross-loading or device shift back in the day. The fact that accidents were rare demonstrates that the theoretical failure points were 1 in 10,000 and, like many accidents, required multiple failures to align. Nevertheless, when top rope soloing on a single device, the climber must always be aware of that ten thousand to one risk, with every fall or sag being a relief when the device locks. Switching up to a two-device system removes that subconscious doubt, meaning the climber has a little more brain power to give to the climb.

2:1 - 2 Devices/One Rope

Description
The climber attaches two TRS devices, one primary and one secondary; one is placed above the other on the climbing-line. This set-up gives the climber redundancy in case one device fails, and can replace other problematic and perhaps illusory ass-saving techniques, such as catastrophe-knots.

Set-up
Attaching two TRS devices to a climbing-line should be simple. Just clip both of them into the belay loop, and away the climber goes. Well, it isn't, and doing it incorrectly can negate any safety advantage the climber thinks they have — one plus one, quite easily coming to zero.

Select the right device
First, the climber needs to select which device will be their primary and which is their secondary. The primary device is the one that will be loaded first, while the second acts as a fallback or redundancy in case the primary fails to grab the rope.

If both devices share the same mechanism, such as two eccentric devices (Petzl Croll and Edelrid Spoc), the choice is easy, as either will work. One of the main advantages of including an eccentric device in a system, especially in the secondary role, is that their action is the most dependable, which is why the Petzl Micro Traxion is a popular secondary TRS device.

But if the climber is using a rocker-arm and eccentric device combination, this requires a solid grasp of the limits and failure points of the rocker-arm mechanism, as assuming they're all the same could kill. Remember, just because they look the same and act the same, doesn't mean they're the same. Whenever two different devices are used, then the non-eccentric should be the primary device, and the eccentric the secondary, as it is better able to resist being depressed by the downward pressure from the primary device above.

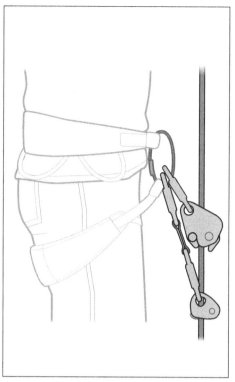

Fig.208

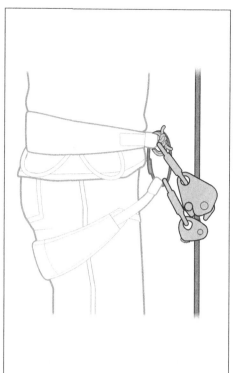

Fig.209

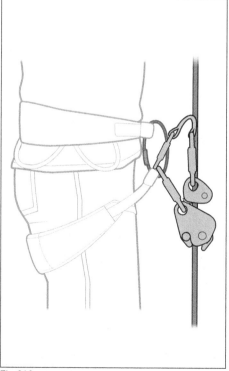

Fig.210

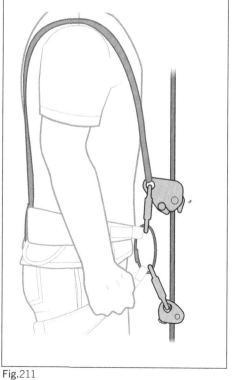

Fig.211

🖋 212
Eccentric (top) + eccentric (bottom) good.

🖋 213
Eccentric (T) + Lever (B) bad.

🖋 214
Eccentric (T) + Rocker (B) bad.

🖋 215
Rocker (T) + Rocker (B) bad.

🖋 216
Rocker (T) + Lever (B) bad.

🖋 217
Rocker (T) + Eccentric (B) Good.

🖋 218
Lever (T) + Lever (B) bad.

🖋 219
Lever (T) + Rocker (B) bad.

🖋 220
Lever (T) + Eccentric (B) good.

Distance matters

Devices must not collide or clash, as this could lead to fouling, blocking, depression, or disabling one or both devices. A gap must be maintained when moving and when weighing the rope, especially rocker-arm and lever devices, as any downward force may disable them.

The best way to achieve this distance is to adopt a high and low set-up, with the primary device on the chest and the secondary on the belay loop.

The reason for keeping this distance is to avoid the downward force of a high primary device that's disabled, sliding down the rope and hitting the secondary device and disabling it also.

An example of this failure point would go like this: the climber attaches a DMM Buddly (rocker-arm) to their belay loop as a secondary device and a Petzl Croll (eccentric) in a low chest position. While climbing, the jaw on the Croll disengages from the rope, and the climber drops down into the Buddy. But instead of being held by the Buddy, the frame of the Croll depresses the Buddy, which stops it from engaging, and the climber falls to the bottom of the climbing-line.

Ways to avoid this type of failure include:

- Use two eccentric devices, as an eccentric device will remain locked if depressed from above.
- Make sure the lower device is an eccentric device, so it cannot be blocked by the upper device.
- Employ a 2:2 system so that both devices have their own rope.
- Use a system where the device remains separate when loaded and unloaded.

The best way to test if a 2:1 system will work is to do a test hang on both from the primary device and then on the secondary, but with the primary still on the rope but disengaged. What the climber is looking out for is the primary device depressing the secondary, which could lead to failure.

Examples

Petzl Croll (P/Chest), Petzl Micro Traxion (S/Belay Loop).

Petzl Micro Traxion (P/Chest), Micro Traxion (S/Belay Loop).

Taz3 (P/Chest), Camp Goblin (S/Belay Loop).

Petzl Rescuecender (P/Chest), Petzl Ascension (S/Belay Loop).

Two devices on a Belay loop

A climber who wishes to avoid using a chest strap can run two devices on their belay loop, but they should be either two

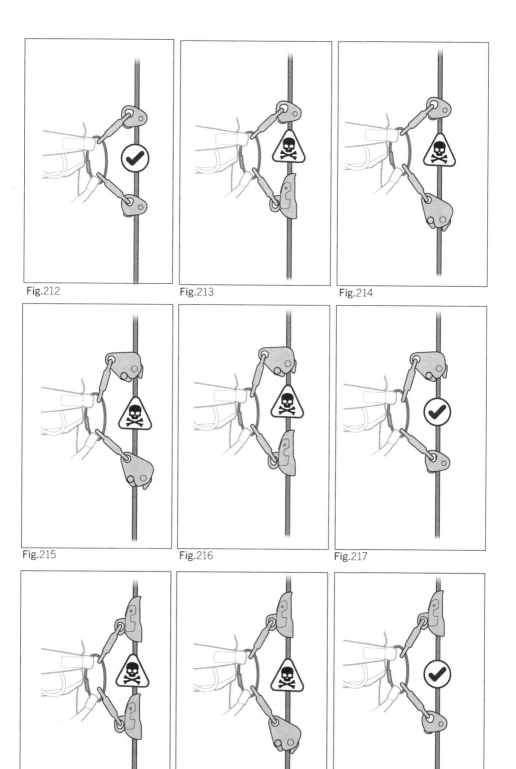

Fig.212

Fig.213

Fig.214

Fig.215

Fig.216

Fig.217

Fig.218

Fig.219

Fig.220

221

An eccentric device is highly aggressive, and will lock if pulled, pressed or grabbed, and will generally always works as long as the jaw is not compromised.

222

Rocker-arm devices will move freely until loaded, but can be disabled if pressed down from above, either by an upper device, or by grabbing the rope above the device before grabs.

223

Lever devices share the same issues as rocker-arm devices.

224

An inertia device will generally work in the same way as an eccentric device.

eccentric devices or non-eccentric devices as primary (P) above the eccentric secondary (S).

Examples

Petzl Micro Traxion (P), Petzl Nano Traxion (S).

Petzl Croll (P), Edelrid Spoc (S).

Petzl Rescucender (P), Wild Country Ropeman (S).

Camp Goblin (P), Kong Duck (S).

Such set-ups will work, but they will clash on the belay loop, so it's messy and why other set-ups exist.

2:2 - 2 Devices/2 ropes

Description
The system uses two ropes, a climbing-line, and a safety-line. The primary device goes on the climbing-line, and the secondary device attaches to the safety-line, acting in the same way as an industrial rope access fall arrester. When rigged correctly, the safety-line and secondary device should not be weighted but act like a reserve parachute for the climber in the event that the primary device fails to grab.

Primary Device Set-up
The primary device can be set in any way the climber sees fit, using either the belay loop or chest method. Which method is chosen will generally be down to what device is at hand. Note, just because a climber has a secondary device as a back-up doesn't mean they can be sloppy with their primary device. Both devices must be set up in a bombproof manner and be fully functional in their own right.

Secondary Device Set-up
The secondary TRS device needs to be positioned so that it does not interfere with the climber, climbing-line, or primary device in ascent or descent.

Lines should not tangle, devices should not clash, and the climber should not be able to grab their safety-line, or secondary device in a panic, as this could easily disable them.

The best way to separate the climber from their safety-line is to rig it to the side of the climbing-line and employ a lanyard or extension to create distance, allowing the secondary to travel close to the climber and catch them if the primary fails.

Here are some things to consider in terms of lanyards and extensions.

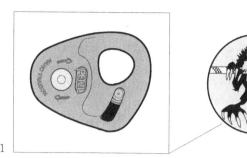

Fig.221

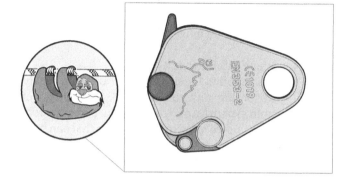

Fig.222

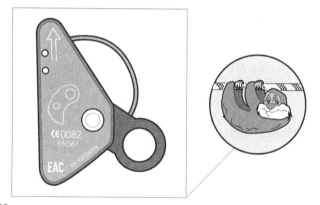

Fig.223

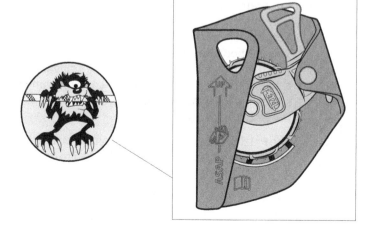

Fig.224

✏ 225
Typical 2:2 system, with
eccentric TRS device
clipped to the belay device
and rocker-arm device on
the safety-line, connected
with a dynamic lanyard.

Margin Call
*Russians have a tradition
when they travel that is worth
adopting in all complex,
high-risk undertakings. Once
packed up and ready to
leave, they stop and have a
cup of tea rather than rush
off to begin their journey.
While boiling the water,
allowing the tea to slowly
brew in the pot, and then
drinking it, there is time to
remember something they
might have forgotten or
something important about
the trip they have missed.
On all my big wall solos, I
always used this 'Russian
tea' approach once I was
set up to lead the next pitch,
undock a bag, or unclip
from a belay to clean a pitch.
Everything was ready to go,
but instead, I would stop.
I would slowly get out my
water bottle, take a drink,
and then another, and just
be present – unrushed – and
give my head some space to
think or see if I was ready for
what was to come. I'd notice
nothing nine times out of ten,
but sometimes I'd notice my
sky hooks still clipped to the
belay, my haul line was not
clipped to my harness, or
my GriGri was threaded the
wrong way around. So, when
setting off to TRS, consider
taking a 'Russian tea' break,
even if only for a sip.*

- Devices that will not slip when shock loaded, such as eccentric and inertia devices, should only be connected by shock absorbing lanyards and extenders.

- Non-slip devices should only be limited to lanyards no longer than 60 cm in length, so as to further reduce the maximum fall to factor 2, although factor 1, or between 0 and 0.9 are ideal. If a static or dynamic element is employed, such a device will likely damage the rope in a factor 1 or 2 fall.

- Rocker-arm or lever action devices that will slip in a high factor fall can be extended via short static extenders under 45 cm, or longer dynamic, or shock absorbing lanyards.

Ideal TRS Devices
Non slipping devices cannot be used safely unless shock absorbing lanyards are used. Seeing as such lanyards are both expensive and designed for industrial rope access, most climbers will want to use a device that can be safely used with dynamic (rope) lanyards, or short static extenders (quick-draws). This means the ideal devices for the safety-line are rocker-arm or lever action devices.

A significant advantage of running two lines, and this style of device, which can be bidirectional, is it allows the climber to move up and down the climbing-line and rock face without restriction. If the climber only has one bidirectional device, it should be placed onto the safety-line to act like a self-tending fall arrester, protecting the climber in ascent and descent.

Failure Points
Each device can suffer some standard failure modes, but the risk of that failure being due to interference between each device would be minor, especially compared to two devices on the same rope.

Alternative
One uncommon set-up is to make both devices primary so that both devices and both ropes are weighted at the same time. This method would only be employed when forced to use two very thin dynamic ropes, which, if used singularly, would risk a ground fall due to rope stretch. Loading both ropes at the same time will reduce stretch by 50%, as the climber's weight will be borne by both ropes.

The Petzl Shunt is the only device on the market that will work with two ropes, so a 2:1 set-up will need to be employed, but with each device clipped into its own line.

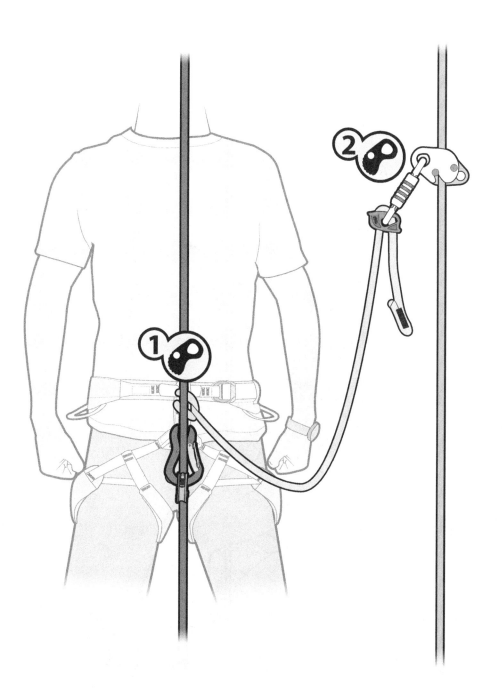

Fig.225

Fig.226

One Rope System

 226

A typical one rope TRS set-up, with two eccentric devices acting as primary and secondary devices.

Margin Call

A one-rope system will always be the go-to system for most climbers, as most climbers only own one (single-rated) rope and even that rope may be shared between two climbing partners. These one-rope climbers will include all novice climbers, as most beginners start with only a harness, rope and belay device. Luckily, a one-rope system is also ideal for beginners or people who don't climb enough to warrant two ropes, as it's the simplest to set up and climb on. Multi-rope-owning climbers will have been climbing for much longer and so have more experience, which helps when trying to get their heads around a two-rope system.

Set-up

The climber builds a solid anchor at the top of the climb; from this, they hang one rope that we call the climbing-line. The climber attaches one or two TRS devices to the climbing-line and starts to climb. At the end of the climb, when they reach the anchor or cannot continue, they will descend the climbing-line to the ground or ascend the climbing-line to the anchor.

Typical Usage

The utility of this method is self-evident and is the most well-established and has been used on all styles of climbing, from large boulders and outcrops to face climbs and multi-pitch routes, even on big walls.

TRS Device Set-ups

With a one-rope system, one or two devices can be used, each set up with its pros and cons.

- Single device

The climber attaches a single TRS device to the climbing-line and then connects the TRS device to their harness. As they climb, the device travels with them. If the device fails to grab the rope and no back-up has been built into the system, the climber will fall to the rope's end or to the ground, whichever comes first, thus demonstrating that it breaks the two-point rule.

Pros

- There is only a need for one rope, one anchor, and one device.
- A well-established system that's easy to understand.
- Fast to set up and escape.
- If a single bidirectional device is used, the climber can achieve a high degree of freedom of movement.
- There is only one device to focus on.

Cons

- No redundant. The climber is dependent on a single rope, anchor, and device.
- Requires catastrophe-knots, which are unreliable.
- Requires a high level of skill in device choice and how to employ it safely.

system
/one_rope

🖉 227
The use of TRS for ice or mixed climbing is limited but is adopted by some hardy climbers who seek to gain experience or train for steeper terrain. However, it's worth noting that while any TRS device can work effectively on a dry rope, once ice begins to accumulate on a rope, there is a risk of devices struggling to catch, particularly eccentric ones.

For this reason, the best primary devices to use in situations where icy ropes may be encountered with TRS are rocker-arm and lever devices. These types are less affected by ice-covered sheaths. It's essential to avoid situations where the moving parts of a device become clogged with ice, which can occur on ice routes at the margin of the freezing point, or sub zero climbs exposed to the typical Scottish style moisture-laden winds.

- Two devices

This method employs two devices on the rope, one above the other, and should — if the devices are chosen and used correctly — be a safe system that can be used without the need for catastrophe-knots. A climber might continue to use catastrophe-knots until they dial their set-up.

Setting up two devices on one rope is covered in depth in the device attachment section.

If a climber wishes to use a one-rope system, then two devices are highly advised and should be the default method for all climbers.

Pros

- Two devices provide almost total security.
- A well-established system that's easy to understand.
- No catastrophe-knots needed.

Cons

- The climber is dependent on a single rope and anchor.
- Climber must be able to set up a two-device set-up that will not see the devices clash.

One rope device back-ups

The classic secondary back-up method when climbing on one rope, using a single TRS device, is for the climber to tie knots into the rope, either catastrophe-knots or clipping bights into their belay loop. This method does not provide an assured back-up, as the climber can still fall a very long way before hitting a catastrophe-knot. Knots can also fail, coming undone when shock-loaded.

It is also possible to clip Figure-8 knots into the harness, so device detachment is not terminal, but this disables the line-ballast, meaning self-tending devices will need the rope pulled through them manually. This manual feeding method is typically only used with assisted braking belay devices (ABD), such as the Petzl GriGri.

Given that a two-device set-up has redundancy built in, the primary back-up is selecting the correct devices to use, so that redundancy is not illusionary. Catastrophe-knots can be used, but with a sound system, they should be unnecessary.

Conclusion

Using just a single device and one rope is best resigned to the dustbin of technique history for all but the most experienced climbers; it only works with a bombproof set-up and a willingness to accept a certain degree of risk. One rope, two TRS device set-up is ideal for everyone else.

Fig.227

Fig.228

Two Rope System

 228

By employing a two-rope system, the climber achieves maximum redundancy, as they will have two anchors, two ropes, and two devices. This comes at the cost of extra weight, rigging, and additional complexity, which may lead to more tangles. Therefore, it requires experience in setting up such a system optimally. However, like all systems, the more you work with it, the better you become at making it work.

Margin Call
Even if you employ a one-line system and prefer the low faff of one rope, on half-rope length climbs, you can still make use of the other half of your rope. By fixing your rope at the halfway mark, you can set the unused section of rope down the crag beside the climbing-line, creating an escape line. This escape line allows you to set up your rappel system while hanging on your primary device, and once transitioned over, remove the devices and descend. If you want to keep this line out of the way while climbing, tie it to the end of the climbing-line, move it away from the route, and then just pull it back when/if you need it.

Set-up
The climber builds an anchor at the top of the climb from which they suspend two ropes: the climbing-line and the safety-line.

The climber attaches their primary TRS device to the climbing-line, with this device being the one that will hold them when they fall or rest. They then connect their back-up device to the safety-line, which will only activate if the primary device or climbing-line fails.

Self-feeding and self-trailing devices are ideal for the safety-line as they don't need monitoring in either ascent or descent; this makes this set-up much safer when climbing and transitioning to descend.

As with the one-rope method, at the end of the climb, when the climber reaches the anchor or cannot continue, they can descend either rope to the ground or ascend the rope to the anchor.

Typical Usage
Anywhere where a climber could use a one-rope system, they can use this two-rope system. Using two ropes also makes this system ideal for very committing and exposed climbs, such as sea cliffs or mountain crags, where ropes have a higher chance of becoming damaged. The need for two ropes can be off-putting, but most single-pitch climbs are less than half a rope length in height, so a climber can often simply double up one rope.

Pros
- Safe, safe, safe!
- Allows bidirectional devices to be employed, such as rocker-arm devices, without the fear of devices disabling each other. This enables the user to have a system that allows them to climb up, down, and sideways, with the device locking onto the rope. This provides the climber with the closest sensation of unencumbered free climbing.
- Panic grabbing both ropes or both devices is very unlikely, which further benefits rocker-arm and lever devices. Having two lines reduces the risk of catastrophic rope failure due to loose or falling rocks.
- Catastrophe-knots are unnecessary.

✎ 229

The two-rope system is directly adapted from industrial rope access, where a higher degree of safety and security is essential. Using a double rope system is logical when working at heights, especially in proximity to abrasive and hazardous structures (although proper rigging should mitigate all terrain hazards). It also serves as a means to create a greater margin of safety against potential lapses in skill, experience, or care, particularly in an industry that often employs individuals with backgrounds in scaffolding rather than climbers and cavers.

The traditional caving single-rope technique for navigating vertical terrain also incorporates a significant level of safety measures, such as redirects and re-anchors. However, it still relies more heavily on the skill and experience of the individual to ensure safety.

- Allows the user to more easily escape the system, as they can attach their descender to the safety-line, weight it, and then rappel. If using a rocker-arm or lever action device, they can simply make the safety-line the climbing/rappel line, and the climbing-line the safety-line, by allowing the rocker-arm or lever device to travel down the rope as a back-up.

Cons

- Two ropes may be needed, so extra weight, bulk and cost – unless the climber sticks to short climbs that can be rigged with one doubled rope.
- Requires a higher degree of skill to rig well.
- Using two ropes requires a bigger learning curve and such a system can be very frustrating to use at first, with ropes constantly getting in the way.

Variation

Some climbers employ an ABD as the back-up on the safety-line, manually pulling the line through as they climb, creating a moving back-up. This method is less safe than a self-trailing device but makes it a little easier to transition to descend and suits a climber who only has one self-tending TRS device.

Back-up methods

This system needs no extra back-up, as the entire system is built around redundancy. Although there is a small risk that a device, rope, or anchor might fail, the chance of both failing would be one in a million, although human errors, such as incorrectly attaching both devices, or building a lousy anchor, can negate even the safest of systems.

Failure points and Effects

The climber can still trash the climbing-line if they lack care and attention.

Conclusion & Personal reflections

This is the new standard for safe and effective TRS, as it offers almost total security throughout all phases of the climb. Additionally, it provides the possibility to maximize the benefits achievable from rocker-arm and lever action devices without the associated drawbacks. When used in this manner, a climber, perhaps employing a Lov Taz3 on the climbing-line and a Petzl ASAP on the safety-line, could have complete freedom of movement right up to the moment they fall. The only real drawback in this perfect scenario is having two ropes in your way, but the more you use a two-rope system, the less noticeable the presence of the ropes becomes.

Fig.229

Fig.230

Pseudo Leading

"Where are the wires?

Robert Angier

✏ 230

The typical pseudo-lead set-up involves the lead climber placing her own protection while being belayed by her partner. Her TRS system consists of a rocker-arm device on a lanyard running on a safety-line set parallel to the route being climbed. While it would be possible for the leader to simply place protection while on a top rope, pseudo-leading brings a much more realistic and challenging experience, akin to being at the sharp end for real.

A non-conventional way to employ a TRS system is as an extra layer of security to a climber who is learning to lead climb when placing their own protection. I call this technique "pseudo-leading."

Learning to lead and belaying someone who is leading can be a steep, and dangerous learning curve. The leader is often unsure whether they can trust the protection they are placing, while the belayer may question their ability to catch a leader if they fall onto that protection. A pseudo-leading system would involve a lead climber roped up as usual, placing their own protection and belayed by a partner, but safeguarded by a safety-line.

By integrating a TRS system, typically consisting of a lanyard device and safety-line, a safer learning environment, as confidence in placing protection on lead climbs is usually established through both placing one's own protection and cleaning the protection placed by others. It also involves having confidence that the belayer will catch you if you fall. Pseudo leading aids in this learning phase.

Once the lead climber and lead belayer have acquired the required level of skill and confidence, they can dispense with the TRS rope.

Margin Call
Although detailed, this book is not exhaustive, aiming to balance between what needs to be known and what's best to work out for yourself. For example, I haven't covered how to set up a TRS rope on a blank roof or overhang or solo stick-clip up a sport route to reach an anchor that cannot be accessed from the top. Such subjects either stray too far from the subject of TRS (stick-clipping up a route is lead rope solo) or can only be understood by a climber who requires no instruction or advice from someone like me. Pseudo-leading strays a little into this category, but I found it very useful when I was only a novice, using it to learn to lead rope solo, which is why I've included it here.

Typical Usage
This technique is typically used on single-pitch climbs with easy access to the top and solid anchors. It can also be employed while training advanced rope techniques: rope climbing, self rescue, rappelling, etc.

Back-up Methods
The primary safety is the lead rope, protection placed and belayer (belay chain), and the TRS system IS the back-up. Don't half-ass either element: solid TRS, solid leading.

Failure Points

The danger with pseudo-leading is that a novice team might do a half-assed job of leading, belaying, and TRS, meaning their assumed reduced risk is actually magnified. Each component of the belay chain needs to be solid.

Conclusion & Personal Reflections:
Yes, it's an advanced technique for novices, but it can be a valuable one if time is taken to do it correctly.

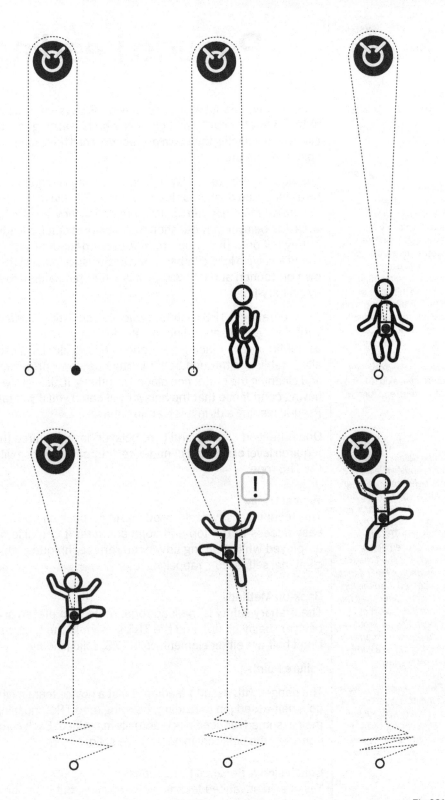

Fig.231

Top Rope TRS

"You know, the feeling that people experience when they stand on the edge like this isn't the fear of falling; it's the fear that they might jump."

Will Emerson

✎ 231

Top rope TRS is a niche technique within a niche, and so it's really only something one should understand, and then ignore.

A top rope TRS is set up the same way as a two-person top rope: the rope goes from the climber up through a top anchor and back down to the belayer. As the climber ascends, the belayer takes in the rope and then lowers the climber back to the ground when they're finished. In a TRS top rope, the climber acts as their own belayer.

In a top rope TRS, with the rope set up for top roping, climber ties into one strand of the rope as usual but then clips the other strand through an ABD (Petzl GriGri, for example), making themselves both climber and belayer. As the climber ascends, they pull the slack through the ABD, and once at the belay, or when they wish to descend – perhaps to practice a move – they fully weight both ropes and lower themselves down.

It is also possible to use a progress capture device, such as a Petzl Micro Traxion, but this negates the ability for the climber to lower themselves via the device once finished, which is the only real benefit of the set-up.

Typical Usage
This method was developed primarily for indoor gym climbing, where top ropes are in-situ, and no auto belay options were available. Unfortunately, this indoor technique has been transplanted into the outdoors when a standard TRS system would be more appropriate.

Back-up methods
As the climber ascends, they can tie knots into the rope, either catastrophe-knots or clipping bights into their belay loop.

Failure Points
The main issue with this system is that it requires manual feeding, which is made even more problematic by the fact twice the amount of rope must pass through the belay device; this increases the workload and the risk of a slack fall. As with all top rope systems, there is the possibility that the climber ties in incorrectly or has the belay device threaded incorrectly. Climbers are regularly injured while top roping, even very good climbers, and all potential top rope failure points apply, plus all the TRS ones as well.

Conclusion & Personal reflections
I include this technique for completeness, but if one wants to top rope safely, then adopt a standard TRS system.

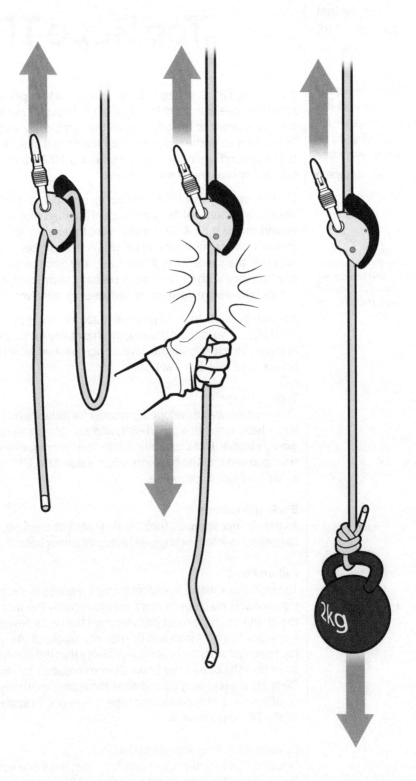

Fig.232

Line-ballast

> *"A bad dancer blames his testicles."*
>
> **Russian Proverb**

 232

Even a self-tending device that moves as lightly as a feather up the rope still requires some resistance to work against. With such devices, the weight of the rope below will eventually be enough to resist lifting, but you still need some initial weight to 'prime the pump.' When using devices that do not self-tend or have a high degree of friction, such as an ABD, the use of a line-ballast becomes crucial; otherwise, the climber must manually pull the rope through the device.

No matter how smooth the mechanism of a climber's TRS device is, even the smallest degree of friction will cause it to lift the climbing-line as they progress rather than travel up it. If a climber wants a free-flowing, self-tending system, this tiny degree of friction needs to be overcome.

Why the friction?
The amount of friction a device exerts is determined by a number of factors, including the following:

- The amount of force the jaws spring exerts. A device with no spring, or a spring that's tired, generes little friction, while a strong spring can create a very 'grabby' jaw.

- The shape of the frame and direction of loading. Some devices will move smoothly when used conventionally but will drag or twist if they are pulled – rather than pushed – up the rope.

- If a device has a rope positioning mechanism, and this is activated, then this will increase friction considerably. Make sure it's disengaged unless it's needed.

- If the device is being used on a rope diameter that is at the top end of the certification, such as an 11 mm rope rather than a 10 mm rope or a rope that has become bloated by age.

Overcoming device friction
The go-to technique for inexperienced climbers is to pull the rope through the device when it won't self-feed. The downside of 'going manual' is obvious; it's distracting, tiring, and, more importantly, exposes the climber to a build-up of dangerous slack.

Eventually, as the climber moves up the rope, there will be enough weight in the dead climbing-line to overcome device friction, but seeing as the closer they are to the ground, the more important it is for the device to travel effectively, the best method for a self-tending system is ballast at the end of the climbing-line.

The weight needed to counter friction depends on the mechanism of the TRS device, which does not only vary between makes and models but even between similar devices, most often due to the age of the jaw spring. Rope thickness and terrain profile also play a part, as the weight of the dead rope lying on a slab is less than on a vertical route.

✏️ 233
Ballast rope.

✏️ 234

Line-ballast set on a friction hitch in order to set the correct distance from the ground.

✏️ 235

Sub two kilogram line-ballast created by a pair of shoes and a water bottle.

Margin Call

I've lost count of the times I've watched someone top rope soloing a climb on which the rope failed to feed correctly through their device, most often a Petzl GriGri. To begin with, they tend to be able to pull in the slack as they go, but once the climbing gets more challenging, their ability to take off one hand to feed the rope becomes diminished, and diminished still by the realisation said slack has already built up for a big lob. Fear of a plummeting fall onto their device gives them such a fright that they try to climb onto some hoped-for sanctuary where they can gain a free hand to pull through the rope, but the further they rise, the more gripped they become, and the further they are from that safe harbour. It's funny to watch — but not to do. To my thinking, no device that requires manual feeding or a heavy line-ballast is a fit for TRS, as what you're doing is not free climbing, but free-climbing AND belaying simultaneously; where's the fun in that?

In my experience, ballast between 1 kg and 2 kg is usually the most effective. Typically, this line-ballast is created by clipping in the climber's approach shoes (a pair of approach shoes weigh between 500 grams and 800 grams) and perhaps a water bottle (1 litre of water weighs 1 kg). The excess rope can also be used as ballast, forming it into a small coil (a 10 mm low-stretch rope weighs around 70 grams per metre).

You can also clip items you may need higher on the climb, such as a cord, whistle, head-lamp etc.

My favourite line-ballast method is to use a rope bag, which I attach to the rope with a friction hitch. I stuff all the spare rope into this, ensuring it's not too heavy, and then adjust its position on the rope with the friction hitch while doing a test hang. With this system, it's also easier to haul up the rope bag and reposition it higher if need be by simply pulling up the bag and then pulling the excess rope through the friction hitch and stuffing it away.

As a rough guide to weight, if one can't lift the ballast with one finger, it's too heavy (unless that climber is Adam Ondra).

The reason for avoiding heavy line-ballast include the following:

- A heavy weight hanging off the climbing-line will constantly tug and bully the climber back to the plumb line. It will be a real hindrance on anything but a vertical laser-like crack.

- Rocker-arm mechanisms require a bendable rope to grab, meaning that on a loaded climbing-line, they may not work correctly or at all.

- The ideal line-ballast should not impede a climber from rappelling the climbing-line while in place; otherwise, they will be forced to haul up the ballast and unclip it.

- On overhanging terrain, the ballast may press the device against the climber, increasing the grab lag and potentially leading to panic grabbing.

The above problems also highlight why it's a bad idea to employ a base anchor, tensioning the climbing-line to the bottom of the route.

Testing

With the line-ballast in place, it's best to do a test hang on the rope to check the line-ballast does not sit on the floor. Then climb up a little in order to check if the weight is correct in order for the TRS device to move smoothly. If it runs without a problem at the bottom of the climbing-line, it will move smoothly up the rope, as the weight of the dead rope will only increase as the climber ascends.

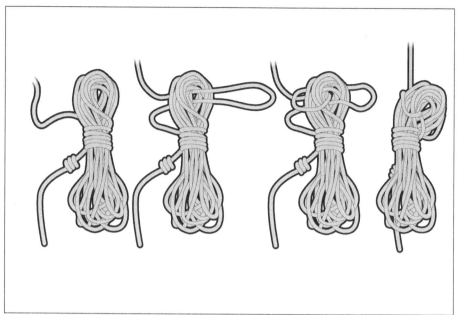

Fig.233

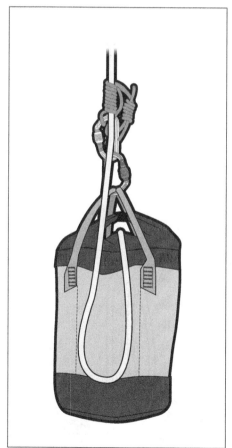

Fig.234

Fig.235

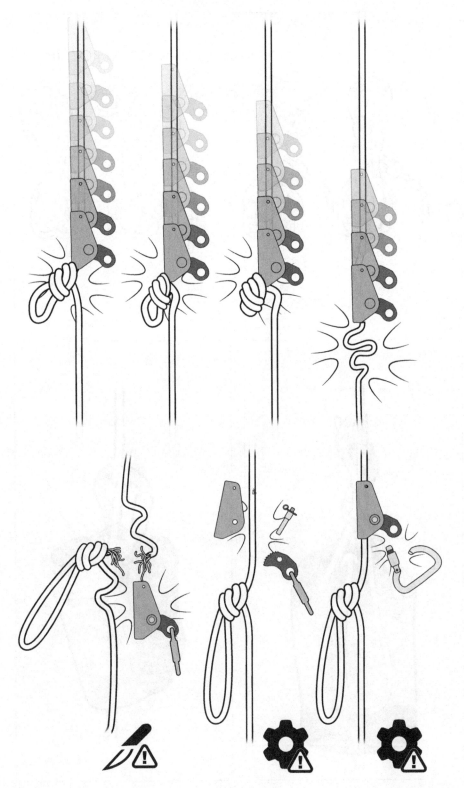

Fig.236

Catastrophe-knots

🖉 236
A device striking a poorly tied catastrophe-knot in a factor 5 fall could cause the knot to fail, or the impact may break the rope, break the device, or the connector.

Margin Call

A catastrophe-knot can save a life, but it could also put a life at risk. A catastrophe-knot can become jammed in cracks and features when you want to pull up your rope, or stick in your rappel device as you descend, but the biggest danger comes from how you view its place within your system. When thinking about using catastrophe-knots, it's vital never to view them as a key element in the system. No, the systems you employ are meant to do you no harm whenever they engage, but there are few such guarantees with a catastrophe-knot. Consider the catastrophe-knots tied into a rappel rope. A climber could fall two hundred feet from the top to the bottom of their ropes and be stopped by those little knots, but if you could see the damage such a fall can do, you'd not view it as being a back-up to anything; it's just a way to retain the body. I say this as too many climbers take the view that they have a two point safety system: (1) their device, (2) the catastrophe-knot, when they do not.

Old school TRS techniques heavily used catastrophe-knots, typically Figure-8 or Overhand knots tied into the dead rope below the climber. The concept is simple: if the TRS device failed to grab the climbing-line and slid down the rope, the device would strike the last catastrophe-knot and check the fall.

This all sounds great in theory, but such catastrophe-knots offer only illusory protection in practice. Here is a short run-down of why that is:

- The knot provides no protection if the climber becomes detached from the climbing device or if the device detaches from the climbing-line, both of which can happen.

- The protection offered is primarily psychological. A free-falling climber, descending twenty metres down the climbing-line, can generate massive energy. Perhaps the knot will stop the climber. It might also be sliced off, inverted, unravelled, or pulled through the device. Who knows?

- A fall is a fall, whether it's during free climbing or down a climbing-line. What are the chances of getting injured before that catastrophe-knot checks the fall? Big falls should always be avoided. Although they might seem casual on overhanging climbs, most TRS climbs are not so steep. Even an edge a few centimetres deep can snap an ankle, while larger ledges or corners can break a back.

- A catastrophe-knot does not count towards the two-point rule.

- The climber will need two hands to tie a Figure-8 or Overhand catastrophe-knot, meaning such knots will not be tied on steep climbs, when climbing at one's limit, or when fearing an imminent fall.

- Is the frame of the TRS device designed to withstand a factor 5 fall — a ten-metre slide down onto a knot?

No, there are far too many unknowns with this method to consider it a bombproof safety system. More often than not, it's a psychological crutch; keeping fingers crossed and hoping for the best is like a parachutist using an umbrella instead of a reserve parachute.

Although both I and others have been saved by catastrophe-knots we've tied and clipped into our harnesses, I have yet to meet anyone saved by a knot merely tied into the rope.

The entire practice of tying catastrophe-knots needs to be replaced by employing a two-device system, either on one rope or two. This will replace that umbrella with an actual reserve parachute.

No Catastrophe-knot Benefits

One major benefit of dispensing with catastrophe-knots is that it makes rappelling the climbing-line back to the start easier, as the climber doesn't have to worry about removing any knots as they descend. These knots can also present a hazard if the climber forgets they're there and a knot jams up against a rappel device, which can prove very challenging for a novice climber.

Effective Back-Up

If a climber wishes to employ a catastrophe-knot system, then here are a few ways to make that umbrella slightly more capable:

- Run the climbing-line through a steel quick-link (7 mm or 8 mm), clipped to the belay loop below the device. Unlike the frame of a TRS device, this will withstand a high-factor fall as long as the catastrophe-knot does not unravel or collapse. A quick-link is also more rope-friendly than the harder, narrower edges of many framed devices, which could cut a rope. Such a back-up will also protect the climber from device detachment. Connect directly to the belay loop or extend.

- Learn to tie a Clove hitch one-handed into a karabiner racked on the harness, then simply unclip the karabiner and hitch, providing a solid stop back-up that will not collapse.

- Tie Overhand knots into the rope with oversized bights (the loop formed by the knot), as these will be more resistant to collapse and inversion. A karabiner can be clipped into these bights to create a solid stop.

- Regularly tie knots to reduce fall distance. Don't untie lower knots; at a minimum, have two knots below — one as a back-up and the one below as a second layer of protection.

- Clipping knots into the belay loop is the only method that stands a good chance of working, but it impedes self-tending, which introduces another risk. If there's no suitable secondary device, the climber could use an ABD, pulling the rope through it as they climb, creating a running back-up. However, this is definitely in the "better than nothing" category.

 237
The Slip knot is a useful knot to employ sometimes, but can be limited by the action of the line-ballast, causing it to release prematurely. This problem can be reduced by making your Slip-knot as tight as possible, or by tying-it off as shown. One of the biggest advantages of the Slip-knot is that even if it jams into a device, or descender, it can still be released by a sharp tug.

 238
Employing a quick-link as a knot catcher creates a more dependable way to catch a knot compared to a TRS device.

 239
A knot catcher can be attached directly to the belay loop, or via a short lanyard.

240
A one handed way to tie stopper knots is to clip clove hitches into karabiners racked on the harness.

Fig.237

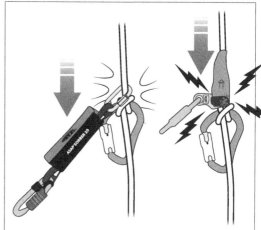

Fig.238

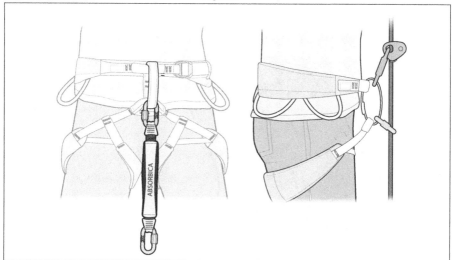

Fig.239

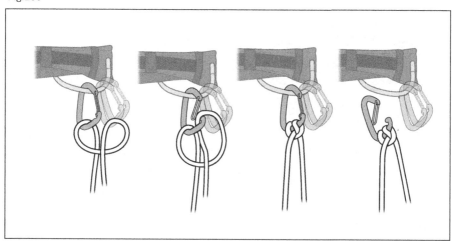

Fig.240

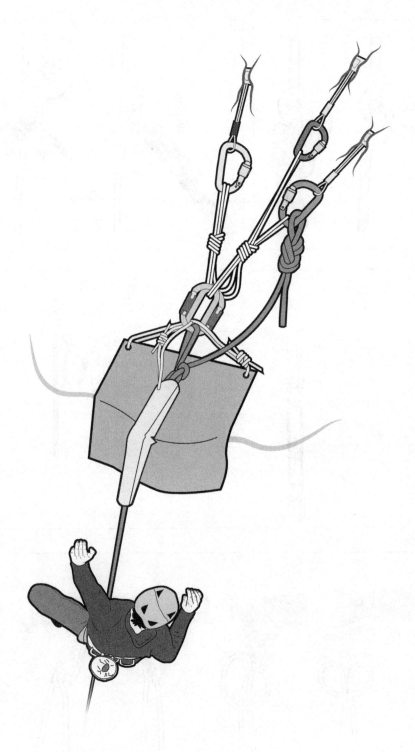

Fig.241

Rigging

"With a piece of rope, you can do magic."

Philippe Petit

✎ 241
Very simple TRS anchor created from three solid nuts, an equalising quad sling and a two locker masterpoint. The rope this protected by both a rope sleeve and a rope mat.

Margin Call
I define a solid climbing anchor as one that can hold five times the expected load, so would an 80 kg climber need a 400 kg anchor? Unfortunately, the anchor must be built to withstand all possible loads, including the force of a rather stupid climber who climbs above the anchor and then falls or falls with a huge amount of slack in the system. Such a loading could (theoretically) be around 10 kN, so you'd need an anchor that could withstand a whopping 50 kN. Is that even possible? Well, the weakest parts of your anchor can hold at least 10 kN (nuts), while everything else will hold 20+ kN (karabiners, slings), but everything is doubled or tripled, so it's possible. The weakest link would be the rope (15± kN), but seeing that we know that's not going to snap in the real world (we hope), it's safe to assume that 5:1 is what needs to be aimed for, even if it's not achievable. It's going to be the thought that counts.

It's beyond the scope of this book to cover the entire subject of how to rig safe and functional belay anchors. Instead I will simply cover the basics of anchor building and TRS specifics.

The TRS Anchor

It doesn't matter how perfect a climber's device is, how well it's set-up, or how careful and well thought out the redundancy, if the main anchor fails the first time it's weighted. Almost as bad is employing an anchor that does not inspire total confidence, because even a shadow of a doubt each time the climber sags on the rope is going to spoil the TRS experience.

One of the biggest issues for a lot climbers, especially novices, or those who have little experience of multi pitch climbing, is that they're really not that good at creating solid belays. They can pull things together to look like how a belay should look, but not what a solid belay can do. Yes, they can make a belay that will hold a second who needs a rest, but they will not be so confident in what they can construct to withstand a factor-2 fall, a leader falling direct onto the anchor.

So, before a climber even begins to get into rigging TRS anchors, they need to be good at making train stopping belay anchors.

Belay Anchor versus TRS Anchor

In many cases, a belay anchor is built with the belayer placed between the anchor and the expected load, such as a falling leader or second, the unwritten hope being that the belayer will somehow stop the anchor itself from being fully loaded; a probable throwback to the days when "the leader must not fall!". A belay anchor also tends not to have a fixed direction of loading in all phases of the climb, meaning the belayer could be yanked down, up, sideways, or all three.

Although the ideal belay anchor is supposedly equalised, following the SERENE methodology (Strong, Equalised, Redundant, Efficient, No Extension), the entire force will be in the real world and in real-life falls often come on to a single anchor point. The fact that it's rare for a belay anchor to fail — but not unheard of — means, although imperfect, the methodology works.

242

Less than body weight loads on the anchor will occur on less than vertical ground. These loads will be further reduced by terrain features, which will also soak up some of that load. This is not an excuse to make shoddy anchors, but rather about understanding that the angles and terrain of a climb effects what the anchor has to deal with.

243

A typical load on an anchor will be bodyweight, so between 60 to 80 kilograms, with the climber's ideal TRS set-up, and vertical terrain, reducing the fall factor to a fraction above 0.

244

On overhanging terrain, and swinging falls do not increase the falling climber's force, but such falls will generally be instantaneous, which can cause sudden changes in rope position at the far end of the system.

245

A climber falling onto a secondary device on a lanyard could generate between a 1 to 2 factor fall, but the TRS anchor and system should be designed to handle such forces.

246

The highest, most dangerous anchor loads will happen when a climber allows a great deal of dead rope to build up above their TRS device, leading to very high factor falls. Never the less, even if other parts of the system may fail, the anchor should not be one of them.

The main TRS anchor, on the other hand, will have a very narrow and certain vector of loading. The loading angle is easily determined, so creating a fully functioning SERENE anchor is much easier.

Unlike a belay anchor, where it's desirable not to load the anchor, a rigging anchor is almost always loaded. This means that there is no room for the kinds of sketchy anchor points a climber may work with on a belay, but rather the rigging anchor must be rock solid, be it an oak tree, two glue-in bolts, or five equalised nuts. If a climber feels nervous rapping off their top anchor, then it's not an anchor.

Forces on the TRS anchor

Like any climbing anchor, it must be built significantly stronger than any potential load it will be asked to hold, which is generally achieved by a single anchor point being able to hold the entire maximum load, and then double, triple, or quadrupling those points, then linking them all together. This means an anchor constructed from three large DMM Wallnuts buried deep in solid cracks is viable, but not five micro cams wobbling in shallow sandy slots. Each piece should be good enough to be a single anchor in itself. If that's not possible, then move on.

Expected and abnormal anchor loading can be split into these categories:

Sag catch: This loading occurs when climbing on less than vertical ground when the climber allows the rope to take their weight, but most of the weight is borne by the rock.

Full catch: If the climber rests on the rope on steeper ground, the anchor must hold their total weight. Many typical TRS falls would fit into this category, as the climber is not really falling, but they just sag onto the rope, or the climber grabs the rope to avoid a hard catch. A body weight load will also occur when rappelling, rigging the ropes, or escaping the system.

Drop Catch: This is harder than a full catch, but not significantly, and occurs in the time and distance it takes for longer connectors to load the TRS device, so around a 30 cm to 60 cm fall, so factor 1 or less. This kind of fall is well within the limits of a TRS system but can still generate a double body-weight load. This kind of fall would also cover falling onto a secondary device when running two devices on the same rope.

Emergency Catch: I would categorise this as a semi-factor 2 fall of between one and two metres, and it would generally only happen when falling onto a secondary device on a safety-line. With a well set up system, the climber should not feel a hard fall but more of a swing, with the body, harness, rope, and connectors taking up the slack. This will apply a significant

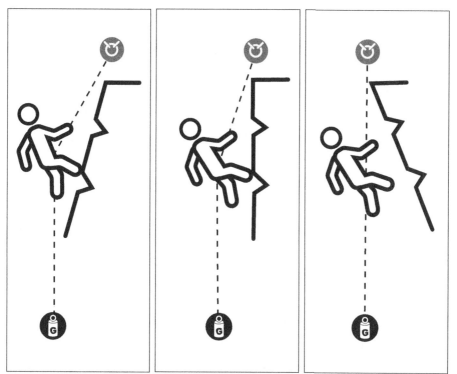

Fig.242

Fig.243

Fig.244

Fig.245

Fig.246

force to the anchor but should be within the safety margin of a TRS rigging system.

Catastrophic catch: This is the worst-case loading, such as when a climber has allowed a great deal of slack to build up in the live rope, creating a very high factor fall. It could also include falling down the climbing-line to a catastrophe-knot. In such a fall, there are several links that could fail, which is why system redundancy is vital, but the anchor should not be one of them.

Setting up the top anchor

How the top anchor is set up depends if one line or two ropes are being employed, so either a climbing-line alone or a climbing and safety-line. These ropes will be hung from one or two masterpoints, built from equalised anchor points (tree, boulder, bolt belay, or matrix of natural protection), using cord, rope, or slings. The ideal anchor is one made using just rope itself.

The climber will build a style of anchor they are most comfortable with, and although a cordelette method with a fixed angle of loading is probably the default, constructing an anchor with a self-equalising masterpoint is ideal, with a quad or equallette allowing the masterpoint to self-adjust to the actual - rather than imagined - direction of loading.

Two-point Rule

Just as a climber should never trust their life to just one point, it's worth noting that sometimes that point might be up the anchor chain. For example, I've seen climbers use two TRS devices on a sturdy 11 mm low-stretch rope but only anchor that rope via a Figure-8 knot clipped to a single locker.

The two-point rule should apply to the entire system, especially to parts of it that are out of sight and must be trusted totally. What this means is never rely on one knot, one karabiner, one anchor, but only on paranoia.

The Masterpoint

The masterpoint can either be set off the face of the climb, meaning the climbing-line will be running over the top edge of the climb, or set on the face, meaning it's the top anchor's rigging that will be going over the edge, not the climbing-line.

The first method has the advantage of allowing the climber to rappel from the top anchor more easily, as well as climb all the way to safe ground (ideally to safe ground) but does leave the rope exposed.

🖊 247
Four point cordelette anchor with twin locker masterpoint. Note that further redundancy is created by tying off the end of the climbing-line to the strongest anchor point.

🖊 248
Equalette anchor made from cord.

🖊 249
Alpine Butterfly and Figure-8 knot used on two bolt belay.

🖊 250
Single rope used to create two lines (note middle mark).

🖊 251
Bunny Ears Figure-8.

🖊 252
Asymmetric Double Bunny Ears Figure-8 knots creating a two line system when using a single rope.

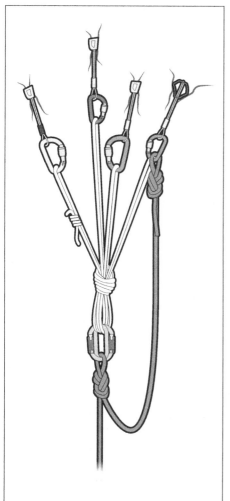

Fig.247

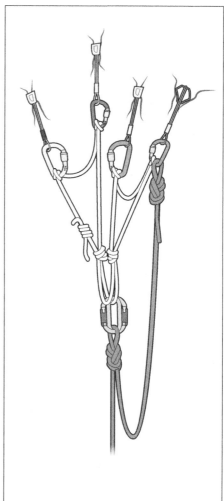

Fig.248

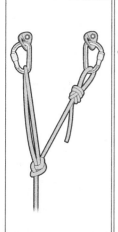

Fig.249

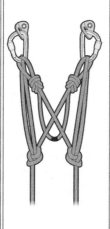

Fig.250

Fig.251

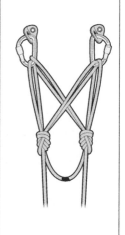

Fig.252

253
A meandering line that zigzags around the fall line of the anchor can lead to many dangerous swings, causing a climbing-line to saw backwards and forwards at the anchor.

 254
An off the face master-point makes life easier for the climber, but can lead to dangerous sawing actions on the rope. This problem can be reduced by employing good edge protection.

🖉 255
A below the edge master-point tends to be much more stable, and even though the anchor strands may face some abrasion, this should be minimal as they should remain fixed in place. Although less prone to damage, a rope mat is still advisable.

The second method is harder to rappel, as it's below the climber but is far more rope-friendly.

Both methods require edge protection, but I'm a fan of the second method.

When rappelling a below-the-edge masterpoint, it's best to pull up the climbing-line, attach the descender and back-up, tie off the device, grab the top anchor, climb over the edge, release the device, and descend. A lanyard can be clipped into the masterpoint as a back-up to the above, but should never be trusted alone if there is any chance of a factor 2 fall.

The ideal connectors for a masterpoint, the link between rope and anchor, should provide 100% security, even if they end up being cross-loaded or loaded over an edge or the action of the rope unlocks them.

To these ends, I would go for either double lockers with gates opposed (twist-locks ideally) or quick-links, ideally steel, as they won't get trashed against the rock. A steel rappel ring could also be used, as this would be unbreakable, with the rope being tied directly into it or clipped in with lockers.

Ropes are much more likely to get abraded when tied into knots as they stand proud against the rock, so it's worth giving them special attention. It is important to make sure the masterpoint and line knots are protected by a rope protector or mat, but an alternative is to thread the top of the climbing-line through a 2-litre plastic bottle with the bottom removed or through a heavy-duty fuel funnel. These rope protectors will get trashed, but that's the point.

Setting the Anchor

Single Line
Build a top anchor and create a masterpoint by attaching the end of the rope to this masterpoint, ideally using a knot such as an Alpine Butterfly, which is easy to untie. However, to fulfil the two-point rule, the end of the climbing-line should be run back to the strongest individual anchor point. This ensures that even if the masterpoint were to fail, the climber would not be in danger.

Two Lines
When using a climbing and safety-line rope, it's essential to keep the ropes apart to avoid tangling or compromising the devices. I suggest using two cordelettes or a rigging rope to create two asymmetric masterpoints for each rope. If the climber has good rigging skills, they can use the ends of the climbing rope to connect to the anchors, forming an anchor

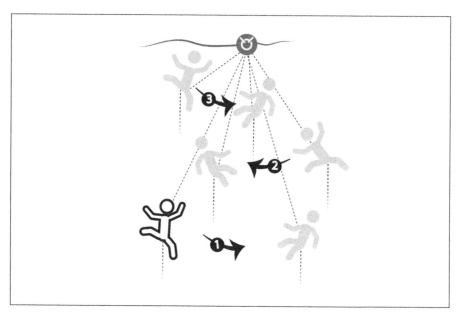

Fig.253

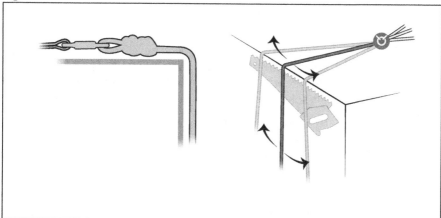

Fig.254

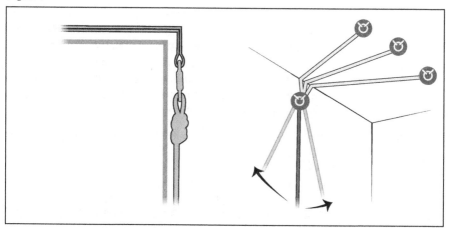

Fig.255

matrix with no weak links, such as extra karabiners, slings, cords, etc. Alternatively, a single masterpoint can be used with a re-anchor or re-direct on the safety-line lower on the pitch.

Failure Points

As with any complex anchor, there are countless ways individual anchor points or connectors could fail, which is why redundancy is built into all anchors. Even if half of the anchor fails, or even two-thirds, the anchor can still be relied upon. Don't hang your life from single anchor points unless they're train stoppers.

256

Rope stretch should be factored in to a climbers safety calculations. For example, a skinny dynamic rope may drop a climber 3 metres on rope stretch, which is enough to break a ankle, a back, or a skull.

Death Yo-Yo

One misnomer is that sharp edges cut ropes when weighted, but this is not true unless the edge is as sharp as a knife blade; rather, a cut event is caused by the climber's movement. The weighting and unweighting of the rope, such as using rope ascenders or repeated falls or swings, creates a yo-yo-ing, see-sawing, or sawing action, which will eventually cause the rope to disintegrate.

257

The maximum stretch takes places at the very point that the ground is closest.

One of the primary reasons thick low-stretch ropes are employed in industrial rope access, versus skinny dynamic ropes, is to reduce such rope-cutting events. But such events still occur, so the low-stretch rope is not a fix, just a part of the solution.

258

One way to reduce rope stretch if thin dynamic ropes are the only option is to use two lines, as this should halve the drop.

If the climber treats their rope with respect and does not view it as a steel cable, but rather a bunch of twisted nylon fibres, then they will have a good foundation for both a long-lasting rope and life, and not end up cutting both short.

259

Even if using a two rope system, a fall off 1.5 metres onto your ass can still injurious, so it's best top be prepared to carry a bouldering style fall rather than hope the ropes will catch you.

The rope should also not be viewed as a swing or bungee, and whenever it is loaded, all movement should be smooth and not jerky.

The reason for avoiding dynamic ropes, especially the thinner ropes, meaning both thin single ropes (9.5 mm and down) as well as half ropes (9 mm to 7 mm), is their inbuilt stretch properties magnify movement. This results in a far greater sawing effect, which, when the rope is shoelace-thick, makes a bad combination. This is not to say that a static rope is immune to sawing, only that it is much reduced.

Treat the rope as if your life depended on it, because it does.

Shift

Regarding TRS top anchors, one potential failure point to consider is that the angle of loading is generally certain. If that angle changes suddenly or is miscalculated, it could undermine the anchor and the rope. The primary danger is that the

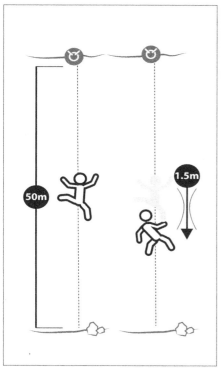

Fig.256

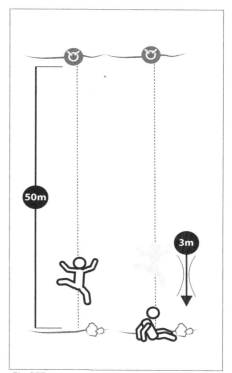

Fig.257

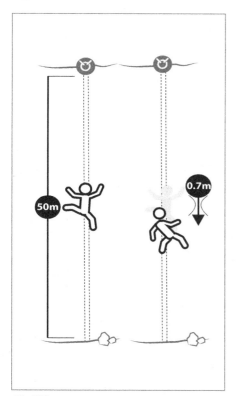

Fig.258

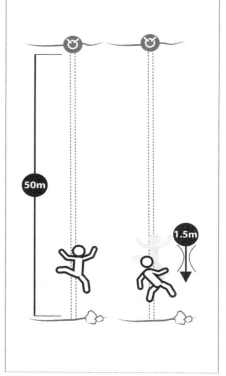

Fig.259

260

When rappelling the lines, employ a back-up friction hitch, stopper knots, and make sure the ends reach the ground.

 261

Some multi pitch crags can feature several belay points on other routes which may cause a climber to miss the one they're rigging down to. This can lead to a climber going too far and either hitting the ends of their ropes, or rappelling off the ropes!

 262

Climbers should always be cognisant of the terrain they're on, the location of the anchor, the plumb line, and what risks they're exposed to if they swing. Also note that the lower a climber is on the rope, the greater the swing, the greater the damage when they crash into something.

Margin Call

A point I try to pass on in a lot of my writing is the importance of avoiding the "Oh shit!" moments in climbing, that moment in which you're about to die (or think you are), you know why, and it's your fault. I've had many of these moments, especially early on. An example would be transferring from one rappel rope to another, 800 metres up, only to discover the new rope was just the tangled end of the rope I'd been on (I fucked up, I fell, I lived). TRS is ripe for 'OS' moments, and the best way to avoid them is to give each thing you do a fraction more time before you do it.

rope could saw across the edge of the crag as the angle shifts or saw back and forth during swinging falls. This sawing action can quickly destroy the rope, leading to a life-threatening fall to the ground.

Short Fall
When hanging ropes down cliffs, perhaps cliffs that have not been climbed on before, the climber must make sure the ropes reach the bottom before rappelling, and always tie stopper knots in case they're wrong.

Ground Strike Stretch
All ropes will stretch, be they low-stretch or dynamic, and the more unanchored rope above a climber, the greater distance they will fall. This can result in a ground fall when close to the ground, the stretchier the rope, the higher the climber must go before being out of the danger zone.

The angle of the rock also plays a part. On a slab, a slip or fall will place a lower load on a rope compared to vertical or overhanging ground, as a percentage of the load will be taken by the rock itself. On steep ground, the rope will be required to absorb the full weight of the climber.

For example, if a climber is trying to boulder out the start of an overhanging route with a 9.5 mm dynamic rope running straight to the anchor 25 meters above, if they fall in the first 3 meters, they stand a good chance of landing on their arse.

Such falls can appear funny to bystanders, but they can also be life-changing, resulting in a bruised or broken coccyx or worse. Conversely, a climber falling on a 60-degree slab using an even stretchier 9 mm dynamic rope may not stretch the rope enough to even notice.

If faced with this potential rope stretch problem, and a climber does not have a heavy-duty low-stretch, they should consider doubling up ropes to create two climbing-lines so the load is held by both. The use of re-anchors can also significantly reduce the overall stretch of a thin line by decreasing the amount of stretchy rope in the system.

Keep it Tidy Up Top
When rigging anchors, only life-supporting ropes should lead over the edge, such as the climbing-line or climbing and safety-line. Avoid allowing rope ends or loops of slack to hang over the edge, and keep all loose ends tied to the main anchor to prevent accidental mistakes. Keeping ropes tidy also applies to climbing hardware and equipment to avoid gear landing on heads due to movement of the rope, wind, or other factors.

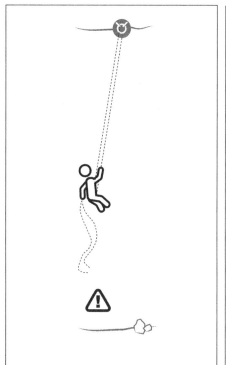

Fig.260

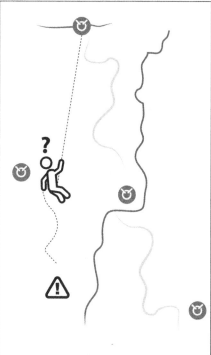

Fig.261

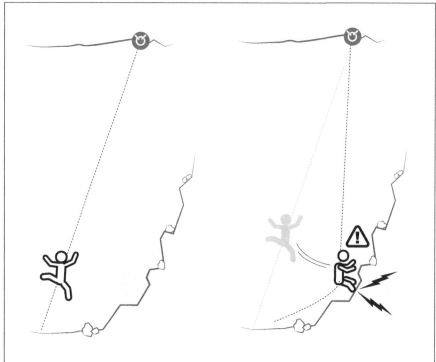

Fig.262

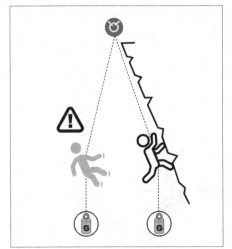

Fig.263

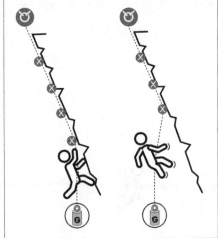

Fig.264

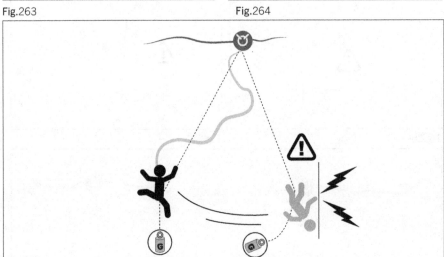

Fig.265

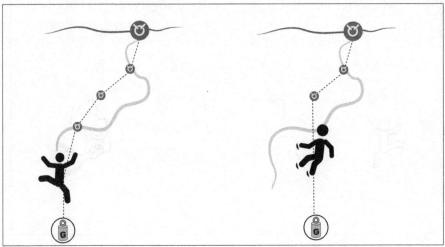

Fig.266

Sub Anchors

 263
On overhanging ground a fall will see the climber swing out into space, potentially impacting trees or other objects.

 264
By using re-directs on steep ground the climber will eliminate dangerous swings.

🖉 265
Routes that begin offset to the anchor can lead to dangerous swings, either into the ground, or into rock features.

🖉 266
By employing re-anchors and re-directs, the climber limits the risk of dangerous swings.

Originally developed by cavers and later adopted by industrial rope access technicians, re-anchors and re-directs are used to keep ropes away from the rock, establish clean drops, and re-align ropes on zig-zagging pitches to avoid damaging edges. They are also ideal for rigging climbs for TRS.

When used in TRS, unless used as a secondary anchor to the top anchor, this kind of anchor will be climbed to, the rope unclipped from it, and then the climber will continue either removing the anchor or leaving it in place for another attempt, re-fixing it when descending.

Re-anchors

A re-anchor connects the climbing-line directly to an intermediate anchor via a knot, essentially fixing it to a mini anchor. This anchor can consist of one solid piece or several, but it should be unquestionably bombproof.

A typical re-anchor has the rope attached by an Alpine Butterfly knot, as it's much easier to untie once loaded compared to a Figure-8. Although this is ideal, such knots require two hands to untie, making them less suited to steep TRS.

A Clove hitch is perhaps the easiest full-strength knot one can remove one-handed, and it will unravel once removed, but only if it hasn't been loaded (otherwise it'll be too tight). Clipping a free karabiner into the Clove hitch can make it easier to loosen a tight Clove hitch before unclipping, but it's still not ideal.

A better alternative is a Cow hitch, which is a Girth hitch in which only one strand is loaded, as this is strong enough for typical TRS loads and can be tied and untied one-handed. If the hitch has been loaded, this can be loosened easily by just using a thumb to press down on the loop of the Cow hitch. A Cow hitch is not a fully fixed hitch, as the rope can slip, but a fully fixed version can be made using a Pedigree Cow hitch, as this is just as easy to untie one-handed, but stops a hitch from slipping.

An unconventional option is to forgo a full-strength fixing knot and use a hitch that will take a substantial amount of load but not its entirety, with the payoff that it can easily be unclipped one-handed. The best hitch to use is a Munter hitch, which, although a belaying hitch, locks down on the karabiner when loaded. The drawback is that the rope above the hitch leading

🖋 267
Alpine Butterfly re-anchor.

🖋 268
Cow hitch re-anchor.

🖋 269
Munter hitch re-anchor.

🖋 270
Super Munter re-anchor.

🖋 271
Friction hitch re-anchor.

Margin Call
If you have big wall ambitions, learning to employ sub-anchors and re-directs while rigging for TRS will give you a few extra arrows for your big wall quiver. Just as these techniques were developed initially by cavers venturing into – and out of – the deepest caves without abrading their ropes, the same is true of climbers scaling giant walls. Re-anchors and re-directs are vital to fixing ropes over multiple pitches, allowing you to move safely up and down them. I've also used these techniques on alpine climbs, setting scary thin dynamic ropes (8 mm), allowing us to fix up from a good ledge rather than sit on each other's knees all night, confident the next day to climb the ropes from solid re-anchor to solid re-anchor.

to the anchor will also be loaded, although much less so than when using a re-direct (this is really a re-anchor-re-direct).

Another unconventional option is a slip knot, which works a little like the Munter hitch in that it's semi-fixed, but can be harder to unclip one-handed after loading.

For pitches that are tricky to rig, one option is a friction hitch, as they can be attached to a loaded rope.

Re-directs

A re-direct or deviation acts like a re-anchor; only the rope is not fixed to it, only clipped into with a karabiner or quick-draw, acting like a running belay. Its sole duty is to direct the rope where it needs to be. This is ideal when the climber can't afford to battle knots as they climb. It also helps to maintain the full dynamic properties of the rope, although this is also a drawback as it could lead to abrasion higher up the rope if multiple falls are taken.

The utility of re-directs is a reverse of the climbing norm, where the leader attempts to minimize rope drag but rather tries to magnify it; this means using short quickdraws rather than long and placing anchor points to create multiple acute angles in the rope path to the re-anchor.

Remember that the more acute the angle, the greater the load on the karabiner, with a 90-degree bend in the rope equating to an approximately 50% reduced load on the top anchor. A typical example of a pitch with multiple re-directs would be an overhanging bolted climb, where the rope has been clipped into each bolt via quickdraws, and the climber unclips as they go.

When to Employ Sub-anchors

For TRS, these techniques can be employed for the following reasons:

- The pitch is indirect, such as on gradually traversing climbs or routes that ascend in steps: climb up, walk left, climb up, step right, etc. The use of one or several intermediary anchors can chunk up a climb, meaning any swings will be minimal.

- They can also be used on steep and overhanging climbs to avoid big swings out from the rock.

- They can be integrated into the main anchor and used to bypass loose or abrasive cliff tops.

- If forced to climb on sub-optimal, highly dynamic 'sport' ropes, when wear is magnified by the dynamic yo-yo-ing

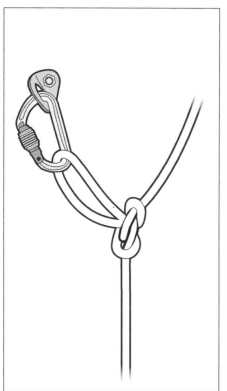

Fig.267

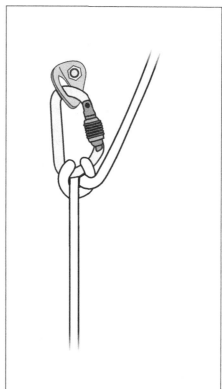

Fig.268

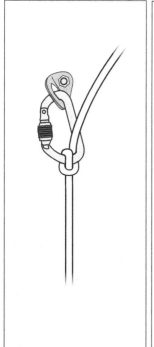

Fig.269

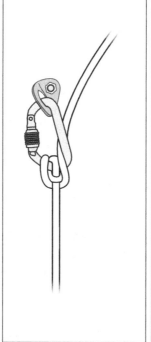

Fig.270

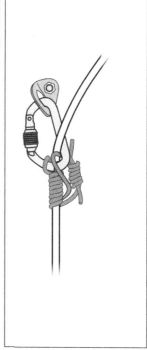

Fig.271

🖉 272
A mix of re-anchors and re-directs on different styles of route.

on the rope, re-anchors can "chunk" up the rope, making it less stretchy.

- If the top anchor is offset from the start of the route by a considerable distance, a fall low down on the climb could result in the climber swinging into the ground, increasing the risk of a ground strike.

- Higher on the climb, such swings are equally dangerous, causing the climber to barrel across the rock, smashing into rock features or corners. The swing must be tamed.

- One of the significant unseen risks of swinging or having the rope travel sideways across the rock face is dislodging rocks from above the climber and damaging the rope.

- Re-anchors and re-directs help a climber adopt a vital no-swing mindset.

Setting Sub-anchors

Re-anchors and re-directs are best set by rappelling the line of ascent first and placing these anchors at problem points, such as below sharp edges, away from loose rock, and rope-snagging features.

Re-anchors should be viewed like full high-strength anchors, as they will be taking the total weight of the climber, while re-directs are more like running protection, so single pieces.

Re-directs are easy to place on rappel; just position the anchor point, clip in a quickdraw, and then attach the climbing-line above the descender. If the climb is steep, using a long quickdraw (30 cm) or sling (60 cm) can make this easier.

Re-anchors are harder to clip, as the rope will often be loaded and will need unloading to tie a knot and clip it into the re-anchor. If the climber can stand in balance, this process is easy, but invariably, if the climber needs a re-anchor, they won't be able to stand in balance.

The following options can be used for connecting the climbing-line to a re-anchor. All require being "hands off," so they require a back-up friction hitch, and I would also advise tying off the descender, using a catastrophe-knot, or an ABD:

- **Footloop method**: With the re-anchor built, clip a footloop (120 cm sling) into the re-anchor, and stand in it to unweight the climbing-line. A lanyard, short sling, or linked quickdraws can be used to connect the climber to the re-anchor. Allow some slack to travel through the descender, tie a knot, and connect this to the re-anchor, then continue down.

- **Two-device method**: This works around the fact that many climbers will have two descenders, their tube device

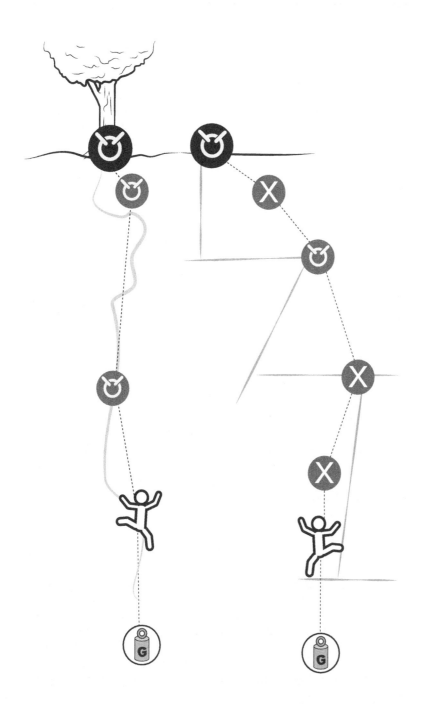

Anchor   Re-Anchor   Re-Direct

Fig.272

273

A selection of re-directs. Note, it's OK to clip a rope into the far end of a quick-draw, and have it run across the nylon sling – as seen in the third image – as the rope is not moving, but fixed.

274

A re-direct should be avoided if it must handle acute load-ings, and a re-anchor should be employed instead.

275

A failed re-direct could lead to a dangerous swing, or even trigger other pieces to fail.

276

If poor re-directs are employed when rigging a climb, this may lead to a cascading failure result-ing in a ground fall.

277

Employing a re-anchor in a pitch can act as an insurance policy against re-direct failure.

and ABD. Build the re-anchor and while hanging on the climbing-line, tie the fixing knot (Alpine Butterfly) below the descender and clip this into the re-anchor, leaving enough slack in the rope the descender is on, so it's possible to rappel below the re-anchor. Take the second descender, ideally an ABD, and connect this to the rope below the re-anchor, pulling it tight to the knot. Now rappel down into the loop of rope above the re-anchor until the second descender is taking the weight of the climber. Remove the other descender and continue down.

- **Friction hitch:** The climber builds a re-anchor and connects a friction hitch to the climbing-line above their descender. They swing in and clip the hitch to the re-anchor, then, with one hand on the rope above the hitch and the other holding onto the re-anchor, take their weight off the climbing-line for a second, and allow a little of the rope to spring back through the friction hitch, then re-weight the rope. The hitch should now hold the climbing-line.

Failure Points

When tying re-anchor connector knots, a little slack must be left above the knot, as too little slack, when tied to a loaded rope, can cause the rope to spring back a little, leaving the re-anchor unweighted, which can lead to it being pulled side-ways. At the other extreme, don't create big dead loops of slack, as this will magnify a fall if the re-anchor fails or when it is detached from the re-anchor. One of the big advantages of low-stretch ropes is that they create fewer spring-back issues.

The main danger from re-anchors and re-directs is forget-ting to detach the climbing-line from the said anchor when climbing past them, easily done when in "the zone." When using an eccentric device, once the anchor is passed, the rope will come tight on the device, reminding the climber to stop; but if the climber is using a bi-directional device, it may just start feeding out the live rope, increasing the possible fall distance with every foot climbed. The issue here, apart from the obvious one of climbing on a big loop of dead rope, is that the dynamic properties of the climbing-line reduce to zero the closer the climber gets to the re-anchor, so any such fall will be severe.

A similar issue can happen if the climber unclips the rope from a re-anchor but forgets to untie the knot, as this will jam in the device and stop the live rope from passing through the device, leading to another slack fall.

There is also a small risk of a shortfall or swing if an anchor point fails while the rope is loaded, so don't have any acute angles between re-anchors or re-directs.

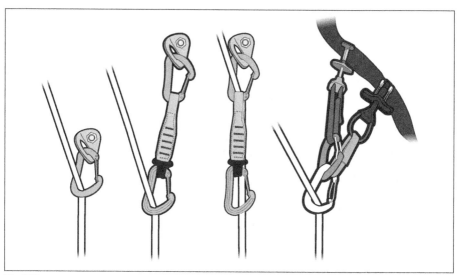

Fig.273

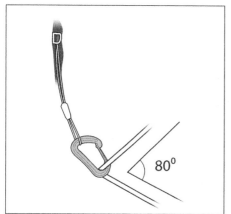

Fig.274

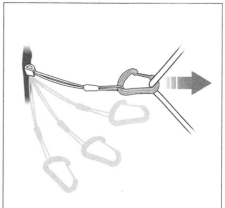

Fig.275

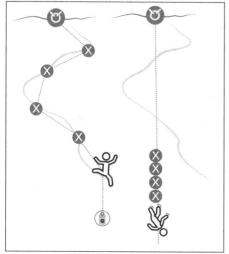

Fig.276

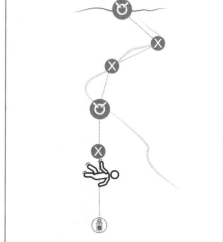

Fig.277

Fig.278

Escape

 278
Climber 'Batmaning' up the climbing-line. This technique takes some practice, but is a very good way to cover short distances, perhaps to pull past a crux section. When 'Batmaning', it's vital to check that the climbing-line is still running through the TRS device, otherwise the climber risks a very long and hard fall.

Sooner or later, a climber will find themselves unable to progress up the line they've fixed. There are countless reasons why, including the obvious ones, such as exhausted arms or battered toes, reaching one's limit of skill and ability, or simply losing one's nerve. If the climber is using TRS to push their technical limits, they will eventually reach a dead end and be unable to continue climbing. When this happens, the climber will invariably be left hanging on their climbing-line with a number of choices. They can rest a while and then try again when their arms have more strength, attempt to solve a puzzling sequence, or they can decide to call it quits and return to the ground.

Safety

A key to escaping the system is disconnecting oneself from one system to another, but if care and focus aren't applied or corners cut, that next system might be life support. When switching around devices, which will include disconnecting them from the harness or rope, always maintain the two-point rule. This is most easily achieved by tying a catastrophe-knot in the climbing-line below you and attaching it to your belay loop. This knot can be an overhand or Figure-8, or if you want to be able to remove it one-handed, a slack Clove hitch. If no karabiner is available for clipping, learn to tie a Bowline into your belay loop using a bight of rope. When tying the catastrophe-knot, one must always leave enough slack above to operate your devices, including tying off descenders. The use of a catastrophe-knot will negate any line-ballast, which means rope climbing will require manual feeding initially or will need removing before descending. Another safety point would be to have a plan for what to do when you're hanging in space without any escape equipment.

Methods of Escape

How the climber returns to the ground depends on numerous factors, but it can either be a simple process that requires minimum effort or a complex one that calls on all the climber's technical skills. Below, I will outline the most common ways to escape your TRS system in order of complexity.

- **Climb up:** The climber may be stopped by the rock ahead, but can they climb around it? Is it possible to traverse left or right or tension the climbing-line a little and move to an easier line? By climbing around the problem, the climber might be able to save time and hassle, reach the top, and then reset the climbing-line or de-rig and descend.

- **Climb down:** If the climber is using a bi-directional system, they can simply reverse and down-climb back to the start. This is easy on less than vertical climbs, and on steep climbs, it's generally possible, perhaps with a few rests.

- **Climb the Rope:** For marooned TR soloists, switching to a rope climbing system is fairly simple if they are using some form of rope grab. There are improvised "guerilla" methods and full rope climbing systems, with the improvised methods being faster for short stretches but less strenuous and faster for long pitches.

- **Rappel:** Transitioning from ascent to descent is trickier than climbing the rope, as the climber will likely not be using a TRS device that can switch easily from an ascender to a descender. Remember, learning rope climbing should not be attempted for the first time in a high-pressure situation. Invest time in practicing the basics before venturing into more complex scenarios. When descending, the climber must go through a number of steps. First, they need to set up the rappel, and then they have various options depending on the system they are escaping from. Using these methods and techniques, climbers can safely escape their TRS systems and make their way back to the ground when they encounter obstacles or reach their limits. Proper training, experience, and preparation are crucial for effectively dealing with these situations.

Climb the Rope

Luckily for the marooned TR soloist, the fact that they are using some form of rope grab makes switching to a rope climbing system fairly simple. The system that is adopted can either be an improvised "guerilla" or a full rope climbing system, with the improvised methods being faster for short stretches but far less strenuous and faster for long pitches.

Guerilla Style
The following systems are quick, dirty, and non-standard, and they require skill and experience in knowing when they are appropriate.

Batmaning
Very often, a climber will be stopped by a crux move that cannot be passed, but they know there is easier climbing just beyond it. Rather than escaping the system, one option is to just pull up on the rope a little, allowing the TRS device to follow. This is done like in the old Batman TV shows, with the

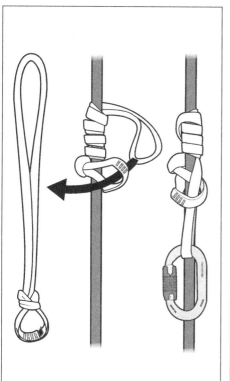

Fig.279

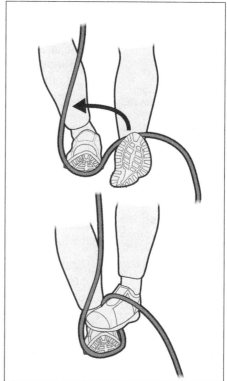

Fig.280

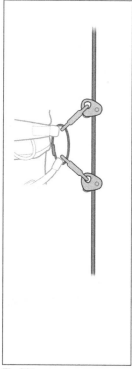

Fig.281

Fig.282

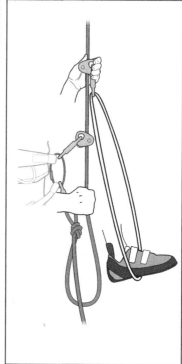

Fig.283

284
The climber attaches
a ABD below both TRS
devices rather than tying a
catastrophe-knot. Not that a
catastrophe-knot can also be
tied, as well as the ABD could
be locked off. In this scenario
a stopper knot is tied onto
the rope below the ABD.

285
The secondary device is
removed and racked.

286
A foot loop is added on
the live rope using a friction hitch, or the racked
secondary device.

287
The climber unweights the
primary device and dis-
engages it from the rope,
and transfers onto the
ABD, and now rappels.

288
Rather than rappel, the
climber moves the attached
TRS device up the rope, and
ideally connects a lanyard to
the TRS device, which is now
acting as a top ascender.

289
A foot-loop is now clipped
into ascender and the
rope can be climbed.

feet on the wall and the hands pulling up on the rope. As the climber moves up, the TRS device should continue to protect them and provide rest if needed. Pulling up on a single strand of rope on anything less than vertical rock is easier than one would imagine, and pulling up on both lines is even easier. As soon as the crux is passed, the climber can resume climbing normally.

Improvised
Due to the TRS device being an ascender, holding the weight of the climber, all that's required to climb the climbing-line is some way of allowing the legs to power the climber up the rope. In the above Batman style, the legs are using the rock to propel the climber, but on steeper ground, the climber needs a greater degree of traction over the rope. This can be achieved in the following ways:

- Create an S-wrap in the rope below the TRS device and step up using this. This is not a fast technique, but can be used for short stretches of rope climbing.

- Tie a friction hitch above or below the TRS device to create a foot-loop and use this to climb a short distance. Some may imagine that you can climb a whole rope length using a TRS device and a friction hitch, which you could, but it would be a slow, strenuous, and sweaty ascent.

- If the climber is running a safety-line and secondary TRS device, this can just be left to run as normal as they climb.

Mechanical rope climbing
If the climber is carrying the right gear or knows how to adapt the gear they're carrying, they can set up a dedicated rope climbing system using ascenders, allowing them to fly up the rope in no time. The more rope climbing one does, the faster the transition will be, and the faster the rope will be climbed. A climber running two TRS devices can easily switch a secondary device into foot ascender mode and use this with the primary as the body ascender, or they may carry one or two other devices for ascent. Such devices could include micro and full-size ascenders, or an ABD.

Rope Climbing Training
It's beyond the scope of this book to cover rope climbing, but it's a good idea for a climber to begin learning this skill, with all its subtleties and dangers, before they find themselves stuck on the climbing-line. Yes, it's possible to know the theory and to have read all the books, but a hundred feet off the ground is not an ideal classroom. Instead, invest a day to practice the basics.

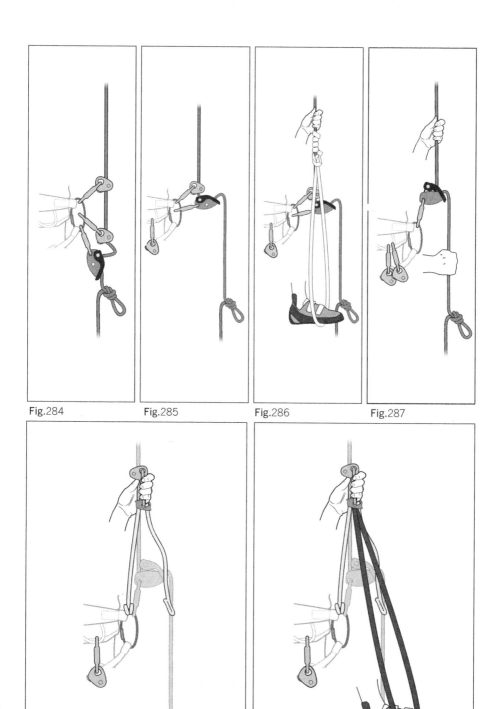

Fig.284   Fig.285   Fig.286   Fig.287

Fig.288   Fig.289

Climber ties catastrophe-knot and connects it to belay loop.

The climber connects a belay device, and removes secondary device and racks it.

Belay device is tied off.

Foot-loop is attached above the TRS device with either a friction hitch or the racked TRS device.

The foot-loop is weighted and the TRS device disconnected.

295
The tied off belay device is weighted, the friction hitch pulled down and removed, the catastrophe-knot untied, then the belay device unlocked and the climber descends.

Rappel

Transitioning from ascent to descent is far trickier than climbing the rope, as generally the climber will not be using a TRS device that can switch easily from being an ascender to a descender.

TRS Rappel Device

If the climber is using a TRS device that can both work as a rope grab and descender, such as the Taz devices, all that's required is to remove or disable the secondary device on the climbing-line and rappel. If the secondary is on the safety-line, then this should travel down the rope as a rappel back-up. It's worth noting here that in my experience, many climbers will carry out their first rappel with such a device at the point they need to escape, so generally, with zero grasp of how the device functions in descent. Some mechanical devices can be very hard to rappel on, requiring a higher degree of force than expected, especially when using very thick ropes. Other devices can have a hair trigger and can drop a climber onto the deck before they know what's happening. And so, when choosing a device that works as both an ascender and descender, I recommend practicing using it as such before you hang your life off it. Do several rappels with it and climb several ropes before you use it as a TRS device.

Ascent to Descent Process

If the climber has to transition from ascent to descent, then they must go through a number of steps, keeping in mind the two-point rule at each step. Several factors will aid or hinder this process:

- Don't try and escape this system one-handed. In fact, if you're trying to escape one-handed, stop what you're doing, as you're probably doing something sketchy and dangerous. This is a two-handed process.

- I repeat, if you're straining, you're probably doing something sketchy. Let something hold you in position that allows you to set up for your escape.

- The more secure the climber's connectors, i.e. triple twist lock, anti-rotation rubbers, bridge cord etc, the more time and care will be needed to unclip the TRS device. Such processes come down to practice, and anger and frustration will be unhelpful to that process and will undoubtedly lead to dropping your TRS device, or the climber. It's best to always adopt the soloist's mindset, and acknowledge that almost every problem you encounter is a problem of your own making, most of all the fact it was your choice to go and dangle off a cliff all by yourself.

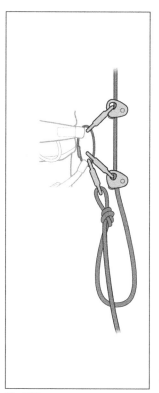

Fig.290

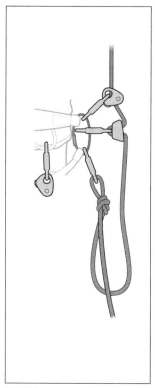

Fig.291

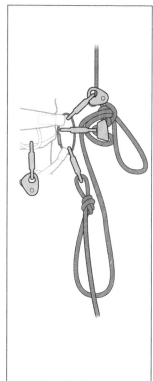

Fig.292

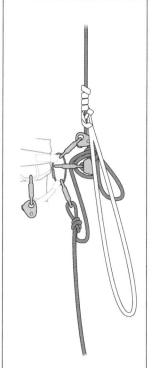

Fig.293

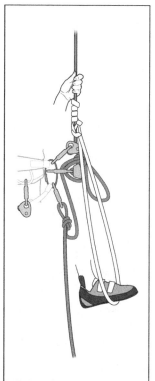

Fig.294

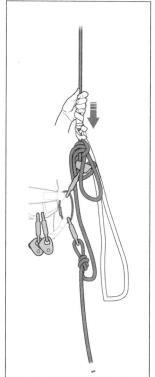

Fig.295

Margin Call

I love the term 'catastrophe-knot'; it just sums up what such a knot is for. In an ideal world, this term would replace the more common 'backup knot' in most places where it's applied. The thing about such a knot is that – once taught – it will used by novices on every occasion in which it should. It will also be used by the highly experienced because they probably owe their lives to one. Those in the middle who think they're too good for such things are often missing, the same people who don't use a friction hitch as a backup when rappeling or think helmets are for wimps. These are the kinds of people who think it's OK to hang their lives – and the happiness of the people who love and care for them – of a single friction hitch as they transition, or think people who think about redundancy in their system need to 'man up'. The truth is that although many things can kill a climber, or worse, the most tragic is the triad of complacency, arrogance, or hubris. So, next time you think you can save five seconds by skipping that catastrophe-knot before you escape the system, just tie the damned knot.

- A climber who is familiar with how their connectors work should be able to unclip them when they need to be unclipped. If the climber can't, then they should not be up there, or simply need to take a little more time and care.

- Having an adjustable lanyard will make the transition far smoother, as it will act like a third arm, which is a very helpful thing to have.

- Place all escape gear, such as hitch loops, slings, rope grabs, and karabiners where they are easily accessible before you make your escape. This could be on your dominant hand side of your harness, or are the very back, where either hand can reach it.

- All escape gear can be placed on one karabiner that can easily be touch identified, such as an extra large, unusually shaped snap link, a wire gate oval for example. The downside with this approach is if it's fumbled and dropped, it's all lost. If the climber is clumsy, then spreading the escape kit is a good idea, as is carrying spares.

- I'll repeat myself again, don't make your escape the first time you've used friction hitches or climbed a rope.

- The steeper the ground, the more skill required, as well as some small degree of balance, fitness, and strength.

- Above all, focus, focus, focus, until the end.

Traditional Escape
No one escape is like another, but below is the boilerplate way of doing it.

01. The climber pulls up an arm's span of dead rope from below the TRS device and ties a catastrophe-knot and clips this into their belay loop with a locker. Some climbers may believe simply tying a knot into the rope may act as an effective stopper knot, but in a complex transition, a novice climber may make the terminal mistake of total disconnection from everything but the ground.

02. When tying the catastrophe-knot, there must be enough slack to attach a descender and tie it off, hence an arm's span of rope.

03. The climber attaches their descender to the loop of dead rope formed between the catastrophe-knot and primary TRS device, attaching it to their belay loop with a locker.

04. The descender should be pulled up tight to the TRS device as possible so the climber does not drop down too far as they switch from one device to another.

05. The descender can now be tied off in a suitable manner, such as a Munter Mule Overhand.

06. A back-up rappel friction hitch can now be attached to the rope below the descender.

07. The climber now removes any secondary TRS devices on the climbing-line. If the device is self-trailing and sits on a safety rope, then it can be left in place in order to act as a trailing back-up.

08. The climber must now unweight the primary TRS device. If they are standing in balance, this is simple as the device will already be unweighted. If not, a rope grab or friction hitch, connected to a foot-loop, must be placed above the device. Using this, the climber unweights the device and unclips it from the rope.

09. Released from the primary TRS device, the climber can now lower down carefully onto their tied-off descender.

10. Hanging from the descender, the climber removes the primary TRS device and catastrophe-knot and rappels down to the ground.

ABD Variation

If the climber has access to an ABD, such as a Petzl GriGri, they can usually forgo tying off the device and just go with a catastrophe-knot. Some climbers may forgo clipping the knot into their harness, believing the ABD will jam into the knot, but as discussed before, a disconnected knot is not a safe-guard against a disconnected climber. How would an ABD fail? Well, a climber may fail to clip an ABD into their belay loop as intended, but instead clip it into a belt loop, chalk bag strap, or the plastic harness racking. Such a terminal error will only be discovered at the final step, when the climber sits back on the ABD in the false assumption they're safe.

An ABD is a very useful tool for TRS escape, as it can also be rapidly switched to ascent mode by moving a TRS device above it and clipping on a foot-loop.

One paradox with an ABD is that it generally flouts the two-point rule and will most often be used without a back-up, such as a friction hitch. Although this may be the case when rappelling, when transitioning, a catastrophe-knot should be employed until it's time to rappel.

Final thoughts

Just as there are countless variations of TRS set-ups, so too are the variations of escape, with each type of device offering up different methods of escape. But however you make that great escape just take your time, keep two points of contact, and you'll make it.

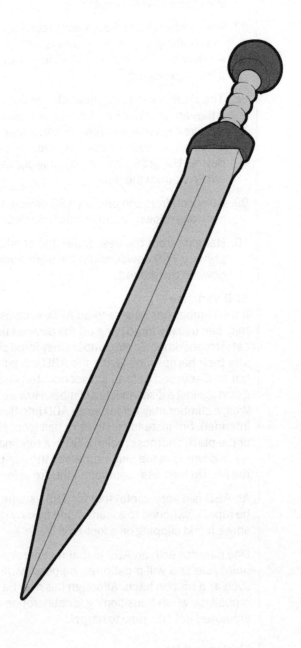

Fig.296

Final Thoughts

✎ 296

The Roman wooden gladius, or rudis, was used to train legionnaires and gladiators how to fight. The sword had no live edge that could cut, which made training safer, but it was also often much heavier than a steel gladius. Training with a heavy sword and full armour was an ideal way to develop strength, stamina, and skill to control the blade for fights that could last for minutes, hours or even days.

Having written several books that have mined the Kirkpatrick's brain and having finally reached the end of writing this one, I've come to a conclusion that I'd like to share.

In the past, people saw me as a brave/fearless/foolhardy/ stupid/incompetent/dangerous climber. Sometimes, I'd do a slide show, and the person who thanked me afterwards would say, "I hope you're alive long enough to come back and give us another one". I thought it was funny, a joke, but it wasn't. I mistook concern for admiration. As I got older, I began to see the lives of other climbers, my heroes, in the same light, that exhilarating feeling of watching the slow-motion death of someone remarkable but perhaps only a hero due to the carelessness with which they held their own lives. People who live near-death lives, one mad and crazy stunt and near miss after another, will eventually fail to wriggle free from its bony fingers.

So, what was I back then? Was I brave or foolhardy or stupid or incompetent or dangerous? It would be nice to pick just one, but I was all of them (but not all simultaneously). But mainly, I was just wildly ambitious.

Now I'm older; I've reached an age in which people sometimes call me a 'legend', which is in no way accurate, in fact I'd class myself as an anti-legend. If I was to deserve such status, it would only be that some climbers are self-aware enough to save themselves from themselves, to go from hero to has-been, to legend (the ideal is to become a "...whatever happened to?" rather than a "did you hear what happened to...").

How I avoided dying in my dangerous days was to pay attention to all technical aspects of climbing. In the pre-Internet, I read everything I could and talked to anyone sharing their knowledge. I quickly realised I could die in many ways, but it would not be that if I could become an expert in the technical stuff.

And so all my technical books have built on that foundation, that survival knowledge, death wriggling stuff — but as a result, it can often appear to be a little too concerned with dying. Doom written. In this book, the reader might get the impression that TRS is far too dangerous to practice or give it up, not realising how at risk they'd been all these years. The truth is, TRS is safe if you know how risky it is, but risky if you think it's safe. I don't write these books to be a doom monger but to trap the doom within these pages, like a spell, so you, the reader, are armed with the knowledge to be safe, so one day, you can be the kind of legend who tells others not to do what they did.

Fig.297

Last Word

A pair of old dog eared running shoes met me as I pulled over the top the wall, sat together, like dogs waiting their master. A week before we made the climb, the owner of these shoes had hiked up here alone, up the long zigzagging trail, probably in the dark, his seventy metre rope in his pack, looking forward to a day of top rope soloing a thousand feet above the valley floor.

He'd turned left at Angel's Landing, the tourists already gathering no doubt, hoping to reach the top in time for sunrise, but he'd made his way up the last section of track, to the top of the Moonlight buttress.

Perhaps he took off his sweaty running shoes right here, left them neat for going home, and moved around in feet bare to the cold sand and stone as he rigged the rope. The sun probably still hid as he set off down, the soft rock made hard by winter, what moisture it held, bonding it together tight.

He'd have tip toed down the first pitch, the route's last, easy 5.7, and short as a pitch could be. He'd have short fixed into the bolts and carried on into the black steep.

Below was a pitch more meaty, 12a, the exposure now full power, just a finger crack splitting the buttress. Did his GriGri warm his hand as he descended? Perhaps he fingered the holds as he went, inserting tips and toes, spying for solid nuts and cams. Here and there he'd have seen the chalk marks, the ticks, where others had been. Some had climbed onsight, ground up from the valley bottom, and taken many falls doing it, while others had worked it top down, like him, on a rope, both in order to make the impossible a little more possible, but mainly just for something fun to do.

Another belay would have appeared, and he would have attached the rope to this too. With so much rope left why not carry on further, another 12a to top rope solo, a long rope bonus.

What happened next we'll never know. A team lower on the wall saw someone,fall past them. His body was found at the base after falling a thousand feet. Was he top roping or still rappelling when he fell? When the rescue team retrieved his rope they found no stopper knot, and a GriGri clipped to his harness.

And so a week water I looked down at his ratty running shoes, dusty, already fading, waiting patently for their owner, who, in making just one mistake, would never come back.

Fig.298

Appendix

"Your love of glory must conquer your will to survive; or why fight at all?"

Bring Up the Bodies,
Hilary Mantel

 298
Pseudo Leading.

Fig.299

Certs

✏ 299
Industrial climbing helmet.

Margin Call
When I worked in an outdoor shop, we had a very lightweight helmet from a nameless brand that one day fell from the ceiling where it was hung, and broke apart. The hard plastic shell of the helmet detached from the polystyrene inner. Inside, at the very apex of the helmet, was a thick coin of plastic. Its role was evident, which was to allow this flimsy helmet to pass its CE test, which involved the ability to resist penetration at this point. Sure, this little disk helped it get a pass, but if a rock hit either side of a 5 cm area, it would probably fail. For me, this was a wake-up and showed that manufacturers were not always designing products with the end user in mind, to make them as good as they could, but instead were designing them to pass an often arbitrary test.

All climbing hardware is stamped with a European certification mark starting with "EN" followed by a sequence of numbers. Whilst many climbers might overlook this mark, deeming it just another instance of needless bureaucracy and red tape that bears no relevance to them, it is essential to comprehend these certifications. They offer insights into the strength of a device, its intended use, and its resilience to misuse.

It's worth noting that all tests are conducted with ropes of both the maximum and minimum diameter for each type of rope as specified in the manufacturer's guidelines.

EN_892 - Dynamic Ropes

Climbing ropes that can be used as part of a dynamic climbing system are divided into three categories: single, half and twin.

Static elongation test: (1) An 80 kg mass is hung from one strand of single or double rope, but two stands of twin rope for 10 minutes. (2) Then rope is then rested for 10 min. Now 5 kg for 1 minute (3), then finally 80 kg for 1 minute (4). Static elongation is tested between phase 3 and 4 and elongation must not exceed 10 % for a single rope or 12 % for a half rope. The value of this test is you don't want a rope that's so stretchy you'd hit the ground when you hung from it.

Sheath Slippage: A 2000 mm length of rope is tested. The rope must be pulled evenly through a testing device that simulates a belay plate. The sheath may not slip more than 1 %. Anyone who's climbed on really old climbing wall ropes will understand the issue of sheath slippage.

Dynamic elongation test (drop test): A mass is dropped from a height of 4,800 mm to replicate a factor of 1.7 fall, with the following weight: Single rope/twin rope: 80 kg, half rope: 55 kg. A single rope must transfer no more than 12 kN, with a minimum of 5 falls (all single ropes will far surpass this before breaking).

EN_1891 - Low Stretch Ropes

Low-stretch ropes, most commonly called 'static' ropes, are broken into category A and B. A can be considered as standard, while B is a lower standard, which is required for the thinnest technical ropes, such 8 mm caving ropes.

Knotability: Two single overhand knots are tied one metre apart and a 10 kg mass is hung from the rope for 60 seconds. A test cone is then inserted into the eye of the knot, which must not exceed 12 mm. This tests how flexible the rope is, and eliminates strong but impossible to knot ropes.

Static Elongation Test: A 50 kg load is hung from the rope for 5 minutes, then 150 kg for further 5 minutes. Elongation must not be more than 5 %.

Sheath Slippage Test: A 2250 mm sample of rope is pulled through an apparatus that mimics rope devices and actions, such as rappelling with a descender. The rope passes through the device five times, and type A ropes must now have a sheath slippage of more than 1 %, or 1.5 % for type B ropes.

Static Strength with Terminations: A Figure-8 knot is tied at either end of a length of rope and must withstand a force of 15 kN for type A ropes and 12 kN for type B ropes, for 3 minutes.

Static Strength without Terminations: The rope is wrapped around two bars and pulled, so without any knots, and must be able to withstand a force of at least 22 kN for type A ropes and at least 18 kN for type B.

Fall Arrest Peak Force: A 100 kg mass is suspended for type A ropes, or a 80 kg for type B ropes from rigid anchorage point. The mass is raised by 600 mm and allowed to free-fall and the peak force is measured. The peak force must not exceed 6 kN.

Dynamic Performance Test: A 2000 mm length of rope suspends with a 100 kg mass for type A ropes, or a 80 kg mass for type B ropes. The mass is raised by 1000 mm, and allowed to free-fall, replicating a factor 1 fall. The test is repeated five times. The test specimen has to withstand at least 5 falls.

EN_353-2 - Personal Protection Against Falls (PFPE)

This test pertains to fall arresters that move along a fixed or permanent line. The device progresses as the climber ascends and descends the line, engaging only in the event of a fall.

Dynamic test: The apparatus undergoes a dynamic drop test with a 100 kg weight, released after being elevated to the full extent of the device's lanyard, thus pulling the device up the line, simulating a factor 2 fall. During this evaluation, the device must activate within 1 metre, allowing a maximum arrest force of 6 kN, without inflicting damage to either the device or the rope.

This stringent assessment elucidates why the majority of fall arresters are solely certified for 10.5 mm ropes and above.

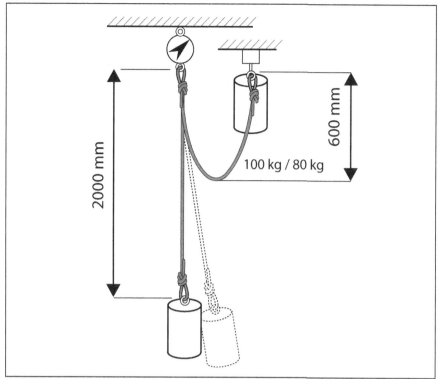

2000 mm

600 mm

100 kg / 80 kg

Fig.300

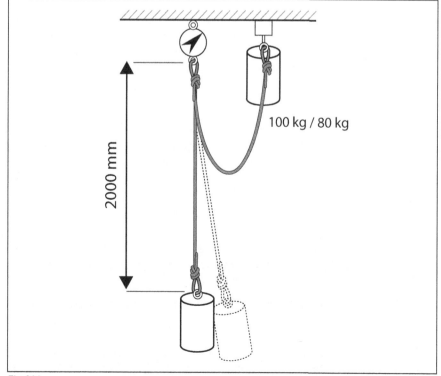

2000 mm

100 kg / 80 kg

Fig.301

This is particularly the case for rocker devices which encounter a notable amount of slippage upon being shock-loaded. The dynamic test accentuates a reason behind the inadequacy of the Petzl Shunt, which could potentially slip several metres when subjected to intense shock-loading.

It is also noteworthy that this test allows for an "energy-absorbing element": a shock-absorbing lanyard. To achieve a pass, this lanyard must possess a length sufficiently short to diminish the impact force exerted on the device; for instance, using a 60 cm shock-absorbing lanyard rather than a 150 cm rope cow's tail.

Incorporating a shock-absorbing link between the climber and the fall arrest underscores its fundamental importance in an efficient fall arrest system, absorbing the peak force, thus reducing the force applied to the rope to 6 kN or under. If such a force was applied on an eccentric rope clamp, it would culminate in a damaged rope.

Static strength: The device is obligated to endure a static load of 12 kN, and the lanyard 15 kN, for a duration of three minutes without any breakage. This particular test isn't performed on a rope, since most devices would commence damaging the rope at half of this load; to illustrate, a 10.5 mm rope begins to degrade at 6 kN when a force is channelled through an eccentric jaw.

Corrosion resistance: The concluding test assesses a device's resilience against corrosion caused by salt-water. While this criterion primarily caters to industrial needs, it could be pertinent for climbers TR soloing on sea cliffs.

EN_567 - Rope Clamps

This mountaineering standard is obviously one of the most significant tests for TRS. It stipulates that a rope clamp must be constructed in such a manner that releasing the rope requires the execution of at least two distinct actions. The tests are conducted as follows:

Design testing: This evaluates the functionality of a rope clamp: can the rope be manually inserted and taken out? Does the apparatus glide effortlessly in one direction whilst obstructing in the other? Furthermore, is it possible to connect a karabiner to the frame?

Tensile test: This assesses the strength of both the jaw and the frame when subjected to suboptimal loading, the kind typically encountered when a climber has made a grave mistake. The frame, jaw, and karabiners are required to withstand a brief static force of 2 kN without sustaining damage, for instance, the frame warping or the pin securing the jaw breaking away.

Push test: This crucial test gauges the device's locking mechanism (safety catch/trigger) by exerting a 0.4 kN force against the jaw, directly pressing upon the locking mechanism. In practical scenarios, such a force is encountered when the device is in an inverted position.

Breaking strength: This is a direct tensile test performed on the device using the rope (covering both Min and Max diameters). The force is administered four times on fresh sections of the rope, and a pass is deemed successful when the rope remains undamaged.

EN_12841 Rope Adjustment Devices (PFPE)

This European standard pertains to personal fall protection equipment, specifically focusing on rope access systems. Devices are classified as per the following categories:

Type A: Back-up devices serving as a fail-safe on an independent line.

Type B: Ascenders and rope adjusters facilitating vertical movement on a static line.

Type C: Descending devices designed for working lines.

The subsequent tests are executed:

Locking: The device is suspended 1 metre from the anchor point, and a lanyard of 0.4 metres in length, holding a 5 kg weight, is affixed to it. The weight on the lanyard is then elevated by 0.4 metres and subsequently released. The device must instantly engage its locking mechanism and remain in that state.

Minimum working strength test: With the device hanging from the rope and in a locked position, an initial force of 1 kN is applied. This force is then augmented to +1 kN for Type A devices, 4 kN for Type B, and 3 kN for Type C. This exerted force is sustained for 3 minutes. For Types A and B, the device shouldn't slide more than 100 mm, and for Type C, no more than 300 mm.

Dynamic test type A: The rope adjustment device is affixed to an anchor line positioned 1 metre beneath the force-measuring apparatus. A testing weight of no less than 100 kg is connected via a 0.4 metre lanyard and hoisted to a height equivalent to twice the lanyard's length.

Upon releasing the test weight, the peak force encountered is measured. The maximal braking force should not surpass 6 kN, and the braking distance must be contained within 2000 mm.

Dynamic test and capacity reserves (Types A, B, and C): The device is fixed to an anchor line 1 metre below the anchor point. A weight of 100 kg is tethered to the device using a 0.4 metre lanyard. This weight is hoisted by 0.4 metres, aligning it with the device, and is then let go.

The rope adjustment device must not detach from the anchor line, and the braking distance should not exceed 2000 mm. Subsequent to the dynamic assessment, the test weight is enhanced, without subjecting it to shock, by 3 kN. The device should endure this increased weight for a period of 3 minutes.

Descent velocity type C: In congruence with the EN_341 descender test for the 'Operating force Test', this evaluation scrutinises the descender's capability to function securely. Crucially, a device should not attain temperatures above 48°C and must exhibit no indications of causing the rope to melt.

EN_15151-1 Assisted Braking Devices

This mountaineering standard pertains to "semi-automatic" mechanical braking belay devices, encompassing ABDs such as the Petzl GriGri, Edelrid Eddy, and similar products. The subsequent tests are conducted:

Blocking Load: A force of 2 kN is exerted on the braking device, which it must resist for a duration of 60 seconds. A maximum slippage of 300 mm is permissible through the braking device. Consequent to the test, neither the braking device nor the rope should exhibit any damage.

Dynamic Performance When Belaying: An 80 kg weight in free fall is introduced to the braking device. This procedure is replicated thrice. Upon completion of the tests, the rope must remain secure (a fresh braking device can be employed for each individual test). Based on the average derived from the three trials, the rope's slippage should not exceed 1500 mm.

Static Strength: With the braking mechanism engaged and locked, the device ought to withstand an exerted force of 8 kN for a span of 60 seconds. The rope entering the device is secured with a stopper knot to prevent it from inadvertently feeding into the device. Under these conditions, the device should neither fracture nor release the rope.

EN_15151-2 - Manual Belay Devices

This mountaineering standard encompasses manual belay devices, inclusive of tube style devices (such as the Black Diamond ATC and Petzl Verso) as well as plaquette style devices (like the Petzl Reverso and Black Diamond ATC Guide, among others). The subsequent tests are undertaken:

Static Strength: For a single rope configuration (with twin rope registering at 7 kN across two strands and half ropes at 5 kN on one strand), a force of 7 kN is required to be exerted on the braking device for a duration of 60 seconds. This test is to be executed for every attachment point on the device.

Static Strength of Additional Attachment Points: The braking device is secured using the supplementary attachment to the test apparatus. The rope is affixed using a 10 mm pin. A force of 8 kN is exerted on the rope for a span of 60 seconds.

EN_341 - Descenders (PFPE)

This standard represents a comprehensive set of tests covering both industrial manual descenders and automatic descenders. It's worth noting that although we, as climbers, may refer to a belay device as a descender, in truth, any descending function is untested beyond the crossover tests of manual belay devices (EN15151-2).

Dynamic Elongation Drop Test 1: The device is attached to an 80 kg mass and suspended from 4 metres of rope. Subsequently, the device is lifted by 0.6 metres and dropped from the side to mimic a swinging fall. The device must retain the mass without releasing the rope.

Dynamic Elongation Drop Test 2: The same procedure is enacted, but in this instance, the device remains stationary, replicating its function when lowering an individual from a fixed point. The mass is suspended 4 metres beneath the device, then elevated and dropped from a height of 0.6 metres.

Function Tests: The device undergoes a battery of environmental tests to ensure its functionality in both high and low temperatures, and in wet and dry conditions.

Descent Energy Test: This assessment verifies the device's capability to securely hold the mass during descent, ensuring that the device doesn't exceed a temperature of 48 °C in the process.

Static Strength Test: The device is set up in a hauling configuration, with one strand anchored to the ground, while a 12 kN load is applied to the other. This evaluates the attachment point and the frame. The device is required to maintain this load for a duration of 3 minutes.

Operating Force Test: This assessment ensures that a loaded device (with an 80 kg mass) can be actuated to descend by applying a force (by pulling the handle) that does not exceed 0.45 kN.

EN_354 - Lanyards (PFPE)

Flexible, separate connecting elements in personal fall protection systems.

302
EN_12841 Lock test

303
EN_12841 Dynamic test and capacity reserves.

304
EN_567 - Rope clamp tensile test.

305
EN_567 - Rope clamp push test.

306
EN_567 - Rope clam breaking strength.

Dynamic strength test : A 100 kg mass is hung from the lanyard using 2 metres of dynamic rope; it is then lifted 4 metres and dropped to simulate a factor 2 fall. Subsequently, a 3 kN force is applied for 3 minutes.

Static strength: The lanyard must withstand a 22 kN force for 3 minutes.

Slippage: An adjustable lanyard must not slip more than 50 mm when subjected to a 3 kN force for 3 minutes.

LIMITATIONS OF TESTING

When applying strength ratings to real-world applications, it's crucial to understand that all EN strength markings are inherently limited and should only be used as a guide. The device tested to attain the marking stamped into its side, demonstrating its strength and the confidence you gain from those marks, was a brand new device in factory-fresh mint condition, devoid of any bangs, dents, drops, or abuse. Its moving parts were not clogged with sand or mud, nor worn down by years of use, with axles bent, bearings shot, or teeth gummed up.

Additionally, if the device in question is intended for ropes, the ropes utilized in the tests will be brand new and specifically chosen to be the ideal size to achieve the maximum strength in the test. Again, they aren't faded or furry, degraded from constant use, or decades old and fixed in place, ravaged by seasons of ice and snow, summer sunshine, and autumn wind.

The rope laboratory is also not typical of the conditions a device will face in the real world. Yes, there are measurements, angles that can be calculated, and forces over time, but how do you test for a shifting boulder that runs over your ascender, or a block of ice that strikes your rope, or the nibble of a rat, or the electric splash of lightning?

When it comes to material strength, it's only ever a guide, a snapshot in time. The device is more ready for its test than it will ever be again in its life. Yes, it's great that your new device attachment point could hold a train, but the moment you start using it, that strength may well degrade. Plus, it won't be stopping a train that will probably lead to failure.

One thing to take away from this is not to equate high initial strength as a sign that a device will last indefinitely, especially not a device that is destined to be as lightweight as possible. There is a reason why you don't fly on 1950s vintage jet airliners.

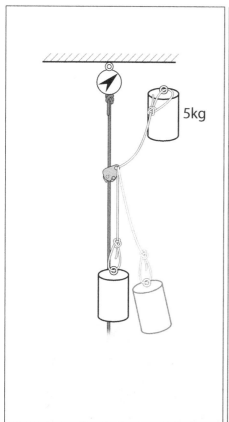

Fig.302

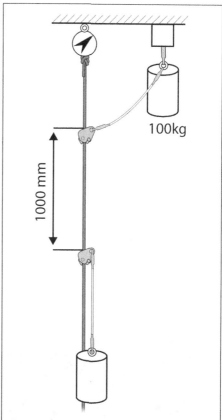

5kg

100kg

1000 mm

Fig.303

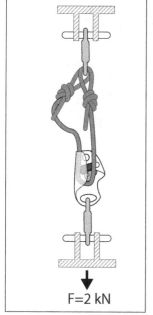

F=2 kN

Fig.304

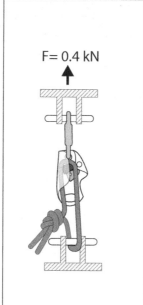

F= 0.4 kN

Fig.305

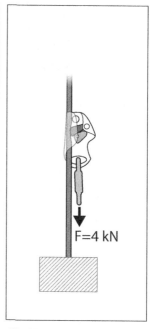

F=4 kN

Fig.306

Fig.307

Limbic hijack

"Is there someone inside you?"

The Psychiatrist

✏ 307
H&K MP5K

In the military and law enforcement, water sports, and aviation, the effects of instinctual panic responses, how one reacts to a real and imagined threat — are now well understood. These effects are combated in several ways: safety methodology and protocol — such as not having your finger on a trigger; simulation training, which reduces the shocks that can trigger such a response; and education, how instinctual responses can hijack a person's brain and perhaps kill them or others. But for some reason, even though these same issues affect climbers and kill and injure climbers, there is zero interest in the subject. Why?

In Australia, between 1992 and 2010, 103 would-be rescuers were drowned, pulled down by the person they were trying to rescue. The mechanics of such a tragic event are well understood: the drowning person goes into an automatic drowning response in which they no longer attempt to swim or tread water or try and seek help from others (shouting, waving) but instead will involuntarily focus only on keeping their mouth above water by pressing down with their hands while holding their heads back. If anyone gets close to someone in this state, they will instinctively grab at them to save themselves, even if this results in both drownings. This panic response is well understood within life-saving, so swimmers are now taught, "Reach or throw, don't go". This panic response is also mirrored by how people needlessly die in rip tides, the survival instinct and the panic response to swim to shore rather than swim parallel to it and escape.

One climbing story of a panic response is my own. I was working in a climbing and caving shop, and one day, an expert caver — Moose — who worked there offered to show me how a Petzl Stop worked. The shop had a climbing wall, so we climbed the ladder up into the rafters of the shop where a static rope hung down next to it, and he supervised me attaching the Stop to the rope and then the devices to my harness. Once fully loaded, he told me to wait, climbed back down to the floor, and told me to pull the red handle on the device and rappel down. Now, I knew how to rappel, and I'd used a GriGri before and assumed I'd depress the red handle and descend slowly and gracefully down under control. "OK, down you come," said Moose. I pressed the handle. Whoosh. I hit the ground, landing on my feet. What had happened was rather than a slow and controlled descent; the second I pressed the handle, the device had zero control over the rope, and I just dropped like a stone.

To make matters worse, rather than control my descent with my control hand on the dead rope, I let go and grabbed the rope above the Stop while my other hand was clamped down on the red handle in a death grip. Moose looked at me. I looked at Moose. I held up my hand, glassed and burnt from holding onto the rope, and Moose just high-fived it and laughed.

Other manifestations of irrational and counterproductive panic responses in climbing include letting go of the break strand when belaying to stop yourself face-planting into the rock, failing to release your hand when squeezing an ABD to give out slack and then the leader falls, inability to move – frozen in your tracks – when rocks, or snow, is coming towards you. Apart from belaying, TRS is perhaps the climbing activity most vulnerable to such panic responses, with accidents often being due to the climber grabbing – and so disabling – the thing that is supposed to keep them from hitting the ground. Rather than a drowning man pulling their rescuer down, it's a falling climber pulling their safety device down with them.

Many terms are used for the issue of a dangerous outcome to an automatic response, which in this case is falling, but perhaps the most easily digested is Daniel Goleman's 'Limbic hijack'. In such a 'hijack', the limbic system, the emotional, impulsive, and instinctual part of the brain, temporarily overwhelms or 'hijacks' the rational and thoughtful part of the brain, particularly the pre-frontal cortex. This part of the brain deals with complex cognitive processes (thinking!). Unlike some forms of limbic hijacking, such as a pilot's brain losing all ability to think, gravity makes any such hijack extremely fast (9.8 m/s2) and unforgiving. Before your pre-frontal cortex returns online and you snap out of it, you or someone else probably hit the deck.

Anti-Hijack Techniques

The more a climber climbs, the more experience they gain, and the less hijackable their brains become. One reason for this is that experience, which, as Mark Twain reminds us, comes from making bad decisions, is the experience of being hijacked before. They are also more comfortable in situations and environments that can trigger such a response in someone new to such experiences and places. But how can you excel in anti-hijack protection?

- **Become an expert in the tools of your trade.** A climber belaying for a thousand hours with a belay plate is much less likely to be hijacked in the first hour of using a Petzl

GriGri. A climber who has never used a belay plate and has been handed a GriGri for the first time is dangerously exposed to a hijacking. The climber with a thousand hours on both devices should be hijack-proof. So, when using new tools and devices, be aware that you are vulnerable, pre-plan how you might get hijacked, and take steps to avoid that happening.

- **Maintain your skills**. Safe practices become automatic when you're constantly climbing. Still, the risk of hijack can creep back if you have significant gaps between doing them, especially if they have not yet become automated. One reason is you can't fool yourself, and a sense of non-automation, or feeling a little out of control, can stimulate a panic response.

- **Train it out**. A climber escaping the system for the first time could easily end up grabbing a friction hitch in such a way as to cause it to slip, panic, and let go of their rappel device and fall to the ground. A climber who has practised climbing ropes on friction hitches, practised multi-self rescue scenarios, rappelled with a back-up hundreds of times and knows every friction hitch inside and out would not be so easily hijacked. When training for TRS, train appropriately and simulate expected scenarios and unexpected critical events.

- **Be aware of your surroundings and environment**. If you're climbing in the wet, the ground is sandy, or it's dark, or there are other climbers nearby, could this increase the risk of a hijack? If you're rappelling down a cliff in the rain, and your feet slip, might you put out your brake hand to stop a face plant? If you can anticipate a threat, you can generally find a way of avoiding it.

- **Avoid complacency**. If you read in this book that X device can be turned off by panic grabbing, don't just assume that would never happen to you. Rather than being complacent, be quietly vigilant and adopt a healthy expectation and suspicion for things going wrong.

- **Adopt an anti-hijack mindset**. If you study these issues and understand how they might affect you and others, you can reduce their likelihood and reduce the impact if they occur. Having done a lot of scary stuff, I can now keep the "I'm going to die" blind panic at bay because I understand just what it is that I'm feeling. If all else fails, when you feel that hijacker's gun put to your head, just count to ten, breathe slowly, and wait until you're free of it.

- **Fitness**. I have a theory that the fitter and stronger you are — or feel — the more able you are to fight off a limbic attack. The opposite is also true: when you're tired and beaten down, it's much harder to put up a fight.

Index

A

ABD 83
  failure points 84
assisted breaking device (ABD) 8
  Belay assist devices 8
attachment 161
autoblock 95

B

batmaning 218
belay Loop 161
bungee sash 144

C

Camp Goblin 60, 62, 66, 115
Camp Matik 84
certification 233
  EN_341 descenders 239
  EN_353-2 fall protection 234
  EN 354 lanyards 240
  EN_567 rope clamps 236
  EN_892 dynamic ropes 233
  EN_1891 low stretch ropes 233
  EN_12841 rope adjustment 237
  EN_15151-1 ABD 238
  EN_15151-2 - Manual Belay 238
chest ascender 46
chest slings 143
cliff safety 26
climbing-line 9
cordelette 200

D

dead rope 9
death yo-yo 204
devices 31
  Camp Goblin 115
  failure points 43
  Modifications 43
  MT RollNlock 121
  Petzl ASAP 113
  Petzl Micro Traxion 109
  Petzl Nano Traxion 109
  Petzl Shunt 101
  rocker-arm 59

Taz Lov3 117
Trango Vergo 119
DMM Buddy 60

E

eccentric 45
  Chest ascender 46
  Failure Points 54
  Handled Ascender 46
  Micro 48
  Non-Handled 48
Edelrid Eddy 84
escape 217

F

FB friction hitch 96
forces 198
French Prusik 95
friction 189

G

Gibbs 43, 69, 70
GMD 91
Grand Wall uAscend 60
GriGri 83, 84, 86, 119
ground strike 206

H/I

handled ascender 46
hitches 95
  Failure Points 95
ice climbing 178
inertia 75
introduction 15
ISC Rocker Mk.1 60

K

Kong Back-up 62

L

lanyards 141
lever 69
  Failure Points 69, 75, 79
link cord 147
live rope 9

M/N

Mad Rock Safegaurd	84
masterpoint	200
mechanics	43, 75
ABD	83
Eccentric	45
GMD	91
Hitches	95
Lever	69
Rocker-Arm	59
Wedge	79
micro ascender	48
neck elastic	144
nomenclature	8
non-handled	48

P/Q

Petzl ASAP	113
Petzl ASAP LOCK	76
Petzl Croll S	107
Petzl Micro Traxion	109
Petzl Mini Traxion	50
Petzl Nano Traxion	109
Petzl Neox	84
Petzl Reverso	91
Petzl Shunt	33, 59, 69, 70, 101, 109, 113, 236
positioning sling	143
progress capture pulley (PCP)	50
pseudo leading	185
quad sling	200
quick-link	133

R

rappel	222
rigging	197
rocker-arm	59
Failure Points	62
RollNlock	121
rope climbing	220
rope & cord	137
rope pad	154
rope protection	153

ropes	149
rope sleeves	153
rope systems	
One Rope System	177
Two Rope System	181

S

safety	25
safety trigger	50
Schwabisch friction hitch	96
self-rescue	217
self-tending	9
self-trailing	9
single rope technique (SRT)	9
sub anchors	209
Setting	212

T

Taz Lov3	40, 62, 117
tools	125
top rope soloing (TRS)	8
top rope TRS	187
Trango Vergo	119
TRS Anchor	197
two-point rule	26

W/X

wedge	79
Wren Silent Partner	76
x chest sling	144
xt hitch	95

Bio

Special Thanks

- Yann Camus
- Stéphane Dupont
- Waldo Etherington
- Clint Flitcher
- John Godino
- Callum Martin
- Ryan Block
- Ryan Jenks
- Mark Stevenson
- Craig Spaulding
- Clinton Szady
- Gary Storrick

The US magazine 'Climbing' once described Andy as a climber with a "strange penchant for the long, the cold and the difficult", with a reputation "for seeking out routes where the danger is real, and the return is questionable, pushing himself on some of the hardest walls and faces in the Alps and beyond, sometimes with partners and sometimes alone."

Climbing since the age of five, Andy's speciality is big wall climbing and winter expeditions. He has climbed El Cap over 35 times, including 5 solo ascents, and 2 one-day ascents, skied across Greenland, put up new routes in Antarctica, and spent a month on the Eiger North face in winter, and Denali in winter (without getting up either).

Andy is also an accomplished writer, with books such as: 'Psychovertical', 'Cold Wars', and 'Unknown Pleasures', being viewed as modern adventure classics. His instructional books: *1001 Climbing Tips*, *Higher Education* and *Down* have also helped many climbers achieve their goals, have more fun trying, and stay a little safer when they don't.

Andy lives in Connemara, on the wild West coast of Ireland.

Books

- **Psychovertical**, *Hutchinson, 2008*
- **Cold Wars**, *Vertebrate, 2011*
- **Me, Myself & I**, *Kirkpatrick, 2015*
- **1001 Climbing Tips**, *Vertebrate, 2016*
- **Unknown Pleasures**, *Vertebrate, 2018*
- **Higher Education**, *Kirkpatrick, 2018*
- **Down**, *Kirkpatrick, 2021*

Note: several of these books have been translated into various languages, including French, German, Spanish, Polish, Russian, and Korean.

Films

- **Cold Haul**, *Fresh Lettuce, 2004*
- **Suffering Andy**, *Slackjaw, 2006*
- **Winter Patagonia**, *Posing Productions, 2008*
- **Psycho Vertical**, *Light Shed, 2018*

Book Stuff

Book Info

ISBN 978-1-9997005-5-3

Design and Production: Andy Kirkpatrick

Published and distributed by

Andrew Kirkpatrick Limited

Ireland 2023

First Edition

Music used in the production of this book

Secret Life, *Brian Eno and Fred Again*

The King, *Nicholas Britell*

Untrue, *Burial*

Tusk, *Fleetwood Mac*

Mulatu of Ethiopia, *Mulatu Astatke*

Dirty Harry, *Lalo Schifrin*

Live with Ginger Baker, *Fela Kuti*

Contact & Social

If you want to get in touch, contact me via my website, email or whatever social media I've not yet deleted.

🌐 andy-kirkpatrick.com

🔖 andykirkpatrick.substack.com

✉ books@andy-kirkpatrick.com

📷 psychovertical

Made in the USA
Monee, IL
13 June 2024

59875224R10138